SAGE was founded in 1965 by Sara Miller McCune to support the dissemination of usable knowledge by publishing innovative and high-quality research and teaching content. Today, we publish over 900 journals, including those of more than 400 learned societies, more than 800 new books per year, and a growing range of library products including archives, data, case studies, reports, and video. SAGE remains majority-owned by our founder, and after Sara's lifetime will become owned by a charitable trust that secures our continued independence.

Los Angeles | London | New Delhi | Singapore | Washington DC | Melbourne

OBSESSIVE COMPULSIVE DISORDER

OBSESSIVE COMPULSIVE DISORDER

A NEUROPSYCHOLOGICAL APPROACH

EDITED BY
PRITHA MUKHOPADHYAY
SREEMOYEE TARAFDER

Los Angeles | London | New Delhi
Singapore | Washington DC | Melbourne

First published in 2018 by

SAGE Publications India Pvt Ltd
B1/I-1 Mohan Cooperative Industrial Area
Mathura Road, New Delhi 110 044, India
www.sagepub.in

SAGE Publications Inc
2455 Teller Road
Thousand Oaks, California 91320, USA

SAGE Publications Ltd
1 Oliver's Yard, 55 City Road
London EC1Y 1SP, United Kingdom

SAGE Publications Asia-Pacific Pte Ltd
3 Church Street
#10-04 Samsung Hub
Singapore 049483

Published by Vivek Mehra for SAGE Publications India Pvt Ltd, typeset in 10.5/13 pt Sabon by Zaza Eunice, Hosur, Tamil Nadu, India and printed at Chaman Enterprises, New Delhi.

Library of Congress Cataloging-in-Publication Data

Names: Mukhopadhyay, Pritha, editor. | Tarafder, Sreemoyee, editor.
Title: Obsessive compulsive disorder: a neuropsychological approach / edited by Pritha Mukhopadhyay, Sreemoyee Tarafder.
Description: New Delhi, India: SAGE Publications India Pvt Ltd; Thousand Oaks, California, USA: SAGE Publications Inc., 2018. | Includes bibliographical references and index.
Identifiers: LCCN 2018022459 | ISBN 9789352807314 (hardcover: alk. paper) | ISBN 9789352807321 (e pub 2.0) | ISBN 9789352807338 (e book)
Subjects: LCSH: Obsessive compulsive disorder.
Classification: LCC RC533 .O26427 2018 | DDC 616.85/227—dc23 LC record available at https://lccn.loc.gov/2018022459

ISBN: 978-93-528-0731-4 (HB)

SAGE Team: Abhijit Baroi, Guneet Kaur Gulati, Shobana Paul and Ritu Chopra

To

The Department of Psychology, University of Calcutta (estd 1916)—where psychology started its journey in India more than 100 years ago

CONTENTS

LIST OF TABLES

LIST OF FIGURES

LIST OF ABBREVIATIONS

AVDTR	audiovisual display time reproducer
BDD	body dysmorphic disorder
BDI	Beck Depression Inventory
BGT	Bender Gestalt Test
BPD	borderline personality disorder
CBT	cognitive behaviour therapy
CCG	community control group
CGs	control groups
COWAT	Controlled Oral Word Association Test
CPEPA	Centre with Potential for Excellence in Particular Area
CS	Conditional Stimulus
CSTC	cortico–striatal–thalamic–cortical
DB	Digit Backward
DBS	deep brain stimulation
DEP	depressive disorder
DF	Digit Forward
DLPFC	dorsolateral prefrontal–circuit
DM	decision-making
DSM	Diagnostic and Statistical Manual of Mental Disorders
DZ	dizygotic
ECA	Epidemiologic Catchment Area
EF	executive functions

EEG	electroencephalogram
EHI	Edinburgh Handedness Inventory
EPQ	Eysenck Personality Questionnaire
ERP	exposure and response prevention
FDR	first-degrée relatives
FSH	follicle stimulating hormone
FTMS	failure to maintain set
GHQ	General Health Questionnaire
GSR	galvanic skin response
HA	harm avoidance
HRSD	Hamilton Rating Scale for Depression
HYP	hypochondriasis
ICD	International Classification of Disorders
IGT	Iowa Gambling Task
IPD	idiopathic Parkinson's disease
IPDE	International Personality Disorder Examination
IWM	internal working model
LH	luteinizing hormone
LNS	Letter Number Sequencing
LOI	Leyton Obsessional Inventory
MCQ	Metacognition Questionnaire
MDD	major depressive disorder
MMSE	Mini-Mental State Examination
MRI	magnetic resonance imaging
MSE	mental status examination
MZ	monozygotic
NAOP	National Association of Psychology
NEO-FFI	NEO Five Factor Inventory
NEO-PI	NEO Personality Inventory

NOCC	number of categories completed
OBQ	Obsessive Beliefs Questionnaire
OCD	obsessive compulsive disorder
OCPD	obsessive compulsive personality disorder
OCPTs	obsessive compulsive personality traits
OCSD	obsessive compulsive spectrum disorder
OFC	orbitofrontal cortex
PCLR	percent conceptual level response
PE	perseverative error
PNPE	percent nonperseverative error
PPE	percent perseverative error
PPR	percent perseverative response
PR	perseverative response
PSI	Processing Speed Index
RT	Reaction time
SAPAS	Standardized Assessment of Personality Abbreviated Scale
SD	standard deviation
SEM	structural equation modelling
SMRA	Stepwise Multiple Regression Analysis
SNST	Stroop Neuropsychological Screening Test
SPSS	Statistical Package for the Social Sciences
S-REF	Self-regulatory Executive Function
SRIs	serotonin reuptake inhibitors
SSRIs	selective serotonin reuptake inhibitors
SST	Serial Subtraction Test
TAF	thought–action fusion
TCFC	trials to complete first category
TCI	Temperament and Character Inventory

TEF	thought–event fusion
TOF	thought–object fusion
TOL – DX	Tower of London Drexel University
UD	unipolar depression
US	Unconditional Stimulus
WAIS-III	Wecshler Adult Intelligence Scale-III
WCST	Wisconsin Card Sorting Test
WFD	workforce development
WHO	World Health Organization
WMI	Working Memory Index
YBOCS	Yale Brown Obsessive Compulsive Scale
YBOCS-SC	Yale Brown Obsessive Compulsive Scale Symptom Checklist
5HIAA	5-hydroxy-indole-acetic-acid

FOREWORD

For more than a century psychologists have been trying to understand OCD in terms of its diagnosis, aetiology and prognosis. It was since the case history of 'Rat Man' was reported by Freud in 1909 that OCD has remained a fertile area of research in clinical psychology. The Rat Man was indeed a lawyer fantasizing about being tormented by rats. The lawyer was very fearful that terrible things may happen to his father and his lady friend. Freud personally treated him regularly for three months and sporadically afterwards, using his method of psychoanalysis. The lawyer had partial relief but was never cured completely. Research in the area of OCD has come a long way from the days of Freud, who incidentally was the contemporary of Girindra Shekhar Bose, the first psychoanalyst in India. OCD is now taken as a spectrum of neuropsychological disorders treated by a combination of psychotherapy, cognitive behaviour therapy (CBT) and pharmacological drugs. There is a vast body of knowledge today about the role of cortico-striatal-thalamic-cortical circuit. Hollander (2013) while bringing out DSM-V expanded the scope of OCD as a spectrum of disorders, introducing the continuum of 'compulsive–impulsive' along which the disorders vary. Impulsivity implied deficient mental control and premature act at one end of the continuum, the other being rigidity and over-control. A term 'obsessive compulsive spectrum disorder' was introduced to cover a wide range of OCDs. That has given research a new direction in this area. But even today it is looked upon as a mysterious disease, and we have a long way to go in deciphering the origins and true character of this disorder. It is still considered, as in Freudian days, that OCD can be managed by psychotherapy and drugs, but there is no cure.

The present book on OCD, edited by Professor Pritha Mukhopadhyay and Dr Sreemoyee Tarafder, is a comprehensive work comprising a series of studies. Professor Mukhopadhyay set up a neuropsychological laboratory in the Psychology Department of University of Calcutta in 2000, and the present book is the culmination of this team's research on OCD in the last 15 years. She and her students conducted a series of studies over this long period and have come out with salient findings on obsessive compulsive behaviour. This work has set a new direction and approach in the study of OCD. The implications of her findings are worth considering for the management of this disorder. In seven chapters of this book, the editors have examined OCD patients from psychological, physiological and neurological perspectives. The book also focuses on the prognosis and other ramifications of OCD.

As many aetiological studies show, OCD is on rise in India. It should be noted that most of the aetiological studies are conducted in urban areas and few in rural areas. The reported studies are mostly clinical observation rather than demographic surveys. A gross estimation shows that around 2% to 3% of the population suffers from OCD in India, which includes both mild and severe cases. OCD often manifests in late adolescence, and the disorder continues for lifetime with intermittent remission. In recent decades, OCD has been on the rise, and we are still in the process of understanding its prognosis and various ramifications. One of the reasons for lack of reliable data about OCD is its overlap with obsessive compulsive personality, obsessive compulsive spectrum and related symptoms. Another difficulty is that children with OCD often hide their symptoms and are shy of talking about it. This leads to delay in diagnosis of the disorder.

OCD is a chronic disorder and can only have symptomatic relief. Obsession implies repetition of the same thought, imagery or idea for long period of time and compulsion is repetition of some action over and over again. It becomes a disorder when patients have no control on their thinking and behaviour, and suffers distressing anxiety. Some of the important manifestations of obsession are fear of causing harm to someone else, fear of harm inflicted to self, fear of contamination, need for symmetry or exactness, sexual and religious fixation, fear of behaving unacceptably and anxiety of making a mistake. The consequent compulsive behaviour may be cleaning, hand washing, checking, ordering and arranging, hoarding, asking for reassurance and mental acts such as counting, silent word repetition and rumination. It is a mentally disabling condition, varying from person to person and severity varying even within the same person at different times. In most severe condition, it may completely take over the thinking faculty and activities, such as in case of a possessed person. As a mental health disorder, it should be understood that there is no treatment of the disease, only symptomatic relief is possible.

It is characteristic of OCD that it often gets associated with other disorders such as depression, suicidal tendencies, eating disorders (such as bulimia), anxiety attack and sexual perversions. Then the situation becomes even more complicated and threatening. According to WHO, suicide will be the number one killer disease by 2030, and OCD will play an important contributory role in that. Containing OCD becomes all the more urgent in such cases. Children with autism have greater probability of developing OCD.

The main thesis of the work reported in this book is that repetitive thinking along with associated faulty neural network leads to multiple cognitive deficits. It contends that there is a symbiotic connection between brain and behaviour. Neurological dysfunctioning is both cause and consequence of OCD. It is reported that OCD patients are slow in responding to conflicting and nonconflicting situations. They follow their internal rule—disregarding external instructions—and this choice does not arouse any guilt. Information processing speed is found to be the potent predictor of severity of the disorder. Higher-order cognitive activities such as planning, intention, coordination and integration (called executive functions) are severely impaired in the condition of OCD. These and other findings reported in this book render it a valuable contribution in the field of OCD.

Ajit Kumar Dalal
Retd Professor of Psychology,
University of Allahabad

ACKNOWLEDGEMENTS

Pritha Mukhopadhyay

Throughout my life, I have acknowledged to myself that the only best friend of my life is my mom. My mother, Mrs Pranati Mukherji, who is no more with me, but is always there. It is she who made me what I am today. But for the first time in my life I am formally acknowledging, 'Mom, I have no words to express the insight, love and support you've given me'.

My sincere gratitude to my department, the Department of Psychology, University of Calcutta, for providing me with all the facilities to carry out my research work with my students and research scholars. I am thankful to Centre with Potential for Excellence in Particular Area (CPEPA) for providing me with the infrastructure to do the research and also with an academic impetus to disseminate knowledge in a greater sphere by providing a peaceful ambience.

I have no words to express my thanks to Professor Ajit Dalal who has given me inspiration and guidance from the time I communicated to him about this attempt to write a book based on our own research. I am thankful to all the doctors, Professor Gautam Bandyopadhyay, Dr Jai Ranjan Ram, Dr Satyajit Ash and Dr Abhijit Hazra, who have sent patients to us and helped us as and when necessary. We continuously felt their support throughout the course of our work. I am delighted to mention that my students and research scholars—Ms Ananya Mondal, Ms Piya Saha, Ms Ayoleena Ray, Mr Kaustav Manna and Ms Doyel Ghosh—helped me at every step in making tables, formatting texts, charting graphs and correcting typographic errors.

To Sreemoyee, I will just say that the comfort of cognitive symbiosis that you have provided to me cannot be expressed in words—if I would start a thought, you'd finish it for me and that is perhaps the reason why we worked so well together. I am thankful to all the authors who have contributed to the book— Mrs Suvosree Bhattacharya, Dr Sujata Das, Professor Shyamal Kumar Das, Dr Dinaz Bilimoria, Ms Parmeet Soni and Mrs Nilanjana Chatterjee. Without their contribution and cooperation, the book would not have been possible. I extend my thanks to the editorial and production teams of SAGE India for their continuous guidance and monitoring for publication of the book.

This work could not be made complete with all the workload I have to undertake as academic and administrative responsibilities of the department and the university. But I am ever so grateful to my husband, Professor S. K. Ghoshal, who always stands beside me in any of my academic endeavours and helps me to improve my knowledge at every step. My daughter, Ms Sayari Ghoshal, her concern for me, her tolerance and her ability to never place her need before mine and always smiling. I do not know how to say my thanks to her.

Sreemoyee Tarafder

An absence that makes its presence felt at every juncture of my life is that of my mother. When I graduated from college, my mother had gifted me a book, and on its inside cover she had written words of encouragement for me that I cherish till date. When our book is being published, she is not around to hold it in her hands, but I know what she would have said, and I know what I would have felt. So, to begin with, I thank her—my mother, Sanghamitra Tarafder—a woman of immense wisdom and empathy who taught me all about unconditional love and instilled in me the love for academia. This is your dream, Maa.

I know that this book would not have been possible without the driving force of my supervisor and mentor Professor Pritha Mukhopadhyay. The book is the result of her tireless efforts and rigour that made all of us put in our best. She is my co-editor for the book, and I feel honoured to share the title credits with her. I remain 'limbically yours, Mamie'. It was good to work at the CPEPA lab over endless cups of tea and food (being supplied by Ananya and Pia), interspersed by some invigorating conversations with Ma'am, her students and scholars.

I have received a lot of help from Dr Dinaz Jeejeebhoy—my co-author and guardian angel. Rupam Banerjee, Navnita Bose, Priyanka Roy, Parmeet Soni, Suvosree Bhattacharya—I really appreciate their inputs and comments at various stages of the work. Had it not been for Professor Gautam Bandyopadhyay, Dr Jai Ranjan Ram, Dr Satyajit Ash and my teachers—Professor P. K. Chattopadhyay, Debabrata Biswas, late Saugato Basu, Professor Nilanjana Sanyal, Prasanta Kr. Roy among others—I would have perhaps not acquired an insightful understanding of OCD.

I thank my inner circle of love—*DJLPS* (my soul sisters Dona Pal, Jayshree Sarda, 'Lalti', Priyanka Bhattacharyya and Priyanka Thapar)—for keeping the dream alive in me. My friends kept me afloat through difficult times and the last two years have not been easy; hence, a big thanks to 'Mangsho-Mishti-More', Trina, Srinayana, Priyanka, Pushpita, Sayantan, Souvik, Anuttama and Jhuma for your hand-holding. I am also indebted to my workplace—West Bengal State University, the Honb'le Vice Chancellor Prof. Basab Chaudhuri and all my departmental colleagues for ensuring that I could devote time to the book. My students at WBSU are my source of suste-nance, they provide me with immense joy and satisfaction. I feel humbled by the love that they shower on me and they must be thanked for keeping my spirits high. My friends from work—'Mureer Tin', especially Dr Kausik Bandyopadhyay, needs special mention for guiding me about the publication process. I am especially thankful to Abhijit Baroi, Guneet Kaur Gulati and team SAGE for beautifully guiding us all through the journey.

Words cannot express the admiration that I feel for my father Sri Apurba Kumar Tarafder, who always inspires me with his infectious workaholism. And my family—brother Abhishek, his wife Gargi, niece Aritri, uncle Sameer Mitra and father–in-law, Sri Aditya Kr Chatterjee—for providing the holding environment.

I thank my husband, Dr Siddhartha Chattopadhyay, for being my cherished friend and for making the frame of my life so beautiful with his steady and nurturing presence, encouraging me to become the best that I can be.

INTRODUCTION
The Research Journey

Pritha Mukhopadhyay

He who has a why to live for can bear almost any how.

Friedrich Nietzsche

If what you have chosen to do in life is important, you may suffer and the path may not be easy and encouraging, but never doubt the reason why you are going through it all. It is with that 'why' that one is able to find sustenance and salvation. Carrying out research work in India is not an easy task. The infrastructure, the academic budget, the laboratory, journals, scholars—almost none of it is optimally conducive to empirical research work. Yet, if your rigour and thirst for knowledge and discovery will not let you rest, you just have to make do with 'almost any how'! This book is our attempt to highlight the research work that has been carried out in my neuropsychology laboratory for the last 15 years, with very limited resources. This book talks about my journey and that of my scholars, about our insights that developed around obsessive compulsive disorder (OCD) while working with patients. The year 2016 marked the year the Department of Psychology, University of Calcutta (CU) celebrated centenary of the study of psychology in India. In 1916, the first psychology department was established in India by Professor Girindra Shekhar Bose and ever since the legacy of psychology in all its glory has been carried on by CU. I have been lucky enough to study at the prestigious department right from my undergraduate days. I went on to do my postgraduation and PhD from CU. After I joined CU as a faculty, I continued my research in the area of psychophysiology and later it veered towards neuropsychology. From 2000, my main research focus was on neuropsychological studies. Along with my research scholars over the last 15–16 years, we have developed some understanding regarding OCD, which we would like to showcase in a form of a book. The book is also our dedication to the Department of Psychology, CU, joining in celebration of the centenary.

My research journey started after my postgraduate examination in psychology. I started reading whatever book I could lay my hands on, and I read books across disciplines. At that time, I found interesting anecdotal papers on post-adoption pregnancy, though the reason for achieving pregnancy after adoption was not specifically delineated. The articles concerning idiopathic infertility or unexplained infertility attracted my attention more. Why was it unexplained? Was it due to limitation of the prevailing diagnostic tools to ascertain the aetiology of infertility? Perhaps that was not the only reason. I came across many articles that discussed how mild hyperprolactinemia might lead to infertility and tried to associate the mild elevation in prolactin with psychological stress. In spite of normal hormone profile (including luteinizing hormone (LH), follicle stimulating hormone (FSH), oestrogen and progesterone surge), that is, with fully functional cycle and without any structural anomaly in reproductive system, women failed to be mothers with reproductively healthy spouses. Though few studies tried to associate it with psychological dysfunction, their selection of infertile group as free from any anomaly was not beyond question. Owing to the fact that the psyche is not a tangible entity and not as amenable to assessment as hormones, the psychogenic aetiology could not be ascertained. Questions may arise regarding the impact of subjective element of the participant while responding to the questionnaires. Not all participants may mean the same when they denote something as 'severe' in their subjective judgement. Could subjective element of the person therefore have an impact on the outcome measure?

So I tried to link the infertile female's anxiety disposition with her stress hormones—cortisol and prolactin—to search for the link between the two. In addition to high anxiety disposition in these females, the observation of variation in the nature of relationship between these two hormones in infertile and fertile females indicated the possibility of a significant underlying factor leading to infertility associated with stress. After screening the couples for any aetiological factors underlying infertility, our investigation included psychological, psychophysiological and hormonal measures that delineated how psyche could have impacted somatic factors and how the so-called unexplained may be partially explained by the existence of psychological substrates.

It is not a story of how to study infertility and what is the study outcome, but it is the story of a journey that made me learn the way of thinking in research and how to develop a methodology in interdisciplinary research centring around psychology, in search of the root of any pathology.

I tried to find the possible root in psychophysiological system which is the transition point of stress to soma, and its link to the relevant parameters that impede the function of one's reproductive system. I also found how the condition of females suffering from long infertile condition has been reversed, with a warm interaction with the psychologist during investigation which could have a healing effect on the women and some of them achieved pregnancy. Though we cannot put a claim on effectiveness of warm interaction onto achievement of pregnancy, we cannot remain blind to these events also. Reports of post-adoption pregnancy also explain all the life events may not be tested under rigorous research control, but they cannot deny the observed truth.

In search of truth, psychophysiological research helped us to discover that many established findings are not beyond question. Law of initial value is a good index of relationship between one's state of arousal and pattern of response habituation to external stimulation, and we found it to be applicable within a small range of arousal. The law does not hold when one is too calm and maintains a very low arousal state. We further extended our study and found how the recovery time of galvanic skin response (GSR) is related to one's personality disposition (Mukhopadhyay & Mukherjee, 2000).

Those within moderate range of recovery time showed emotional stability on personality questionnaires, signifying they have the capacity to free themselves from prior excitation within an adequate period of time. The group with greater recovery time showed greater dysthymic disposition that explained its inability to easily disengage from prior excitation, possibly indicating intrusion of greater subjectivity in interpreting the reality. This could also be substantiated from the findings of shallowness of information processing in the group with very quick recovery time as it correlated with their impulsivity. This adventure with psyche–soma relationship fostered my interest to probe into brain–behaviour relationship.

As the years progressed, I started working with different groups with neurological problems in search of psychological sequelae of the disorders. We observed how the patients with frontal lesion showed perseveration, that is, they failed to disengage themselves from previous set on the simple Bender Gestalt Test (Mukhopadhyay, Mukherjee, Chowdhury, Gupta, Basu, & Dutt, 1999). With brain lesion cases, we found how the wrecked neural network leads to multiple cognitive deficits. In brain lesion cases (Dutt, Das, Hazra, Basu, Das, & Mukhopadhyay, 2008), we observed how with minor changes in test demand, activation of different neural patterns are initiated. In our work with Wisconsin Card Sorting Test (WCST) to assess set shifting, the most damaging effect of left frontal lesion was observed in terms of perseverative response (PR), where the patients received feedback in an ambiguous situation (Mukhopadhyay, Dutt, Das, Basu, Hazra, Dhibar, & Roy, 2008). But in terms of perseverative error (PE), the maximal negative impact was found to be in the function of the right frontal lesion. Perhaps the verbal mediation was the key requirement in coming out of ambiguity in case of PR; hence the left frontal involvement was more; but greater role of right frontal than the left in PE suggests the greater demand of sustained attention and monitoring in attention set shifting function with clear feedback in an unambiguous situation.

Though set shifting difficulty is not restricted to frontal area of brain as it was claimed before, frontal region is considered as the epicentre of the neural circuit responsible for attention set shifting function. With this context, we took up the study with the Parkinson's disorder, having fronto-striatal involvement. There too the set shifting difficulty has been noted. Thus the cognitive deficit which we usually observe in brain lesion cases with perseveration is owing to disruption in information processing system as a result of impairment in link between anterior and posterior parts of the brain (Mukhopadhyay et al., 2008), leading to dysexecution. It prompted us to think that the cognitive deficit could also have an equal impact on the information processing system.

Then we went on to study the psychiatric groups where deficits in cognition are at the root of the psychopathology. Our investigation started with OCD.

In this book, we will first emphasize the conceptualization and assessment protocol of OCD so that the clinician can study the patient with full acumen. Throughout the book we look at cases to see how the disposition of obsession characteristics causes functional alteration in brain that interferes with optimal neuropsychological functioning. Additionally, we looked into how neuropsychological dysfunction interacted with dysfunctional metacognitive beliefs to maintain the disease process. While doing so, we also discovered how the obsessive compulsive trait is an endophenotypic factor by studying the first-degree relatives (FDRs) of patients with OCD. In spite of mostly deficient executive functioning, more functional metacognitive belief structure and efficient trial and error response selection (as measured on nonperseverative error on WCST) works as a protective factor that stalls the development of disease process in FDR. Our work with the FDRs made us curious about the status of metacognition and executive functions in patient groups where compulsivity and impulsivity is present. This led us to compare patients suffering from OCD with patients diagnosed as having borderline personality disorder (BPD), two diametrically opposite groups on compulsivity–impulsivity dimension of obsessive compulsive spectrum disorder (OCSD). The same neuropsychological manifestation with opposite underlying dynamics is a learning experience for the scientist. It is an experience of discovery at every phase of clinical assessment and therapy.

With this conceptual background we most humbly present this book based on our experimental work from 2000–2015.

Chapter 1 is an introductory chapter that gives a comprehensive view of OCD. It is a chronic and potentially debilitating condition that affects nearly 1% to 3% of the population worldwide. OCD has become a leading candidate for empirical studies designed with two objectives: first, to focus on understanding the phenomenon from different perspectives and second, to devise effective and efficacious treatment procedures for the condition. A thorough understanding of the mechanisms that maintain the disorder is considered pivotal in devising effective treatment for it. The first chapter is an attempt to gather and integrate information from different perspectives pertaining to disorder to form a strong basis for understanding the complex etiological factors related to OCD.

Chapter 2 deals with the art of case history taking and conducting mental status examination of patients to maximally understand OCD, interspersed with case examples. The specifics highlighted in the chapter in terms of MSE will be helpful guidelines for clinicians. The chapter also discusses assessment tools that can be used to study different dimensions of OCD in terms of symptom severity, beliefs, cognition and personality. Since the interpretation of test results do not depend on cross-sectional performance alone, and has to be correlated with clinical/behavioural observations, the chapter discusses in detail how a clinician should go about it. The chapter also provides guidelines to enhance processes and skills necessary for developing clinical acumen.

Chapter 3 highlights the beginning of our journey with OCD in our neuropsychological laboratory back in 2000. There were very limited studies back then that had investigated disorder-specific impairment of cognitive functions in OCD by comparing it with other clinical groups. By then it was understood that cognitive deficits are a common feature in patients with OCD, but the results of most of the studies in this area were inconsistent, and it was difficult to draw a comprehensive picture of the cognitive status of patients with OCD based on them. Specifically, our first study was designed to study the cognitive domain of selective and sustained attention in two disorder groups—OCD and Idiopathic Parkinson's Disease—to make a comparative evaluation of the function in the two diseases and to examine whether attention is differentially affected. Basal ganglia has the ability to inhibit an already initiated response, and therefore IPD was selected as a clinical control group (CG) since it is a disorder of basal ganglia. In view of the fact that patients with OCD face similar issues, their comparative analysis was done, helping us to infer that the subthalamic nuclei of the basal ganglia may be a common site of dysfunction in the disorders. Thirty right-handed, non-depressed patients with OCD and 33 patients with IPD were selected for the study. They were administered the 'A' Random Letter Test, Digit Forward (DF) and Digit Backward (DB) Test, 20–1 backward counting and 40–3 Serial Subtraction Test. Parametric statistics was employed to determine group differences, if any. Results showed that compromised attentional ability was observed in both the groups in comparison to their matched normal controls. Comparison between the OCD and IPD groups indicated inferior performance of the OCD patients on tasks of attention.

Chapter 4 looks into the entire gamut of executive functions along with domains of metacognitive beliefs and personality factors in patients with OCD. Patients with OCD (n=75) along with respective CGs comprising the community control group (CCG; n=75) were matched on age, sex and education. They were assessed on Yale Brown Obsessive Compulsive Scale (YBOCS), General Health Questionnaire (GHQ), Beck Depression Inventory (BDI), Leyton Obsessional Inventory, Neo Five Factor Inventory (NEO FFI), Metacognition Questionnaire (MCQ), WCST, Controlled Oral Word Association Test (COWAT), Processing Speed and Working Memory subtests from Wecshler Adult

Intelligence Scale III (WAIS III), N-Back Tests and Tower of London DX (TOL – DX) Test to measure severity of obsessions and compulsions (OCD group), psychiatric morbidity (in CGs), subjective level of distress, obsessive symptoms and traits, personality structure, metacognitive deficits, executive functions such as set shifting, fluency, speed, working memory and planning, respectively. The comparative evaluation of the findings indicated that the OCD group significantly differed from its respective CGs in terms of depression, metacognition, personality and executive functions. Obsessive personality traits emerged as the highest contributory factor for bringing about obsessive symptoms in the study group.

Chapter 5 is a continuance of the aforementioned study and explores the endophenotype of OCD by studying probands with OCD and their unaffected FDRs to identify neurocognitive markers in terms of impaired cognitive flexibility, motor inhibition, decision-making and behavioural reversal. The study, highlighted in the chapter, not only compared the probands and FDRs on executive function tasks but also in terms of obsessive traits and metacognitive belief. The study was carried out with 50 dyads of patients with OCD, their FDRs and matched healthy controls. There were no statistically significant differences between patients with OCD and their unaffected FDRs on neurocognitive domains of obsessive traits, set shifting, planning, processing speed and working memory which were impaired, as compared with their respective CGs. Significant differences on domain of metacognitive beliefs were noted between FDRs and probands along with unique association pattern of the traits and executive functions in the OCD group. The finding of the present study upholds executive dysfunction to be endophenotypic marker for OCD and identifies metacognitive beliefs as protective factors for unaffected FDRs of OCD probands which prevent manifestation of pathology in them.

Chapter 6 discusses other disorders of the obsessive compulsive spectrum. The characteristics of the disorders under obsessive compulsive spectrum range from ego-syntonicity, poor insight and risk-seeking behaviour on one end and ego-dystonicity, good insight and risk-avoidance behaviour on the other end. The symptom manifestation of the disorders is exclusive in their own right, yet as the disorders move from compulsivity towards impulsivity many symptoms overlap. The chapter discusses our study in which we investigated whether or not personality and neuropsychological disposition are different for the three groups, namely, OCD, BPD and OCSDs (hypochondriasis [HYP], body dysmorphic disorder [BDD], OCPD), in comparison to a community sample. All the three study groups were high on the trait of neuroticism, but differed in their expression of the trait where it was observed that patients with OCD are risk-aversive, perfectionistic and guilt-ridden; those with OCSD are overtly anxious and are prone to distress and worry; and patients with BPD displayed disturbances in uncertainty about self-image, their aims in life and internal preferences. Further, it was noticed that all the three patient groups performed poorly on WCST in comparison to the community sample. The nature of impairment in the disordered groups showed similar patterns of impairment of set shifting capacity and in terms of taking decisions regarding response selection and shifting of attention. Thus, although the overt manifestations of the disorders differ, the underlying psychopathology may be similar reflecting their oneness to be conceptualized as OCSDs.

Chapter 7 presents experimentally studied slowness in OCD and compares them with depressive patients with respect to reaction time, feedback utilization, cognitive interference, time perception and decision-making. The studied sample comprised participants from OCD, depressive disorder (DEP) and CCG (N=72). Results indicated that both OCD and DEP performed poorly in comparison to the CG on reaction time, suggesting impairment in RT response inhibition and cognitive interference. With respect to time perception and decision-making, all the groups performed at par with each other. But the DEP group could maximally utilize the feedback, expressed in terms of knowledge of result, whereas OCD group could not utilize the feedback provided to them. The finding empirically establishes the difference between slowness demonstrated by the patients of OCD and patients with depression, causally linking it to their typical cognitive patterns.

The last chapter concludes with a discussion of obsessive compulsive personality traits, as proposed by Freud, from a neuropsychological framework. It provides a model based on our work where we integrate the neuropsychological and psychodynamic understandings of OCD. We analyze each anal character trait suggested by Freud and go on to experimentally explore the neuropsychological correlates of each of these traits, enabling better eclectic understanding of the pathogenesis of OCD. At the very end of this book, we arrive at a juncture that brings us to a holistic understanding of OCD.

References

Dutt, A., Das, S., Hazra, A., Basu, A., Das, S. K., & Mukhopadhyay, P. (2008). Neural network underlying non-spatial attention: Evidence from patients with focal brain lesions. National Conference of Indian Association of Clinical Psychologists, held at Department of Psychology, University of Calcutta.

Mukhopadhyay, P., Dutt, A., Das, S. K., Basu, A., Hazra, A., Dhibar, T., & Roy, T. (2008). Identification of neuroanatomical substrates of set-shifting ability: Evidence from patients with focal brain lesions. *Progress in Brain Research, 168*, 95–104. doi: 10.1016/S0079-6123(07)68008-X.

Mukhopadhyay, P., & Mukherjee, S. (2000). A closer look on the behavioural inhibition system and personality interrelationship: A psychophysiological study. *Journal of the Indian Academy of Applied Psychology, 26*(1–2), 141–146.

Mukhopadhyay, P., Mukherjee, S., Chowdhury, M., Gupta, S., Basu, P., & Dutt, A. (1999). Determination of lobe function in brain damaged and psychiatric patients: Role of Bender Visual-Motor Gestalt test. *Indian Journal of Clinical Psychology, 26*(2), 223–227.

1

Obsessive Compulsive Disorder
A Functional Overview

Suvosree Bhattacharya, Sreemoyee Tarafder and Pritha Mukhopadhyay

The idea of a disease entity is not an objective to be reached, but our most fruitful point of orientation.

Karl Jaspers (1923)

Obsessive compulsive disorder (OCD) is a chronic and potentially disabling condition that has a significant impact on the personal, social and occupational life of the individual afflicted with the condition. It has a prevalence rate of 1% to 3% in the general population. Even in the recent past, it was erroneously believed that OCD is a rare disorder with a prevalence rate of less than 5 per 1000 adults (Coryell, 1981). Rasmussen and Eisen (1990) cite reluctance of patients to divulge symptoms, failure of professionals to recognize the diversity of symptoms manifested, misdiagnosis and failure to screen for OCD in routine mental status examinations as the reasons that account for previous underestimation of the prevalence of OCD. Data from the Epidemiologic Catchment Area (ECA) survey (e.g., Karno, Golding, Sorenson, & Burnam, 1988) suggest that OCD is 50–200 times more common than previously believed and twice as common as schizophrenia or panic disorder in the general population. Epidemiological studies have shown that roughly about 2% of adults suffer from this intriguing disorder. Systematic studies have shown that from one-third to one-half of adult cases with OCD have their onsets in childhood and adolescence (Flament & Cohen, 2002; Jaisoorya, Janardhan Reddy, & Srinath, 2003). Prevalence studies on adolescent OCD have shown varying rates ranging from 1% to- 4%, possibly because of different methodologies, but the rates are similar to those in adults (Flament & Cohen, 2002). The prevalence of OCD among children is from 2% to 4% (Kiejna, Rymaszewska, Kantorska-Janiec, & Tokarski, 2002).

Clinical Picture of OCD

The hallmark symptoms of OCD are obsessions, which are sudden intrusions into consciousness of unwanted thoughts and unpleasant images, followed by a profound sense of dread and a strong desire or urge to complete certain specific behaviours/acts, which are termed compulsions, to bring down the tension. OCD is a complex and heterogeneous condition, with marked disparity in the symptom presentation between two individuals affected by it. There may be various types of intrusive thoughts, images, preoccupations and related rituals and compulsions with non-overlapping clinical presentations.

The diagnosis, treatment and research of such a widely hetero-geneous presentation becomes difficult to handle. Thus, an important concern for researchers in this area has been to simplify the process of diagnosis. Both the *Diagnostic and Statistical Manual of Mental Disorders* (DSM) and the *International Classification of Disorders* (ICD) of WHO have focused on the so-called 'checklist approach', where the mere presence or absence of the symptoms, or a group of symptoms, is enough to make the diagnosis (Abramowitz & Houts, 2005). This approach, although helps in improving diagnostic unreliability, thoroughly discards the functional basis of the condition. The need therefore is for an understanding of the symptoms through the process of symptom formation and not merely through the presence or absence of certain behaviours.

Keeping this in view, in the present chapter, the focus will be to understand the phenomenology of the disorder from the functional perspective.

Obsessions

Numerous investigations have converged to indicate that 80% to 90% of the population at large experience senseless intrusive thoughts, the content of which is indistinguishable from that of the obsessions reported by individuals with OCD (Abramowitz, Schwartz, Moore, & Luenzmann, 2003; Rackman & de Silva, 1978). However, most of the people can brush off such unwanted thoughts, whereas people with OCD appraise them as significant, unacceptable and threatening (Salkovskis, 1985, 1989, 1999). When it occurs, individuals with OCD equate these intrusive thoughts and images with actions. Studies have stated that people with OCD believe that when an unwanted and intrusive thought occurs (e.g., aggressive and assaultive image towards someone), it is equivalent to the behaviour (assault, in this case) being performed and therefore morally reprehensible. Such beliefs lead to the conclusion that thoughts must be kept in check so that as a consequence the feared outcome is prevented (Abramowitz, Whiteside, Lyman, Kalsy, & Tolin, 2003).

Compulsions

The way individuals with OCD manage the distress caused by unwanted and excessive thoughts is by performing compulsive rituals. Performance of such ritualistic behaviours helps in immediate (although short term) reduction of the anxiety and a decrease in an urge to perform the behaviour corresponding to the thought (Hodgson & Rachman, 1972). These rituals can be overt behaviours such as washing, checking, hoarding objects or covert/mental rituals such as praying, counting and forming mental imagery that the patient performs to reduce anxiety. Recently the significance of covert compulsions or mental rituals has also gained prominence. Foa and Kozak (1995) have found that more than 80% of the patients suffer from mental compulsions with or without overt compulsive acts. De Silva, Menzies and Shafran (2003) stated that mental compulsions serve the same purpose as compulsive behaviours to reduce obsessional anxiety. The significant and long-term consequence of these compulsions are that they produce a 'self-perpetrating' cycle of anxiety and ritualizing, and therefore they have a tendency to become repetitive. Two reasons why these ritualistic performances become repetitious are:

- These acts are interpreted to prevent the negative consequences of the thoughts (or catastrophes) from occurring.
- They are ineffective in providing a sense of complete assurance that the feared consequence will not occur.

Since the actual occurrence of the feared outcome can never be verified with certainty no amount of ritualizing will bring about a sense of complete assurance.

Neutralization

Mention should also be made of the mechanism of neutralization. Researchers have found a variety of 'neutralizing strategies' present in OCD that do not exactly match the diagnostic criteria for compulsive acts; however, they possess similar functional utility as that of compulsions. These include reassurance seeking, overanalysing, rational self-talk (i.e., to convince oneself of the unimportance of the thoughts), mentally replacing a bad thought with a good thought, performing a brief mental or behavioural act, intentional distraction and attempts to control unwanted thoughts (Ladouceour et al., 2000a). Investigators have found that neutralizing strategies, like compulsions, are self-perpetuating (Salkovskis et al., 1997). Attempt to suppress neutralizing thoughts led to increased discomfort associated with it and the corresponding urge to continue neutralizing.

A case example of OCD will help us to identify the aforementioned factors:

Case Study

Mrs B, a 34-year-old female, married, graduate, coming from middle class socio-economic status and urban background, living with husband, son of seven years and father-in-law, presented with the complaint of recurrent thoughts about dirt and germs and fear that she will get infected by touching dirty objects around her. As a result, she spent most of her time cleaning and washing things several times before using them, especially kitchen and bathroom items. She is also concerned about guests coming and sitting on the sofa and tries to dissuade them from sitting on the sofa. If they still sit on the sofa, she feels ill at ease thinking how she will manage to clean up after they leave. She finds respite in imagining that the guests are not sitting on the sofa. Since it is difficult to wash the sofa, she uses her moist hands in an attempt to clean the sofa and she makes it a point to thoroughly clean the house to get rid of germs that might have contaminated the house after they leave. She and her family members are very disturbed by her habits. They complained that because of her time-consuming habits, the whole household routine gets disturbed and as a result her husband and son have difficulty maintaining proper schedule for work and school. According to the client, she understands her problem and is distressed by this. But even after trying a lot, she cannot stop her thoughts about dirt and germs and reported that if she wants to stop herself from cleaning, she gets excessive bouts of anxiety and therefore has to yield to the behaviour.

The aforementioned case is an example of a person suffering from OCD having frequent intrusive thoughts of dirt, germ and contamination, and consequently performing compulsive act of washing and cleaning to lessen the anxiety. This is a very typical case with predominant obsessions related to germ and contamination and corresponding washing and cleaning behaviour. However, as has been stated earlier, OCD is a heterogeneous condition with usually more complex and varied symptom presentation. A person with OCD usually has more than one obsession and related compulsions (as seen in the case example, overt compulsion such as washing and covert such as mental images).

This varied and complex presentation makes diagnosis difficult and thus attempts have been made to divide the symptoms into distinct groups or subtypes based on some common grounds such as age of onset, co-morbidity, family history and presence of tic, infections and the like. Investigators have also tried to find symptom dimensions in OCD that will be reliable and replicable across time. The dimensional system can be well understood as potentially overlapping clinical features that falls on a continuum with normal worries related to these thoughts on one hand and extreme and frequent intrusive thoughts on the other and having their first onset in childhood (Leckman, Bloch, & King, 2009). The dimensional concept was first given by Baer (1994) who first factor analysed the Yale Brown Obsessive Compulsive Scale Symptom Checklist (YBOCS-SC), the most widely used OCD symptom scale, to group the symptoms of OCD among the 13 major categories of the YBOCS SC and found three factors that accounted for > 48% of the variance. They were:

1. Symmetry/Hoarding
2. Contamination/Cleaning
3. Pure obsessions

Following Baer's seminal work, Leckman, Walker and Cohen (1997) used the same 13 categories of the Y-BOCS SC on a large sample of over 300 participants. In an attempt to incorporate valid 'traits' they included any OCD symptoms the patients ever experienced in the course of their illness and not only their current status. The results yielded a four-factor model that accounted for more than 60% of the variance. Subsequently, two more noteworthy investigations, first by Summerfeldt, Richter, Anthony, Huta and Swinson (1999) and second by Bloch et al. (2008), involving meta-analyses of existing models involving 5,124 participants, both concluded upon the four-factor model, with similar results in case of children and adults. The four factors are:

1. Forbidden thoughts—aggression, sexual, religious and somatic obsessions with checking compulsions
2. Symmetry—symmetry obsessions repeating, counting and ordering compulsion
3. Cleaning—cleaning and contaminations
4. Hoarding obsessions and collecting compulsions

French researcher David Mataix-Cols and his group (2006) mentioned four distinct symptom dimensions with one more hypothetical dimension that is yet to get sufficient validity. These four dimensions are:

1. Symmetry and ordering
2. Hoarding
3. Contamination and washing
4. Aggression and checking

The hypothetical fifth dimension is somatic/sexual/religious/ mental rituals.

Mataix-Cols and his group (2002) mentioned that these dimensions are overlapping and usually patients do not present with one symptom but more than one or two at a time.

Most studies consistently identified four symptom dimensions. Some studies identified a fifth dimension consisting (in various combinations) of somatic, sexual, religious obsessions and mental rituals ('pure obsessions'), but more research is needed to determine its validity. In most studies, these pure obsessions were highly correlated with checking symptoms and loaded on a single factor named obsessions/checking.

Although the factor analytic model gives us the afore-mentioned OCD dimensions, more research is still needed in this area to prove the dimensional aspect OCD symptoms (Abramowitz, 2005). It should be mentioned here that the factor analytical model does not prove that OCD is dimensional. Factor analysis is only applied to create dimension and thus reduces the heterogeneous presentation of OCD into a more logical approach. The most important points about the dimensional approach are as follows. First, that they are consistent with the severity of the condition of the patient, Second, they are stable in adults but not in children. Third, changes in symptoms occur within but not across dimensions (Mataix-Cols et al., 2002).

A number of studies have been conducted to test the merits and demerits of the dimensional approach, mainly to see if the dimensional approach correlates with other variables such as other symptoms, biometric variables associated with OCD and treatment responses. These investigations have shown that the dimensional approach does have considerable correlation with genetic and biometric factors (Abramowitz, 2005). However, more research is needed to see if the dimensional approach is continuous or it is a categorical concept. Moreover, extensive research in the area of OCD symptomatology is needed to deter-mine the best-fitting dimensional model of OCD.

OCD as a Diagnostic Entity

Until recently, the major theorists were of the opinion that OCD is an emotional disorder with the predominant symptom of anxi-ety. The DSM (published by the American Psychiatric Society) and the ICD (published by WHO) used to classify OCD under the broad classification of anxiety disorder. The main reason for such an approach was that anxiety is a cardinal feature in response to obsessions. Moreover, this anxiety is reduced when the person yields to compulsions. More importantly, other anxiety disorders occur as a co-morbid condition to OCD. But recently with the publication of DSM-V, OCD has been classified under the broad umbrella term of obsessive compulsive-related disorders.

Diagnostic and Statistical Manual of Mental Disorders (DSM) Criteria of OCD

Though it appears similar to ICD-10 criteria, it represents a slightly better definition of OCD. A patient presenting with either obsession, compulsion or both will be diagnosed as having OCD.

DSM-V Diagnostic Criteria for Obsessive Compulsive Disorder (300.3)

A. Presence of obsessions, compulsions or both:
   Obsessions are defined by 1 and 2 or both:

   1. Recurrent and persistent thoughts, urges or impulses that are experienced at some time during the disturbance, as intrusive and unwanted, and that in most individuals cause marked anxiety or distress.
   2. The individual attempts to ignore or suppress such thoughts, urges or images, or to neutralize them with some other thought or action (i.e., by performing a compulsion).

   Compulsions are defined by 1 and 2:

   1. Repetitive behaviours (e.g., hand washing, ordering, checking) or mental acts (e.g., praying, counting, repeating words silently) that the individual feels driven to perform in response to an obsession or according to rules that must be applied rigidly.
   2. The behaviours or mental acts are aimed at preventing or reducing anxiety or distress, or preventing some dreaded event or situation: however, these events or mental acts are not connected in a realistic way with what they are designed to neutralize or prevent, or are clearly excessive.
      Note: Young children may not be able to articulate the aims of these behaviours or mental acts.

B. The obsessions or compulsions are time-consuming (taking more than 1 hour per day) or cause clinically significant distress or impairment in social, occupational or other important areas of functioning.

C. The obsessive-compulsive symptoms are not attributable to the physiological effects of a substance (e.g., a drug of abuse, a medication) or another medical condition.

D. The disturbance is not better explained by the symptoms of another mental disorder (e.g., excessive worries, as in generalized anxiety disorder; preoccupation with appearance, as in body dysmorphic disorder; difficulty discarding or parting with possessions, as in hoarding disorder; hair pulling, as in trichotillomania [hair-pulling disorder]; skin picking, as in excoriation [skin-picking] disorder; stereotypies, as in stereotypic movement disorder; ritualized eating behaviour, as in eating disorders; preoccupation with substances or gambling, as in substance-related and addictive disorders; preoccupation with having an illness, as in illness anxiety disorder; sexual urges or fantasies, as in paraphilic disorders; impulses, as in disruptive, impulse-control and conduct disorders; guilty ruminations, as in major depressive disorder; thought insertion or delusional preoccupations, as in schizophrenia spectrum and other psychotic disorders; or repetitive patterns of behaviour, as in autism spectrum disorder).

Source: DSM-V (American Psychiatric Association, 2013).

DSM-V also makes a provision for specifying whether OCD is presented with good or fair insight, with poor insight or with insight being absent altogether or delusional in nature.

In DSM-V, the concept of OCD has undergone a vast change from being one of the anxiety disorders to being a separate nosological entity in the form of OC-related disorders. This section includes OCD, body dysmorphic disorder (BDD), trichotillomania and two new disorders, hoarding disorder and excoriation (skin picking). The reason for grouping these conditions under the same umbrella term is the common features of obsessive preoccupation and repetitive behaviours present in them. Also, there is a growing body of evidence that emphasize the neurobiological aspects of OCD and aims to group disorders with similar patho-physiological entity under the same group.

This change does not imply that anxiety is absent from OCD, rather anxiety remains a prominent feature in OCD. In many cases, anxiety as such is not reported by the patient in whom prominent obsessions and related compulsions are present. Therefore, it is assumed that these disorders may be having certain distinct pathophysiological mechanisms as well as neural circuitry that are different from other anxiety disorders (Cisler et al., 2009; Fiddick, 2011). Moreover, commonly in OCD, anxiety does not present with the same level of behavioural and physiological arousal as is present in the other anxiety disorders (Goodman et al., 2014). For example, in OCD with exactness/symmetry phenomenon, the patient reports that they perform the rituals until they feel 'just right' instead of feeling relieved or doing it out of anxiety. This sense of inability to inhibit or stop repetitive behaviour until the person feels 'just right' is the reflection of behaviour that follows the dictates of the biological programming. Instead of flexibly modifying behaviour or integrating the environmental input into the behaviour repertoire, the person gets into a repetitive action sequence. This rigid pattern of behaviour develops as a sequel of its survival value at one time point but consequently may lose its survival significance, but remains as a repetitive behaviour without it having a particular necessity in the person's life, and may not be amenable to any form of modification. For example, a person may start having dirt and contamination-related obsessions as a result of a specific life episode, such as a toddler at home who is having frequent bouts of stomach infections due to mouthing objects, but this may continue long after that phase is over with the frequency and intensity of the thoughts increasing or remaining the same over time.

The grouping of OCD and related disorders into a separate nosological entity may be better understood if we understand the concept of obsessive compulsive spectrum disorder (OCSD). The OCSDs are a group of disorders that are said to have certain common and overlapping clinical characteristics as well as common neurobiology, genetics and treatment responses with OCD. The disorders belonging to this group have been divided into clusters based on various paradigms.

- Compulsivity–Impulsivity dimension: The OCSDs are thought to occur along a compulsive–impulsive continuum. The compulsive side consists of those disorders where the predominant feature is harm-avoidant behaviour. Ritualized and repetitive acts are performed in order to relieve the anxiety caused by the perceived harm-related thought. The disorders under this group are OCD, body dysmorphic disorder, hypochondriasis (HYP), depersonalization disorder and anorexia nervosa. On the impulsivity end are those disorders where symptomatic features include reduced sense of threat perception and the behaviours are driven by indulgence of acts with a drive to obtain pleasure, arousal and/or gratification. These include the cluster-B personality disorders, sexual compulsions and self-injurious behaviour. In the middle of the continuum lies the disorder which consists of balance amount of both compulsive and impulsive features such as Tourette's syndrome, trichotillomania and autism.

- Cluster dimension: The OCSDs can also be grouped according to symptom clusters. One cluster consists of disorders of impulse control; this group includes intermittent explosive disorders, kleptomania, pathological gambling, trichotillomania, pyromania, paraphilias and sexual compulsions. Second cluster consists of those disorders marked with excessive preoccupation and concern with physical appearance, body weight or bodily sensations—they include body dysmorphic disorder, eating disorder, HYP and depersonalization disorders. The third symptom cluster consists of neurological disorders such as those having repetitive motor behaviours such as Tourette's syndrome, autism, Asperger's and Sydenham chorea.

- Heuristic model: The heuristic model claims that the disorders falling within the OCSD spectrum have a common pathophysiological mechanism; however, the clinical expression of the different disorders is the result of the differential involvement of either the sensorimotor or cognitive cues. For example, in OCD, the intrusive thoughts lead to compulsive behaviour in order to relieve the anxiety caused by the intrusive thoughts; on the other hand, repetitive behaviours that occur in Tourette's syndrome or autism are the result of sensory intrusions (Leckman, Walker, & Cohen, 1993). According to this view, either sensory or cognitive intrusions are an essential feature in these disorders to give rise to repetitive behaviours.

Apart from the fact that the OCSDs have common clinical features on the basis of which they can be grouped together, it has also been found that these disorders also have similar age of onset, chronicity of clinical course and co-morbidity. Moreover, family and genetic studies have found that people having any of the OCSDs usually have one family member who also has one of the OCSDs (Hollander & Evers, 2004). The current DSM-V without mentioning the spectrum has nonetheless grouped some of the disorders under the nosological entity of OC-related disorders, as has been mentioned earlier. Further research is definitely needed in this area to gather stronger connection between the different disorders, mainly on the basis of the neurobiological and phenomenological mechanisms so that the impression that the groupings are a mere result of similarity in overt symptomology is not portrayed.

Obsessive Compulsive Disorder Criteria for ICD-10

International Classification of Disorders-10 states that a person will have obsessions, compulsions or both for a period of at least two successive weeks to warrant a diagnosis of OCD. Symptoms need not be present for prolonged periods, although the definition specifies at least two weeks. In practice, most patients would have had symptoms for considerably longer periods. It states that symptom should be 'present on most days', although again, in practice, most symptoms are present every day. ICD-10 recognizes three subtypes—predominantly obsessions, predominantly compulsions and mixed type.

Obsession and compulsion share the following features, all of which must be present:

(i) They must be acknowledged as originating within the mind (patient's own thoughts) and not imposed by outside persons; this distinguishes OCD from thought insertion and schizophrenia.
(ii) The obsession and compulsion must be repetitive and unpleasant, and at least one obsession should be acknowledged as either excessive or unreasonable.
(iii) Patient must try to resist thoughts coming into their mind and try to resist performing the compulsive act; resistance to very long-standing obsession may, however, be minimal. At least one obsession that has been unsuccessfully resisted should be present.
(iv) Obsessional thought/compulsion must not be pleasurable in itself, that is, obsessional thought or compulsion provides relief from anxiety but doesn't give patient enjoyment.
(v) Symptoms may cause either distress or some kind of interference with social/individual function, usually by wasting time (ICD-10).

However, ICD-10 criteria do not include a 'benchmark' to which levels of distress/time-wasting can be compared. Moreover, it does not actually state how to make the judgement that the obsession/compulsion is not result of, for example, mood disorders or schizophrenia (Avasthi & Kumar, 2004).

Understanding OCD from Different Perspectives

OCD has now been recognized as a severe, highly prevalent, and chronically disabling disorder affecting between 1% and 3% of the population worldwide (Rasmussen & Eisen, 1992). The clinical phenomenology- and evidence-based support for treatment for OCD have been well delineated across the life span in both children and adults. This vast body of knowledge generated has created the ground for more research needs in the area. It has been felt that the best way to understand and devise effective treatment strategies for any disorder is to understand the development and maintenance mechanisms underlying the condition (Clark, 1997). Such an approach has proved to be effective in a range of psychological disorders (Abramowitz, 1997). A thorough understanding of the development and maintenance of a disorder is very important since reversing these maintenance processes will result in a weakening of 'existing' symptoms (Abramowitz & Houts, 2005). Moreover, it helps to devise strategies to prevent the occurrence of the condition and relapse after successful treatment. In this context, we will be studying in detail the factors that lead to the development and maintenance of OCD.

Brief Historical Perspective

The reporting of obsessive symptoms and ritualized compulsive acts started long back in history. In the early days, it was connected mainly to over religiosity. It was believed that such people were possessed by demons that infiltrated their minds and filled it with impure thoughts and hence they had to perform overly religious acts to rid themselves of sin. This condition was termed 'obsessio', and this explanation predominated in the Catholic dominated European countries during the medieval period (Ellenberger, 1970). It is still, however, a dilemma whether over religiosity predisposed one to OCD or whether it is a form of OCD itself. Cultures that encourage the concept of self-control (in terms of suppressing sexual and aggressive impulses) and where failure to do so leads to sin may promote exaggerated feelings of unworthiness and redoubling of efforts to rise above one's spontaneous impulses. These may lead to obsessional self-criticism and compulsive acts as a way of reproach. With the advent of the reforming Protestants in Europe, however, a change was seen in the conceptualization of the concept of OCD. Writers started describing such people as those in whom irrational fears, mostly of religious origin, became excessive and morbid and led sometimes to total mental breakdown (Stone, 1997).

However, OCD as a medical/psychiatric condition was first mentioned by the French psychiatrist Esquirol in 1838. He coined the term 'monomanie raisonante', a condition in which ones' rational mind is irrationally fixated on some thought or worry to the exclusion of any other thoughts or symptoms (hence 'monomaniae'). Others have also used different terms to describe the condition, calling it 'Folie du doute' (Jean-Pierre Falret, 1890), 'Folie du doute avec delire de toucher' (Henri Le Grand du Saulle, 1875), implying that OCD exists in varying degrees of severity. Pierre Janet (1903) described the condition as developing in stages. He mentioned three stages in which OCD develops—psychasthenia being the first stage in which a person is tormented by excessive doubting about his abilities to the point of having depersonalization, derealization and déjà vu experiences. Second stage is about forced agitation in which repetitive behaviours are the most important expression. OC symptom formation with repeated intrusive thoughts forms the third stage.

These explanations dominated the picture in the early part of the nineteenth century but it was Sigmund Freud and his psychoanalytical explanation of OCD that eventually made a mark which is prevalent in the understanding of OCD till date.

The Psychoanalytical Perspective: Freud and Obsessive-compulsive Neurosis

Sigmund Freud in 1926 wrote that obsessional neurosis was 'unquestionably the most interesting and the most repaying concept of analytic research'. He coined the term 'obsessional neurosis' ('Zwangneurose') and gave the most detailed description of the characteristics of the disorder. The early psychoanalytic writings provide a comprehensive description of the structures and mechanisms responsible for the development of the disorder (Stein, 1997). Indeed, psychoanalytic understanding of obsessional neurosis on the one hand and hysteria on the other hand comprised the two primary sources on which Freud based his understanding of the unconscious and its role in psychopathology. Freud's explanation of obsessional neurosis has evolved over the time in his different writings. The explanation, therefore, has undergone changes with his development of the concepts of psychopathology formation. We have tried to explain his conceptualization of obsessional neurosis as it has been formed with his concepts of psychopathology in his different writings.

Freud described the phenomenology of OCD most extensively in his paper on the famous 'Rat Man' case. Freud used disguised names for all his clients for the purpose of maintaining confidentiality, some researchers claim that this person was actually a lawyer by profession and his name was Ernst Lanzer (Wertz, 2003). However such information is still doubtful. The patient presented with obsessions and related compulsive acts precipitated by the loss of his pince-nez (a kind of spectacle used extensively during that period) together with a story he heard about a man who had been tortured. This story he heard was about a criminal who received hideous punishment: a pot was turned upside down on the criminal's buttock and it contained rats. The rats bore their way into the person's anus. This story made him terrified of rats. He also had other obsessional thoughts that something bad will happen to a lady whom he loved and although his father had passed away some years ago, the client also secretly wished his father would die so he can inherit all the property. These obsessional thoughts hampered his daily living and made decision-making difficult for him.

Freud treated him for around a year and claimed that through the process of treatment he had become symptom-free. Freud postulated that ideas and thoughts of this nature arise from sexual experiences in early life, and when it occurs, the person tries to suppress such thoughts. In obsessional neurosis, according to Freud, the person defends himself against such distressing thoughts by separating it from its affect. Freud stated in 1896 that obsessional ideas are 'transformed self-reproaches which have re-emerged from repression and which are always related to some sexual act that was performed with pleasure in childhood'. The compulsive acts are performed owing to the need to successfully manage the anxiety that emerged as a result of this repression. Freud formulated that Rat Man had sexual experiences in his childhood for which he felt guilt, and feared that his father would find out and punish him. This, according to Freud formed an important basis of his pathology. In this connection, Freud explained the role of unconscious hatred and sadistic impulses in the formation of obsessional neurosis. According to him, the neurotic phenomenon develops from the tussle of a conscious need for affection on one hand and sadistic impulses arising from unconscious hatred on the other hand. In the case of Rat Man, his relation with his father had the same equation—with a conscious need for affection from him, hatred towards his father's punitive ways and his fear of receiving punishment from his father, which left him in perpetual distress.

The concept of unconscious hatred is further elaborated in Ernest Jones' 1913 paper 'Hate and Anal Eroticism in Obsessional Neurosis'. He states that, according to Freud, obsessional neurosis develops as a result of regressive return to the anal phase of psychosexual development. Freud here emphasized the role of punitive disciplining and parental over-control in the anal phase as central to the pathogenesis of obsessional neurosis. The child's natural impulses to eliminate are, in a series of overwrought and harsh disciplining practice, supplanted by parental will to defer elimination (McCann, 2009). Most often the toilet training is initiated and demanded from the child way before the physiological control is achieved and is done in such a severe manner that the child feels totally out of control. In these children, control is forever searched for, but never found (Hertler, 2014). Anal ambivalence arises when, during expulsion, the child treats faeces in a contradictory manner, expelling the matter from the body and at the same time retaining it as if it were a loved object (Fenichel, 1945). In his explanations of the personality features of these individuals, Freud (1908) stated that these people may develop a character triad of orderliness, parsimony and obstinacy.

These traits compel them to do everything on their own because nobody can do it as well as them (Abraham, 1921). (These character traits will be further elaborated upon in the last chapter of the book.)

Psychoanalytic understanding of OCD is not complete without the mention of defences characteristically used in the disorder. We will try to delve into the understanding of the different defences in OCD. We begin by highlighting a case study of a young Indian woman. In his explanations of the symptom formation of OCD, Freud stated that these aggressive and ambivalent impulses break through the defences of repression in the form of unacceptable and intrusive thoughts or impulses (immoral obsessions). When such a thing happens, the patient isolates the feeling and emotion from thought through the defence mechanism of isolation. The thought remains, devoid of its affective value, which is pushed back to the unconscious and thereby one tries to gain control on the unacceptable impulses (Fenichel, 1945; Salzman, 1980). In addition, the client may also seek refuge in philosophical concepts and thoughts and neglect the feeling and emotion that underlies the discomfort, through the mechanism of Intellectualization. The other defence that is commonly used in OCD is that of undoing (Fenichel, 1945), through which the patient systematically completes certain rituals and behaviours to neutralize unacceptable thoughts. Through the process of undoing one tries to atone and make amends for the 'sins committed'. The entire plethora of defences is evident from the case of Mrs P highlighted further:

Case Study

Mrs P, a 32-year-old married female, coming from middle socio-economic status and urban background, and residing with her husband, two daughters and mother-in-law, presented with complaints of intrusive thoughts of dirt and contamination resulting in excessive washing and cleaning together with long hours of praying and frequent checking behaviour. From a detailed case history, it was revealed that these symptoms started insidiously, gaining a steady progress in

(Continued)

(*Continued*)

> severity over a couple of years. During these times, she had undergone a number of abortions which her husband insisted upon because he did not want to have more children and for which he neither displayed any remorse nor tried to provide emotional support to his wife. Mrs P lived in a constant state of turmoil—she felt an excessive sense of guilt because of going ahead with the abortions and committing a sin by killing 'her own children' and agreeing to do so on her husband's insistence. Towards the husband she felt excessive anger for making her do it and guilt because she loved him, and it was her 'duty' to abide by her husband's wishes. This ambivalence was the root of her symptom formation. There was hatred towards her husband as well as towards her own vulnerability in participating in the sinful act, and also the need for love and affection from the husband.

Her excessive involvement in rituals (cleaning, praying, checking) may be thought of as an effort to ward off the unwanted intrusive thoughts from consciousness (undoing)—the process of intellectualization and isolation through which she had tried to separate her intense emotions from the distressing thoughts and channelized it to acts and behaviour to gain control over the situation. Freud stated that undoing and isolation were the two defences that were cardinal to the formation of obsessional neurosis. Esman in 2001 critically analysed the contribution of Anna Freud in the context of development of anal-sadistic traits and its relation to obsessive features. Esman mentioned that Anna Freud reassessed the classical psychoanalytical views and stated the importance of genetic factors as a strong determinant in the development of anal sadistic tendencies. She also mentioned that these inherited anal sadistic character traits determine the person's preference for adopting certain defences over others that give rise to the obsessive features (Esman, 2001).

Later psychoanalytic explanations by theorists differed from the strictly Freudian concept of repression of sexual impulses and formation of defences being the sole explanation for obsessive symptoms. In fact, Freud's emphasis on sexuality was seen to be absurd by certain authors (Stein & Stone, 1997). They shifted from a more sexual explanation to a more psychosocial explanation. Mention should be made of two important proponents of this discipline—Karen Horney and Erik Erikson. As reviewed by Pollak in 1979, Karen Horney opined that obsessive characters were raised by dominating parents who demanded absolute obedience and deference from their children without establishing the necessary love, trust and attachment that is prerequisite for filial allegiance. As a result, although the children obeyed parental demands, they were wrought with anger—anger for being over-controlled and anger for their obedience being made conditional. Horney also theorized that these overcontrolling parents arouse in their children the feeling that the world is unstable and threatening (Hertler, 2014).

Erikson and other ego theorists viewed the formation of obsessive character to overcontrolling and tyrannical parents who bestow approval only when the child conforms to their standard. This rips them of all vestiges of self-determination and autonomy, and increases the self-critical and self-reproaching tendencies in them. Erikson's psychosocial stage of autonomy versus shame and doubt corresponds to Freud's psychosexual anal stage. According to Erikson, at this stage, the child learns to gain control over her body in the form of control over the bowel and bladder movements. This learning helps them to develop the feeling of autonomy, that is, control over themselves and their behaviour. If the child is acclaimed for her achievements, she develops the will to pursue in gaining different skills being naturally motivated following the time table of nature's prescription. She develops high self-esteem and self-worth. On the other hand, if the parents are too harsh and demanding, and her autonomy and initiative are unduly curbed down, it restricts the child's imagination. The child is then afraid of free deployment of thinking and wilfulness, which is found as the root of psychopathology of OCD. The child develops doubt and guilt about their initiative and activities leading to feeling of guilt in case of minimum failure. It reduces their desire for exploration and cultivation of curious enquiry in apprehension of whether it is right or wrong, though it is the basic need for cognitive development. Consequently, their zeal for achievement loses its flow and rhythm that prevents the full blossoming of their potentiality. Here, OCD develops over-conformity at the cost of natural development of wilfulness in cultivating curiosity, taking initiative, intrinsically sensing right and wrong, developing a sense of responsibility and dependability, that is, self-disciplining. The child forms a negative image of self and suffers from low self-esteem. Feelings of guilt and shame regarding their behaviour later develops into negative cognitive-affective schemas about self and the world. Personal responsibility for all actions, perfectionism, uncertainty over outcome and the like forms the root of obsessions later on in life. Instead of the successful resolution of the psychosocial phases, a sense of inadequacy, inferiority, diminished self-esteem develops in them. They fail to develop natural desire for work, feel the pleasure of work completion and pride of doing something well; this may lead to a kind of passivity where they have to drag themselves to do any task which may partially explain their obsessive slowness and rigidity.

Childhood experiences, especially the pattern of attachment with significant others in the person's life has been regarded as the key aspect in the development of adaptive and functional schemas about self and others (Doron & Kyrios, 2005). According to Bowlby (1969, 1973), the emotional bond between the caregiver and the infant in the early days form the basis for this later social, psychological and biological capacities through the construction of internal representations or internal working model (IWMs). IWMs are tacit expectations and attitudes a person holds towards the primary caregiver. These form the basis of his perception of the 'self' and self-worth, and subsequently regulates his expectations and beliefs of whether others around him are trustworthy and controllable (Bretherton & Munholland, 1999; Howes, 1999). In short, it is the parent–child bonding that is fundamental in determining the person's overall perception of self, others and the world.

Thus, although these causal explanations of the psychoanalytical and psychodynamically oriented theories of OCD are a rich source of understanding, many authors feel that it may prove difficult to operationalize and verify them empirically (Pollak, 1979). The question arises, then, that whether these historical views are still relevant in the current understanding and management aspect of OCDs? We find that despite the advances in neurobiology and cognitive behavioural aspects, in the understanding and management of OCD, these dynamic aspects may provide important sources of constructs and hypotheses as was seen in the case of Mrs P described earlier. Second, researchers have stated that despite the success of psychopharmacology and cognitive behavioural management of OCD, there are many cases where psychodynamic psychotherapy is necessary—either as an independent measure or as an adjunct to other modalities (Stein et al., 1997). Therefore, the issue is not whether these explanations are important, but rather, how best to incorporate them in our modern views of this condition.

Recent empirical evidence suggests that psychodynamic psychotherapy is as effective as other more evidence-based therapies such as cognitive behaviour therapy (CBT) with a relatively large effect size. Moreover, the post-treatment outcome of these therapies is far better with less symptom remission compared to other therapies (Shedler, 2010). However, the current literature reveals that there is scanty evidence of any progress in the recent past in the area of psychoanalytic understanding of OCD. This indicates that more work is needed in this discipline to generate more information regarding OCD from a psychoanalytic viewpoint.

Behavioural Approach in Understanding OCD

The behaviour therapy perspective in OCD is developed through a combination of classical and operant conditioning principles working together, especially the two-factor model of fear and avoidance proposed by Hobart Mowrer (1939, 1960). According to Shafran (2005), this model proposed:

> Obsessions are formed when normal intrusive thoughts, images, or impulses become associated with anxiety via classical conditioning so that when an intrusive thought occurs, anxiety increases. The person then learns, via operant conditioning, to reduce obsessional anxiety by escaping or avoiding stimuli that evoke obsessional thoughts. Thus, compulsive behaviour is performed to escape from obsessional anxiety and is negatively reinforced by the reduction in anxiety that it engenders. Moreover, the obsessional anxiety is never extinguished.

An important point to be noted here is that a normally occurring thought/image is getting associated with fear to produce anxiety. Whenever the thoughts/images are occurring, the person is engaging in some act to avoid the anxiety, thus through the process of negative reinforcement, these 'acts' get strengthened as it leads to reduction in anxiety.

The concept of avoidance learning is an important factor in OCD. It is through avoidance learning that OCD is maintained. Thus, it becomes essential to get a thorough understanding of the concept of avoidance learning in order to understand the core clinical concept of OCD from a behavioural perspective. The concept of avoidance learning was first proposed by Solomon and Wynne (1953) with their classical experiment of traumatic avoidance learning. Although Solomon did not propose that their findings have direct linkage to understanding OCD in humans, it still stands as a pioneering work to understand the functional aspect of the disorder.

Solomon et al.'s Experiment on Traumatic Avoidance Learning

The Solomon work on traumatic avoidance was carried out using mongrel dogs, which were placed in a specially built two-chamber shuttle box. The floor of the apparatus consisted of steel grid bars that could be electrified to deliver shock to the animal's feet such that serious injury was prevented, but it was painful and just below an intensity that would produce involuntary muscle movements. During the experimental session, the dogs were placed in one chamber (starting chamber), the lights in the starting compartment were switched off (CS), the grid of the adjacent compartment opened and the lights in the adjacent compartment went on. When the lights of the starting compartment went off, the floor of that compartment became electrified providing shock to the animal (US). The shock remained on until the dog jumped or climbed over the hurdle into the lit compartment, at which point the gate closed and the training trial ended. If after two minutes of shock, the animal still failed to escape the shock, the trial was ended and then restarted after one minute. During the acquisition phase, failure to escape the shock was called a 'shock trial'. Any trial in which the animal got to the other compartment in less than 10 seconds before the shock came on was called an 'avoidance trial'.

It was seen that after a few initial trials most of the dogs learned to avoid the shock with 100% accuracy. Moreover, the animals started jumping as soon as the lights in the starting compartment went off (presentation of CS) and this lead to the concept of avoidance learning through instrumental responding. Importantly, it was observed that the animals had individual difference in their expression of anxiety to the shock, and the more anxious animals learned avoidance responding faster than those with less anxiety. Stereotypical jumping behaviour continued even in the absence of shock. Solomon and his colleagues thus concluded from here that the jumping did lead to 'reduction in anxiety'. According to them, 'The reinforcement of earned avoidance instrumental responses comes about through drive reduction. Early in the learning process when the animal is escaping from shock, the instrumental act removes the US, as well as the CS. Drive reduction then consists of reduction in the intensity of both pain and emotional upset' (Solomon & Wynne, 1953, p. 15).

After this first phase of the experiment, the second, and the most important from OCD point of view, phase of the experiment was conducted to see how the jumping behaviour (avoidance learning) could be extinguished. They designed the experiment by presenting the CS (light off in the starting chamber) with no subsequent shock (US) for a number of trials. Interestingly, they found that although the avoidance learning was completed in about 11 trials on an average for most dogs there was no sign of the learned avoidance behaviours from getting extinguished, even after hundreds of trials the dogs continued to show jumping behaviour with the presentation of the CS indicating the most important formulation that was derived from this experiments, that 'avoidance behaviour once learned is very difficult to extinguish'. Solomon and colleagues also observed some other important facts:

1. With repeated performances the dogs developed their own idiosyncratic pattern of jumping
2. This jumping occurred as part of ritualized behaviour, after presentation of CS, therefore they did not get any time for feeling the anxiety, these responses were routinized and fairly automatic without signs of extended emotional responses and was termed as anxiety conservation hypothesis (Solomon & Wynne, 1954).

Relevance of Solomon's Experiment in Understanding OCD

This classical experiment was important in understanding some of the core clinical concepts of OCD from two important points of view. They gave a functional explanation for the acquisition and extinction of conditioned emotional responses. Later on, after several research ventures this basic concept drawn from the experiments of Solomon et al. were solidified to develop the concept that compulsive behaviour is a form of active avoidance behaviour which leads to anxiety reduction and thus is difficult to extinguish. Their concept may not be appropriate for understanding the aetiology of OCD in humans; in fact, in none of the reports the authors claimed that they tried to explain human OCD through their experiments. The main utility of the concept derived from the knowledge comes in practice when the goal is to extinguish avoidance behaviour. The behaviour therapy models for OCD are based on how to reverse this avoidance behaviour that mainly serves the purpose of anxiety reduction and therefore helps to maintain the core symptom of OCD, that is, ritualized compulsive/neutralizing behaviours.

The behaviour therapy model has shown significant utility in tackling OCD symptoms. Evidence suggests that the most common behaviour therapy model, exposure and response prevention (ERP), is highly efficacious with an estimated 75% of treatment completers improving significantly and remaining improved at follow-up (e.g., Franklin & Foa, 2002). However, there are some limitations of ERP, many people discontinue treatment from fear of confronting the anxiety (Stanley & Turner, 1995); moreover, ERP is found to be non-efficacious when there are covert compulsions (Rachman, 1997). These limitations coupled with the fact that obsessions are cognitive phenomenon and should be understood from that perspective led researchers to investigate cognitive aspects of OCD.

The Cognitive Behavioural Perspective

According to the cognitive behavioural approaches, intrusive thoughts play an important role in the development and maintenance of OCD (Clark, 1999; Kempke & Luyten, 2007; Whittal & McLean, 1999; Whittal, Rachman, & McLean, 2002). Intrusive thoughts are commonly occurring phenomenon in normal individuals, and it passes away without leaving any impact on the person. But in case of people suffering from OCD, the impact of intrusive irrational thoughts becomes overwhelming for the individual owing to their negative appraisals. These negative appraisals lead to feelings of anxiety and compel the individual to perform compulsive/ritualistic acts to get rid of the distress (Kempke & Luyten, 2007). Performing the compulsive acts negatively reinforce the compulsive behaviour and help to maintain the symptom.

Figure 1:1 represents primarily a working model in the understanding of OCD. After a critical incident (trigger), these beliefs and assumptions are activated regarding the meaning of this trigger. This leads to appraisal/interpretation of the triggering incident, which in turn leads to behavioural manifestation (of rituals) and emotional reaction corresponding to it. This often works as a feedback loop which operates to maintain the symptoms. From the case example of Mrs B (mentioned earlier in the chapter), we can say that whenever she is faced with a trigger (dirty objects from kitchen and bathroom), she gets intrusive thoughts of germs contaminating her and as a result she interprets these intrusive thoughts ('I need to be safe and germ-free') as indicators that she needs to act upon it to remove the cause of these distress and relents to compulsive washing behaviour.

According to the model, individuals with OCD symptoms determine how and when to stop the compulsive acts based on their self-formed idiosyncratic rules/criteria. In most cases, these criteria are based on the individual's feeling of 'rightness' achieved after performing the act in a certain way for a certain period of time. For example, a person with an obsession/obsessive thought related to disease may engage in repeated hand washing to remove germs. As the germs cannot be seen, the person may use a feeling of rightness or a specific number of times that his/her hands have been washed as a signal that it is safe to stop the ritual. These types of maladaptive criteria for stopping rituals, in turn, exacerbate symptoms as these arbitrary pattern of dealing leads to exacerbation of symptoms (Myers, Fisher, & Wells, 2009).

Salkovskis' Cognitive Behavioural Theory of OCD

According to Salkovskis (1985), obsessions are formed when people wrongly appraise intrusive thoughts that occur naturally to them. When an intrusive thought occurs these people think that some kind of harm is supposed to take place to them or to

Figure 1.1 *Model Describing the Formation of Compulsive Washing Behaviour in Obsessive Compulsive Disorder*

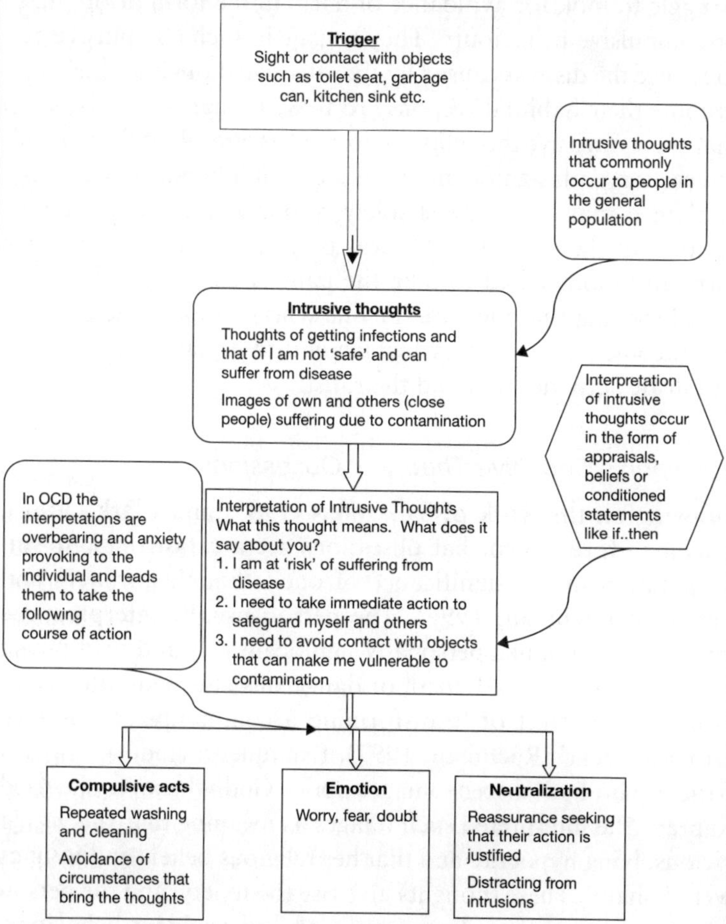

Trigger
Sight or contact with objects such as toilet seat, garbage can, kitchen sink etc.

Intrusive thoughts that commonly occur to people in the general population

Intrusive thoughts
Thoughts of getting infections and that of I am not 'safe' and can suffer from disease

Images of own and others (close people) suffering due to contamination

Interpretation of intrusive thoughts occur in the form of appraisals, beliefs or conditioned statements like if..then

In OCD the interpretations are overbearing and anxiety provoking to the individual and leads them to take the following course of action

Interpretation of Intrusive Thoughts
What this thought means. What does it say about you?
1. I am at 'risk' of suffering from disease
2. I need to take immediate action to safeguard myself and others
3. I need to avoid contact with objects that can make me vulnerable to contamination

Compulsive acts
Repeated washing and cleaning
Avoidance of circumstances that bring the thoughts

Emotion
Worry, fear, doubt

Neutralization
Reassurance seeking that their action is justified
Distracting from intrusions

Source: Authors.

others and that they alone will be responsible for such harms from occurring or in preventing them from occurring (Salkovskis & McGuire, 2003). It is this inflated sense of responsibility for harm to oneself or to others that forms the basis of the person's struggle to look for avoidance of harm in the form of ritualized or compulsive behaviours. They engage in such compulsive acts to reduce the distress caused by the intrusive thoughts which later become their habitual response to these thoughts. It is believed that these intrusive thoughts are formed as a result of the person's interaction with significant others since childhood. When a child is blamed that he or she is solely responsible for the outcome of some of their activity ('He was playing, so the room became dirty and mother had to take the pain of cleaning'), then they start believing that they are the one who is responsible for such an outcome (causes distress) which in turn initiates them to start ritualistic activities to avoid their distress.

Rachman's Cognitive Theory of Obsessions

Drawing on the work of Salkovskis (1985) and Clark (1986), Rachman formulated that obsessions are a catastrophic misinterpretation of the significance of one's thoughts, images and impulses (Rachman, 1997). The person usually interprets the intrusive thought in a personally significant way and as implying that the person is 'bad, mad, or dangerous'. Such an interpretation has the effect of 'transforming a commonplace nuisance into a torment' (Rachman, 1997). Examples include a religious patient who had obscene images about God whenever she tried to pray. She interpreted such images as meaning that she was 'a vicious, lying hypocrite and that her religious beliefs and feelings were a sham'. These thoughts give rise to anxiety, and the person tries to suppress them by neutralizing and avoidant behaviour. Rachman's theory also mentions the cognitive bias of thought–action fusion (TAF). TAF refers to the belief that having an intrusive thought increases the likelihood that a specific adverse event will occur (e.g., 'if I think about someone else falling ill, it makes it more likely that they will become ill').

Purdon and Clark's Cognitive Theory Emphasizing the Importance of Thought Control

In their theory of thought control, Purdon and Clark (1999) stated that (a) faulty beliefs about the importance of controlling one's thoughts and (b) negative misinterpretations of the consequences of failure to control unwanted intrusive thoughts are considered critical to the pathogenesis of obsessional problems. Examples of faulty beliefs include 'I must control every thought that enters my mind, especially negative ones', 'losing control of thoughts is as bad as losing control over behaviour', 'I would be a better person if I could control unwanted thoughts', and 'control over thoughts is an important part of self-control' (Purdon & Clark, 2002). Attempts to control unwanted thoughts through suppression are usually unsuccessful and often lead to a paradoxical increase in the frequency of those thoughts (Rachman, 1998; Salkovskis, 1999).

Cognitive Behavioural Model Emphasizing Danger Expectancies

This is a threat-based model of OCD which states that obsessions develop as a result of appraising the situation as dangerous or threatening, and instead of trying to optimize the danger beliefs the person overreacts and engages in acts to avoid them. Jones and Menzies (1997, 1998a, 1998b) have investigated this model empirically and have attempted to integrate it with Salkovskis' cognitive-behavioural approach by suggesting that the mechanism by which responsibility influences OCD is by impacting estimates of severity of negative outcome (Menzies, Harris, Cumming, & Einstein, 2000). This model has been criticized on the ground that it fails to distinguish between OCD and other anxiety disorders which also has the element of danger perception (Salkovskis, 1996).

Rachman's Cognitive Theory of Compulsive Checking

According to this theory (Rachman, 2002), compulsive checking occurs when people believe that they have a special responsibility to avoid harm but they are unsure whether the perceived threat has been removed or not. Therefore, they go on checking to make sure that the threat has been removed. The intensity and duration of compulsion will depend on the

- Increased sense of responsibility
- Increased probability of harm and
- Increase in the anticipated seriousness of the potential harm

Rachman stated that compulsions recur when the person feels an increase in the sense of responsibility for causing the potential harm, reduction in one's sense self-confidence in tackling anxiety. The theory proposes that by doing compulsive behaviour the person wants to be absolutely sure that they are successful in avoiding harm to oneself and others.

Well's Metacognitive Theory

The effects of thoughts, the need to control them, and beliefs about the importance of monitoring metacognitive theory (Wells, 1997) is based on the principle that 'OCD is a consequence of the over-importance given to thoughts because of underlying meta-cognitive beliefs and processes'. In this model a range of metacognitive beliefs and processes are implicated. Metacognition refers to the beliefs and processes used to appraise, regulate or monitor thinking (Flavell, 1979). According to the metacognitive model, intrusive thoughts or doubts activate meta-beliefs (Wells, 1997) and these beliefs centre on themes of danger and meaning of such thoughts and encompass beliefs about the harmfulness of these thoughts and engaging in perseverative coping strategies such as worry and rumination. Wells (1997, 2000) and Wells and Matthews (1994) proposed a model of OC symptoms in which two domains of metacognitive belief are emphasized:

(1) Thought–fusion beliefs. Three types of fusion have been proposed:

- Thought–action fusion (TAF): the belief that a thought alone can cause a person to carry out, or is equivalent to, an action;
- Thought–event fusion (TEF): the belief that having a thought can cause an event or means that an event has happened and
- Thought–object fusion (TOF): the belief that thoughts or feelings can be transferred into objects. These beliefs are activated by normally occurring intrusions and lead intrusions to be appraised as dangerous or important.

(2) Beliefs about rituals that guide responses to this appraisal have two components:

- Declarative beliefs about the need to carry out rituals (e.g., 'I need to perform my rituals otherwise I will never have peace of mind') and
- Plan or programme for monitoring and controlling action. Part of this plan is a goal which is indicated by a stop criterion or 'stop signal'. Rituals are used to attenuate the appraised consequences associated with the obsessional thought.

These models and explanations form the basis of the cognitive approach in the understanding of the phenomenology of OCD and its management aspects. As an etiological consideration, cognitive-behavioural conceptualization of OCD has generated a large body of empirical support and has led to the development of effective management strategies for OCD. However, most of these works have focused on determining the development and maintenance factors associated with the symptoms and seldom has there been a focus on delineating the underlying vulnerability factors in OCD like the person's concept of himself and perception of others (Doron & Kyrios, 2005). The vulnerability factors that make a person more susceptible to develop OCD are being mentioned herein.

Vulnerability Factors

Some work in the field of cognitive, developmental and attachment areas suggest that a person's internal representation of the self (as suggested by Bowlby) and others form important cognitive vulnerability factors in the development of OC symptoms. Researchers have also found that individual's sense of self-worth is dependent on the person's feeling of competence in several domains, for example, relationship, work life, academics and so on. Consequently, perceived incompetence in those specific domains trigger anxiety and related feelings of threat to self-worth (Harter, 1998). When the individual faces a situation that threatens his sense of self-worth related to these sensitive domains ('If I am not good at this, I am unworthy'), it leads to extreme anxiety. This, in turn, leads to the development of intrusive thoughts and neutralizing behaviours for the management of their anxiety. It has also been found that ambivalent feelings towards different aspects of the self, that is the degree of uncertainty and dichotomy about and preoccupation with the person's self-worth (e.g., I am good or bad, worthy or not worthy) is related to OCD (Bhar & Kyrios, 2000). Researchers have also found that people with OC symptoms have higher degree of ambivalence compared to nonclinical sample. Overall, it can be assumed that parent–child interaction pattern is a very important determinant in the development of self-concept and perception of the world as threatening or non-threatening.

Future research would definitively need to determine the relationship between OC symptoms and specific self and world-view structures. Determining the nature of the association between the self and world representations with respect to core cognitive beliefs (e.g., importance of thought and inflated sense of responsibility) would also be important. Finally, an important area of investigation has to be tackled as to how we should link cognitive behavioural perspective with our progress of neuroscience. These aspects needs more work in order to give us a full and comprehensive understanding of the phenomenon of OCD and would help us to device more effective treatment modes.

Neurobiological Basis of OCD

For a long time OCD had retained its identity as a neurotic condition, and any kind of symptom amelioration was dependent on the successful resolution of internal conflicts through intensive psychoanalytical interventions. However, since the second half of the twentieth century the focus has shifted in search for a more biological basis of the condition. OCD is among the psychiatric disorders with a relatively high rate of heritability. Also, OCD is a genetically heterogeneous disorder and the age of onset of OCD is an important factor that determines familial risk for OCD. According to some authors (Rasmussen & Tsuang, 1986), the lower the age of onset, greater is the possibility that OCD is present in family members. Twin studies show that monozygotic concordance rate is between 53% and 87% and among dizygotic twins it is 22% to 47%). Incidence of OCD and related disorders in first-degree relatives varies between 10% and 22.5% compared to risk in normal community dwellers being 2% to 3% only. However, family history is also absent in a big portion of cases of OCD, especially those with onset at adulthood.

On the other hand, neuroimaging studies have revealed involvement of specific regions of the brain as the pathophysiological mechanism of OCD. Moreover, these findings were supported by studies on cognitive functions (by applying neuropsychological tests) which showed significant deficiency in the areas of attention, memory and executive functions in patients with OCD (Nakao, Okada, & Kanba, 2014). With these advances, the mode of treatment has also undergone massive change. Currently, the most common and effective treatment mode in OCD is pharmacotherapy using selective serotonin reuptake inhibitors (SSRIs) and CBT. Neurobiological studies reveal that intensive pharmacotherapy with SSRIs and CBT bring about changes in the neural networks (Nakao et al., 2014). Functional neuroimaging studies have identified specific regions of the brain such as the orbitofrontal cortex, anterior cingulated cortex, caudate nucleus of the basal ganglia and thalamus as the sites that are found to be disturbed in OCD. In the present chapter, we will be highlighting the neuroanatomical structure that is supposed to be involved in the formation and maintenance of OCD symptoms; also, we will discuss the neuropsychological test findings to highlight the cognitive deficits that accompany the neurobiological abnormalities. We will conclude by highlighting the important aspects that needs further investigation in the current scenario.

Brain Structures Involved in OCD

The neuroanatomical sites found to be closely associated with the pathogenesis of OCD are the basal ganglia, the prefrontal cortex (mainly the anterior cingulated cortex), the dorsomedial nucleus of the thalamus, and certain structures of the limbic system, such as the amygdala and the hippocampus. The basal ganglia is regarded as the main site of pathology formation in OCD (Rauch, Whalen, Dougherty, & Jenike, 1998). Studies have found that abnormal volumetric changes (either increase or decrease in basal ganglia volume) were associated with OCD symptoms (Luxenberg et al., 1988; Robinson et al., 1995; Rosenberg et al., 1997b) although contradictory evidences reports exist (Aylward et al., 1996; Jenike et al., 1996; Stein et al., 1993). Similarly, abnormal volumetric change was also detected in anterior cingulated cortex of OCD patients compared to control (Szeszko et al., 2004). A recent fMRI study suggested that the anterior cingulate may be involved in dysfunctional conflict detection as part of an overactive action monitoring system (hypervigilance towards obsession related themes in the environment) in OCD (Ursu, Stenger, Shear, Jones, & Carter, 2003).

The thalamus plays an important role in information integration and perception (Baxter et al., 1996; Jones, 1997). Evidence suggests that the dorsomedial nucleus of the thalamus is implicated in the pathogenesis of OCD (Alexander, Crutcher, & DeLong, 1990; Cummings, 1993). Apart from these, certain structures of the medial temporolimbic system, such as the amygdala and the hippocampus play an important role in OCD symptom formation. The cybernetic model proposed by Pitman,

Green, Jenike and Mesulam (1987) proposes that the hippocampus plays an important role in compulsive behaviour by maintaining a strong connection with the basal ganglia. Here the role of the hippocampus, mainly the septohippocampus is important as it compares predicted events with actual events. Thus, whenever there is a mismatch between predicted and actual events the septohippocampus directs the attention of the individual to this mismatch so that behavioural control can be enforced. If there is a lesion/dysfunction in the hippocampus, it leads to checking behaviour. The amygdala, on the other hand, is more concerned about conditioned fear response and maintains anxiety and compulsive behaviour in patients (Bechara, Damasio, Damasio, & Anderson, 1995).

Apart from these, certain neurotransmitters have also been found to play an important role in the pathogenesis of OCD. Amongst others, serotonin undoubtedly remains as the most potent neurotransmitter that has been found to play an important role in the pathogenesis of OCD. This view mainly comes from the treatment efficacy result with serotonin reuptake inhibitors (SRIs) (Cartwright & Hollander, 1998; Rosenberg, 2002). The fact that administration of SRI's improves OCD symptoms have led to the formulation of the 'serotonin hypothesis of OCD'. It has been found that serotonin transporter protein (5HTPR) is decreased in OCD patients compared to controls (Bastani, Arora, & Meltzer, 1991; Marazziti, Hollander, Lensi, Ravagli, & Cassano, 1992; Marazziti et al., 1997; Sallee, Richman, Beach, Sethuraman, & Nesbitt, 1996; Sallee, Stiller, Perel, & Rancurello, 1986; Weizman et al., 1986). Another component, the 5-hydroxy-indole-acetic-acid (5HIAA), a primary metabolite of serotonin has been found to be present in an increased level in patients with OCD compared to non-patients (Insel, Mueller, Alterman, Linnoila, & Murphy, 1985; Thoren, Asberg, Cronholm, Jornestedt, & Traskman, 1980). A further evidence of a serotonergic role in OCD is provided by the correlation in decrease in OCD symptom severity and SRI induced reduction in cerebrospinal fluid levels of 5HIAA in platelet serotonin concentration (Flament et al., 1985). Higher pre-treatment levels of 5HIAA is associated with increased severity of OCD symptoms and better response to clomipramine. These findings points to the fact that serotonin does play an important role in OCD and should be regarded as an option that needs further investigation.

Neurocircuits Involved in OCD

Studies suggest that OCD is involved in the metabolic alterations of the activity of the direct and the indirect pathways of the orbitofrontal–subcortical circuits (Saxena & Rauch, 2000). The direct pathway projects from the cerebral cortex to the striatum, then to the internal segment of the globus-pallidus, substantia nigra, pars reticulata (the main output of the basal ganglia) and back to the cortex. The indirect pathway also begins in the cortex and leads to the striatum, to the external segment of globus-pallidus, substantia nigra pars reticulate, and then to subthalamic nucleus, to the thalamus and then back to the cortex. The direct pathway activates the thalamic system and is found to be engaged in the positive feedback loop. The indirect pathway, in contrast, provides negative feedback. The balance between the activation and inhibition of the two pathways determines the function of a number of complex motor functions responsible for facing a number of life situations such as danger, violence, hygiene, order and sex. In OCD, there is a preoccupation with these themes, and it is believed to be mediated by an imbalance between the indirect and direct pathways. For example, a lack of inhibition of the direct pathways (hyperactivity of the thalamic system) may make the patient obsessed about the concept of danger and lead him to be engaged in related ritualistic behaviour.

Deficits in Neuropsychological: Deficits in Neuropsychological Function in OCD

Neuropsychological aspects of OCD have gained focus since the second half of the twentieth century. According to Savage (1998), neuropsychological tests provide an intermediate link between brain dysfunction and cognitive impairment (Savage, 1998). Research evidence points to the fact that cognitive deficiencies occur in OCD especially in the domain of higher cognitive functioning. Studies have consistently shown that patients with OCD have deficits in attention, set shifting and response inhibition. There are also findings that indicate deficiency in planning and decision-making. Working memory and implicit learning was also found to be deficient (Menzies et al., 2008). There is a lot of inconsistent data as to cognitive functioning in OCD patients on areas such as attention and memory (Kuelz, Hohagen, & Voderholzer, 2004) attributing it to myriad factors and confounding patient variables like medication use, onset of illness, selection of controls and comorbid diagnosis. Also, more importantly, studies focusing on delineating the brain regions associated with these deficits yield inconsistent results. All these point to the fact that more extensive investigation is necessary in these areas. In our book, the different chapters will look into different cognitive domains through neuropsychological tools and shed light on these factors. Authors of this book have consistently worked with attention, set shifting, processing speed, planning and working memory in OCD patients and the following chapters will shed light on the same.

This vast body of knowledge as well as the huge amount of inconsistent and discrepant results point to the fact that this area is still inconclusive and needs more extensive investigation. Till recently, a specific brain region, the orbitofronto-striatal loop, was being considered as the most important site responsible for the formation of OC symptoms. However, this region specific deficit is now considered to be a comprehensive explanation of the brain substrate related to OCD. The focus has shifted to studying the whole brain, functionally related to performance of cognitive tasks. Also, it is indicated that more studies should be designed to integrate biological basis (both genetic vulnerability factors and structural abnormalities), cognitive functions and their link with symptom formation in OCD.

Conclusion

The preceding discussion was an attempt to integrate information from various disciplines in the area of OCD to enhance our understanding of the phenomenon of the condition, to provide knowledge as to the areas of research that have been explored till date and how to improvise on that and, most importantly, the information was aimed to provide a groundwork to our understanding of the treatment aspect of OCD, both biomedical and psychological. Current research findings provide evidence as to the role of both neurobiological factors and efficacious psychological management techniques that are widely used as management devices for OCD. However, the need of the hour is to develop stronger collaboration between different disciplines such as psychology, psychiatry, biophysics and genetics for conducting research in this area that will have more credibility and scientific rigour so that the results can be accepted and implemented across various disciplines.

References

Abbruzzese, M., Ferri, S., & Scarone, S., (1997). The selective breakdown of frontal functions in patients with obsessive-compulsive disorder and in patients with schizophrenia: A double dissociation experimental finding. *Neuropsychologia, 35*(6), 907–912.

Abraham, K. (1921). Contributions to the theory of the anal character (D. Bryan & A. Strachey, Trans.). In E. Jones (Ed.), *Selected papers of Karl Abraham* (pp. 370–392). London: The Hogarth Press.

Abramowitz, J. S. (1997). Effectiveness of psychological and pharmacological treatments for obsessive-compulsive disorder: A quantitative review. *Journal of Consulting and Clinical Psychology, 65*(1), 44–52.

Abramowitz, J. S., & Houts, A. C. (Eds.). (2005). *Concepts and controversies in obsessive-compulsive disorder.* New York, NY: Springer Science + Business Media Inc.

Abramowitz, J. S., Schwartz, S. A., Moore, K. M., & Luenzmann, K. R. (2003). Obsessive compulsive symptoms in pregnancy and the puerperium: A review of the literature. *Journal of Anxiety Disorders, 17*(4), 461–478.

Abramowitz, J., Whiteside, S., Kalsy, S., & Tolin, D. (2003). Thought control strategies in obsessive-compulsive disorder: A replication and extension. *Behaviour Research and Therapy, 41*(5), 529–540.

Avasthi, A., & Kumar, D. (2004). Phenomenology of obsessive compulsive disorder. *JK Science, 6*(1), 9–14.

Alexander, G. E., & Crutcher, M. D. (1990). Functional architecture of basal ganglia circuits: Neural substrates of parallel processing. *Trends in Neuroscience, 13*(7), 266–271.

Alexander, G. E., Crutcher, M. D., & DeLong, M. R. (1990). Basal ganglia-thalamocortical circuits: Parallel substrates for motor, oculomotor, 'prefrontal' and 'limbic' functions. *Progress in Brain Research, 85*, 119–146.

American Psychiatric Association. (1994). *Diagnostic and statistical manual of mental disorders* (4th ed.). Washington, DC: American Psychiatric Association.

———. (2001). *Diagnostic and statistical manual of mental disorders* (4th ed., Text Revision). Washington, DC: American Psychiatric Association.

——— (2013). *Diagnostic and statistical manual of mental disorders* (5th ed.). Washington, DC: American Psychiatric Association.

Aylward, E. H., Harris, G. J., Hoehn-Saric, R., Barta, P. E., Machlin, S. R., & Pearlson, G. D. (1996). Normal caudate nucleus in obsessive-compulsive disorder assessed by quantitative neuroimaging. *Archives of General Psychiatry, 53*(7), 577–584.

Baer, L. (1994). Factor analysis of symptom subtypes of obsessive compulsive disorder and their relation to personality and tic disorders. *The Journal of Clinical Psychiatry, 55*(3), 18–23.

Bannon, S., Gonsalvez, C. J., Croft, R. J., & Boyce, P.M. (2002). Response inhibition deficits in obsessive-compulsive disorder. *Psychiatry Research, 110*(2), 165–174.

——— (2006). Executive functions in obsessive-compulsive disorder: State or trait deficits? *Australian and New Zealand Journal of Psychiatry, 40*(11–12), 1031–1038.

Bastani, B., Arora, R., & Meltzer, H. (1991). Serotonin uptake and imipramine binding in blood platelets of obsessive-compulsive disorder patients. *Biological Psychiatry, 30*(2), 131–139.

Baxter, L. R., Jr. (1994). Positron emission tomography studies of cerebral glucose metabolism in obsessive compulsive disorder. *The Journal of Clinical Psychiatry, 55*(Suppl.), 54–59.

Baxter, L. R., Jr., Schwartz, J. M., Bergman, K. S., Szuba, M. P., Guze, B. H., Mazziotta, J. C.,…Phelps, M. E. (1992). Caudate glucose metabolic rate changes with both drug and behaviour therapy for obsessive-compulsive disorder. *Archives of General Psychiatry, 49*(9), 681–689.

Bechara, A., Damasio, A. R., Damasio, H., & Anderson, S. W. (1994). Insensitivity to future consequences following damage to human prefrontal cortex. *Cognition, 50*(1–3), 7–15.

Bhar, S., & Kyrios, M. (2000). Ambivalent self-esteem as meta-vulnerability for obsessive-compulsive disorder. Self-concept theory, research and practice: Advances from the new millennium, Sydney, Australia: Self research Centre (pp. 143–156).

Bloch, M. H., Landeros-Weisenberger, A., Rosario, M.C., Pittenger, C., & Leckman, J. F. (2008). Meta-analysis of the symptom structure of obsessive compulsive disorder. *The American Journal of Psychiatry, 165*(12), 1532–1542.

Bowlby, J. (1969). *Attachment and loss: Attachment* (Vol. 1). New York, NY: Basic Books.

———— (1973). *Attachment and loss: Separation: Anxiety and anger* (Vol. 2). New York, NY: Basic Books.

Bretherton, I., & Munholland, K. A. (1999). Internal working models in attachment relationships: A construct revisited. In J. Cassidy & P. R. Shaver (Eds.), *Handbook of attachment: Theory, research, and clinical applications* (pp. 89–111). New York, NY: The Guilford Press.

Cartwright, C., & Hollander, E. (1998). SSRIs in the treatment of obsessive-compulsive disorder. *Depression and Anxiety, 8*(Suppl. 1), 105–113.

Chamberlain, S. R., Fineberg, N. A., Blackwell, A. D., Clark, L., Robbins, T. W., & Sahakian, B. J. (2007a). A neuropsychological comparison of obsessive-compulsive disorder and trichotillomania. *Neuropsychologia, 45*(4), 654–662.

Chamberlain, S. R., & Sahakian, B. J. (2006). The neuropsychology of mood disorders. *Current Psychiatry Report, 8*(6), 458–463.

Clark, D. (1986). A cognitive approach to panic. *Behaviour Research and Therapy, 24*(4), 461–470.

Clark, D. A. (1999). Cognitive-behavioural treatment of obsessive-compulsive disorders: A commentary. *Cognitive and Behavioral Practice, 6*(4), 408–415.

Clark, D. M. (1997). Panic disorder and social phobia. In D. M. Clark & C. G. Fairburn (Eds.), *Science and practice of cognitive behaviour therapy* (pp. 119–153). Oxford: Oxford University Press.

Cisler, J. M., Olatunjib, B. O., & Lohr, J. M. (2009). Disgust, fear, and the anxiety disorders: A critical review. *Clinical Psychology Review, 29*(1), 34–46.

Coryell, W. (1981). Obsessive-compulsive disorder and primary unipolar depression: Comparisons of background, family history, course, and mortality. *Journal of Nervous and Mental Disease, 169*(4), 220–224.

Cummings, J. L. (1993). Frontal-subcortical circuits and human behaviour. *Archives of Neurology, 50*(8), 873–880.

de Silva, P., Menzies, R., & Shafran, R. (2003). The spontaneous decay of compulsive urges: The case of covert compulsions. *Behaviour Research and Therapy, 41*(2), 129–137.

Dias, R., Robbins, T. W., & Roberts, A. C. (1996). Dissociation in prefrontal cortex of affective and attentional shifts. *Nature, 380*(6569), 69–72.

Doron, D., & Kyrios, M. (2005). Obsessive-compulsive disorder: A review of possible specific internal representations within a broader cognitive theory. *Clinical Psychology Review, 25*(4), 415–432.

Ellenberger, H. F. (1970). *The discovery of the unconscious.* New York, NY: Basic Books.

Esman, A. H. (2001). Obsessive-compulsive disorder: Current views. *Psychoanalytic Inquiry, 21*(2), 145–156.

Fellows, L. K., & Farah, M. J. (2003). Ventromedial frontal cortex mediates affective shifting in humans: Evidence from a reversal learning paradigm. *Brain, 126*(Pt 8), 1830–1837.

Fenichel, O. (1945). *The psychoanalytic theory of neurosis* (Vol. 3). New York, NY: W. W. Norton and Co..

Fiddick, L. (2011). There is more than the amygdala: Potential threat assessment in the cingulate cortex. *Neuroscience & Biobehavioral Reviews, 35*(4), 1007–1018.

Flament, M. F., & Cohen, D. (2002). Child and adolescent obsessive-compulsive disorder: A review. In M. Maj, N. Sartorius, A. Okasha, & J. Zohar (Eds.), *Obsessive-compulsive disorder* (WPA Series Evidence and Experience in Psychiatry) (2nd ed., pp. 147–183). West Sussex: John Wiley & Sons.

Flament, M. F., Rapoport, J. L., Berg, C. J., Sceery, W., Kilts, C., Mellstrom, B.,...Linnoila, M. (1985). Clomipramine treatment of childhood obsessive-compulsive disorder: A double-blind controlled study. *Archives of General Psychiatry, 42*(10), 977–983.

Flavell, J. H. (1979). Metacognition and cognitive monitoring: A new area of cognitive development inquiry. *American Psychologist, 34*(10), 906–911.

Foa, E. B., Kozak, M. J., Goodman, W. K., Hollander, E., Jenike, M. A., & Rasmussen, S. A. (1995). DSM-IV field trial: Obsessive-compulsive disorder. *American Journal of Psychiatry, 152*(1), 90–96.

Franklin, M. E., & Foa, E. (2002). Cognitive-behavioural treatments for obsessive-compulsive disorder. In P. E. Nathan & J. M. Gorman (Eds.), *A guide to treatments that work* (pp. 367–386). Oxford: Oxford University Press.

Freud, S. (1955). Notes upon a case of obsessional neurosis. In J. Strachey (Ed. & Trans.), *The standard edition of the complete psychological works of Sigmund Freud* (Vol. 10). London: Hogarth Press. (Original work published 1909).

Freud, S. (1961). The ego and the id. In J. Strachey (Ed. & Trans.), *The standard edition of the complete psychological works of Sigmund Freud* (Vol. 19). London: Hogarth Press. (Original work published 1923).

Giedd, J. N., Rapoport, J. L., Leonard, H. L., Richter, D., & Swedo, S. E. (1996). Case study: Acute basal ganglia enlargement and obsessive-compulsive symptoms in an adolescent boy. *Journal of the American Academy of Child and Adolescent Psychiatry, 35*(7), 913–915.

Gilbert, A. R., Moore, G. J., Keshavan, M. S., Paulson, L. D., Narula, V., MacMaster, F. P., Stewart, C.M., & Rosenberg, D. R. (2000). Decrease in thalamic volumes of pediatric obsessive compulsive disorder patients taking paroxetine. *Archives of General Psychiatry, 57*(5), 449–456.

Godefroy, O., Lhullier, C., & Rousseaux, M. (1996). Non-spatial attention disorders in patients with frontal or posterior brain damage. *Brain, 119*(1), 191–202.

Goodman, W. K., Grice, D. E., Lapidus, K. A., & Coffey, B. J. (2014). Obsessive compulsive disorder. *Psychiatric Clinics of North America, 37*(3), 257–267.

Gray, J. A. (1982). *The neuropsychology of anxiety: An enquiry into the functions of the septohippocampal system.* Oxford: Oxford University Press.

Hampshire, A., & Owen, A. M. (2006). Fractionating attentional control using event-related fMRI. *Cerebral Cortex, 16*(12), 1679–1689.

Hantouche, E. G., & Lancrenon, S. (1996). Modern typology of symptoms and obsessive compulsive syndromes: Results of a large French study of 615 patients. *Encephale, 22*(Special Number 1), 9–21.

Harter, S. (1998). The development of self-representations. In W. Damon (Series Ed.) & N. Eisenberg (Vol. Ed.), *Handbook of child psychology: Social, emotional, and personality development* (Vol. 3, 5th ed., pp. 553–617). New York: John Wiley.

Hartston, H. J., & Swerdlow, N. R. (1999). Visuospatial priming and stroop performance in patients with obsessive compulsive disorder. *Neuropsychology, 13*(3), 447–457.

Hertler, S. C. (2014). A review and critique of obsessive-compulsive personality disorder etiologies. *Europe's Journal of Psychology, 10*(1), 168–184.

Hodgson, R., & Rachman, S. (1972). The effects of contamination and washing in obsessional patients. *Behaviour Research and Therapy, 10*(2), 111–117.

Hollander, E., & Evers, M. (2004). Review of obsessive compulsive spectrum disorders: What do we know? Where are we going? *Clinical Neuropsychiatry, 1*(1), 32–51.

Horn, N. R., Dolan, M., Elliott, R., Deakin, J. F., & Woodruff, P. W. (2003). Response inhibition and impulsivity: An fMRI study. *Neuropsychologia*, *41*(14), 1959–1966.

Hornak, J., O'Doherty, J., Bramham, J., Rolls, E. T., Morris, R. G., Bullock, P. R., & Polkey, C. E. (2004). Reward-related reversal learning after surgical excisions in orbito-frontal or dorsolateral prefrontal cortex in humans. *Journal of Cognitive Neuroscience*, *16*(3), 463–478.

Howes, C. (1999). Attachment relationships in the context of multiple caregivers. In Jude Cassidy & Phillip R. Shaver (Eds.), *Handbook of attachment: Theory, research, and clinical applications* (pp. 671–687). New York, NY: The Guilford Press.

Humberstone, M., Sawle, G. V., Clare, S., Hykin, J., Coxon, R., Bowtell, R., Macdonald, I. A., & Morris, P. G. (1997). Functional magnetic resonance imaging of single motor events reveals human presupplementary motor area. *Annals of Neurology*, *42*(4), 632–637.

Insel, T. R., Mueller, E. A., Alterman, I., Linnoila, M., & Murphy, D. L. (1985). Obsessive compulsive disorder and serotonin: Is there a connection? *Biological Psychiatry*, *20*(11), 1174–1188.

Insel, T. R. (1992). Toward a neuroanatomy of obsessive-compulsive disorder. *Archives of General Psychiatry*, *49*(9), 739–744.

Jaisoorya, T. S., Janardhan Reddy, Y. C., & Srinath, S. (2003). Is juvenile obsessive-compulsive disorder a developmental subtype of the disorder? Findings from an Indian study. *European Child and Adolescent Psychiatry*, *12*(6), 290–297.

Janet, P. (1903). *Les obsessions et la psychasthenie* [Obsessions and psychaesthenial]. Paris: Felix Alcan.

Jenike, M. A., Breiter, H. C., Baer, L., Kennedy, D. N., Savage, C. R., Olivares, M. J., & Filipek, P. A. (1996). Cerebral structural abnormalities in obsessive-compulsive disorder: A quantitative morphometric magnetic resonance imaging study. *Archives of General Psychiatry*, *53*(7), 625–632.

Jones, E. F. (1997). Cortical development and thalamic pathology. *Schizophrenia Bulletin*, *23*(3), 483–501.

Jones, M. K., & Menzies, R. G. (1997). The cognitive mediation of obsessive-compulsive handwashing. *Behaviour Research and Therapy*, *35*(9), 843–850.

———(1998a). The role of perceived danger in the mediation of obsessive compulsive washing. *Depression and Anxiety*, *8*, 121–125.

———(1998b). Danger ideation reduction therapy (DIRT) for obsessive compulsive washers. A controlled trial. *Behaviour Research and Therapy*, *36*(10), 959–970.

Karno, M., Golding, J. M., Sorenson, S. B., & Burnam, M. A. (1988). The epidemiology of obsessive-compulsive disorder in five US communities. *Archives of General Psychiatry, 45*(12), 1094–1099.

Kempke, S., & Luyten, P. (2007). Psychodynamic and cognitive-behavioural approaches of obsessive-compulsive disorder: Is it time to work through our ambivalence? *Bulletin of the Menninger Clinic, 71*(4), 291–311.

Kiejna, A., Rymaszewska, J., Kantorska-Janiec, M., & Tokarski, W. (2002). Epidemiology of obsessive-compulsive disorder. *Psychiatria Polska, 36*(4), 539–548.

Kuelz, A. K., Hohagen, F., & Voderholzer, U. (2004). Neuropsychological performance in obsessive-compulsive disorder: A critical review. *Biological Psychology, 65*(3), 185–236.

Ladouceur, R., Freeston, M., Rhéaume, Dugas, M., Gagnon, F., Thibodeau, N., & Fournier, S. (2000a). Strategies used with intrusive thoughts: A comparison of OCD patients with anxious and community controls. *Journal of Abnormal Psychology, 109*(2), 179–187.

Ladouceur, R., Dugas, M., Freeston, M., Léger, E., Gagnon, F., & Thibodeau, N. (2000b). Efficacy of a cognitive-behavioural treatment for generalized anxiety disorder: Evaluation in a controlled clinical trial. *Journal of Consulting and Clinical Psychology, 68*(6), 957–964.

Leckman, J. F., Bloch, M. H., & King, R. A. (2009). Symptom dimensions and subtypes of obsessive-compulsive disorder: A developmental perspective. *Dialogues in Clinical Neuroscience, 11*(1), 21–33.

Leckman, J. F., Walker, D. E., & Cohen, D. J. (1993). Premonitory urges in Tourettes Syndrome. *The American Journal of Psychiatry, 150*(1), 98–102.

Leckman, J. F., Grice, D. E., Boardman, J., Zhang, H., Vitale, A., & Bondi, C.,...Pauls, D. L. (1997). Symptoms of obsessive-compulsive disorder. *The American Journal of Psychiatry, 154*(7), 911–917.

Luxenberg, J. S., Swedo, S. E., Flament, M. F., Friedland, R. P., Rapoport, J., & Rapoport, S. I. (1988). Neuroanatomical abnormalities in obsessive-compulsive disorder determined with quantitative x-ray computed tomography. *The American Journal of Psychiatry, 145*(9), 1089–1093.

Marazziti, D., Hollander, E., Lensi, P., Ravagli, S., & Cassano, G. B. (1992). Peripheral markers of serotonin and dopamine function in obsessive-compulsive disorder. *Psychiatry Research, 42,* 41–51.

Marazziti, D., Pfanner, C., Palego, L., Gemignani, A., Milanfranchi, A., Ravagli, S.,...Cassano, G. B. (1997). Changes in platelet markers of obsessive-compulsive patients during a double-blind trial of fluvoxamine versus clomipramine. *Pharmacopsychiatry, 30*(6), 245–249.

Mataix-Cols, D. (2006). Deconstructing obsessive–compulsive disorder: A multidimensional perspective. *Current Opinion in Psychiatry, 19*(1), 84–89.

McCann, J. T. (2009). Obsessive-compulsive and negativistic personality disorders. In P. H. Blaney & T. Millon (Eds.), *Oxford textbook of psychopathology* (pp. 671–691). New York, NY: Oxford University Press.

Menzies, L., Chamberlain, S. R., Laird, A. R., Thelen, S. M., Sahakian, B. J., & Bullmore, E. T. (2008). Integrating evidence from neuroimaging and neuropsychological studies of obsessive-compulsive disorder: The orbitofronto-striatal model revisited. *Neuroscience & Biobehavioral Reviews, 32*(3), 525–549.

Menzies, R. G., Harris, L. M., Cumming, S. R., & Einstein, D. A. (2000). The relationship between inflated personal responsibility and exaggerated danger expectancies in obsessive-compulsive concerns. *Behaviour Research and Therapy, 38*(10), 1029–1037.

Mowrer, O. H. (1939). Anxiety and learning. *Psychological Review, 46*(6), 517–518.

———(1960). *Learning theory and behaviour.* Oxford: Wiley.

Myers, S. G., Fisher, P. L., & Wells, A. (2009). Metacognition and cognition as predictors of obsessive-compulsive symptoms: A prospective study. *International Journal of Cognitive Therapy, 2*(2)(Special Section: Metacognition), 132–142.

Nagahama, Y., Okada, T., Katsumi, Y., Hayashi, T., Yamauchi, H., Oyanagi, C.,...Shibasaki, H. (2001). Dissociable mechanisms of attentional control within the human prefrontal cortex. *Cerebral Cortex, 11*(1), 85–92.

Nakao, T., Okada, K., & Kanba, S. (2014). Neurobiological model of obsessive-compulsive disorder: Evidence from recent neuropsychological and neuroimaging findings. *Psychiatry and Clinical Neurosciences, 68*(8), 587–605.

Nielen, M. M., Veltman, D. J., de Jong, R., Mulder, G., & den Boer, J. A. (2002). Decision making performance in obsessive compulsive disorder. *Journal of Affective Disorders, 69*(1–3), 257–260.

Pitman, R. K. (1987). A cybernetic model of obsessive-compulsive psychopathology. *Comprehensive Psychiatry, 28*(4), 334–343.

Pitman, R. K., Green, R. C., Jenike, M. A., & Mesulam, M. M. (1987). Clinical comparison of Tourette's disorder and obsessive-compulsive disorder. *The American Journal of Psychiatry, 144*(9), 1166–1171.

Pollak, J. (1979). Obsessive-compulsive personality: A review. *Psychological Bulletin, 86*(2), 225–241.

Purdon, C., & Clark, D. A. (1999). Metacognition and obsessions. *Clinical Psychology and Psychotherapy, 6*(2), 102–110.

——— (2002). Mental control beliefs and appraisals in OCD. In R. O. Frost & G. Steketee (Eds.), *Cognitive approaches to obsessions and compulsions: Theory, assessment and treatment* (pp. 29–43). Oxford: Elsevier.

Rachman, S. (1997). A cognitive theory of obsessions. *Behaviour Research and Therapy, 35*(9), 793–802.

Rachman, S. (1998). A cognitive theory of obsessions: Elaborations. *Behaviour Research and Therapy, 36*(4), 385–401.

—— (2002). A cognitive theory of compulsive checking. *Behaviour Research and Therapy, 40*(6), 625–639.

Rachman, S., & de Silva, P. (1978). Abnormal and normal obsessions. *Behaviour Research and Therapy, 16*(4), 233–248.

Rasmussen, S. A., & Tsuang, M. T. (1984). The epidemiology of obsessive compulsive disorder. *The Journal of Clinical Psychiatry, 45*(11), 450–457.

—— (1986). Clinical characteristics and family history in DSM-III obsessive-compulsive disorder. *The American Journal of Psychiatry, 143*(3), 317–322.

Rasmussen, S.A. & Eisen, J.L. (1990). Epidemiology of obsessive compulsive disorder. *Journal of Clinical Psychiatry, 51*(2, Suppl), 10–13.

—— (1992). *The epidemiology and differential diagnosis of obsessive compulsive disorder. Journal of Clinical Psychiatry, 53*(April); suppl: 4–10.

Rauch, S. L., Whalen, P. J., Dougherty, D. D., & Jenike, M. A. (1998). Neurobiological models of obsessive compulsive disorders. In M. Jenike (Ed.), *Obsessive-compulsive disorders: Practical management* (pp. 222–253). Boston, MA: Mosby.

Roberts, A. C., Robbins, T. W., Everitt, B. J., & Muir, J. L. (1992). A specific form of cognitive rigidity following excitotoxic lesions of the basal forebrain in marmosets. *Neuroscience, 47*(2), 251–264.

Robinson, D., Wu, H., Munne, R. A., Ashtari, M., Alvir, J. M., Lerner, G.,...Bogerts, B. (1995). Reduced caudate nucleus volume in obsessive-compulsive disorder. *Archives of General Psychiatry, 52*(5), 393–398.

Rogers, R. D., Andrews, T. C., Grasby, P.M., Brooks, D. J., & Robbins, T. W. (2000). Contrasting cortical and subcortical activations produced by attentional-set shifting and reversal learning in humans. *Journal of Cognitive Neuroscience, 12*(1), 142–162.

Rosenberg, D. R. (2002). Selective serotonin-reuptake inhibitors. In D. R. Rosenberg, P. A. Davanzo, & S. Gershon (Eds.), *Pharmacotherapy for child and adolescent psychiatric disorders* (Rev. and expanded 2nd ed., pp. 223–296). New York, NY: Marcel Dekker.

Rosenberg, D. R., Keshavan, M. S., O'Hearn, K. M., Dick, E. L., Bagwell, W. W., Seymour, A. B.,...Birmaher, B. (1997). Fronto-striatal measurement of treatment-naive pediatric obsessive compulsive disorder. *Archives of General Psychiatry, 54*(9), 824–830.

Sachdev, P. S., & Malhi, G. S., (2005). Obsessive-compulsive behaviour: A disorder of decision-making. *Australian and New Zealand Journal of Psychiatry, 39*(9), 757–763.

Salkovskis, P. (1985). Obsessional-compulsive problems: A cognitive-behavioural analysis. *Behaviour Research and Therapy, 23*(5), 571–583.

Salkovskis (1989). Cognitive-behavioural factors and the persistence of obsessional problems. *Behaviour Research and Therapy, 27*(6), 677–682.

——— (1996). The cognitive approach to anxiety: Threat beliefs, safety seeking behaviour, and the special case of health anxiety and obsessions. In P. M. Salkovskis (Ed.), *Frontiers of cognitive therapy* (pp. 48–74). New York, NY: Guilford.

——— (1999). Understanding and treating obsessive-compulsive disorder. *Behaviour Research and Therapy, 37*(Suppl. 1), S29–S52.

Salkovskis, P., & McGuire, J. (2003). Cognitive-behavioural theory of OCD. In R. Menzies & P. de Silva (Eds.), *Obsessive compulsive disorder: Theory, research and treatment* (pp. 39–58). Chichester: Wiley.

Salkovskis, P., Westbrook, D., Davis, J., Jeavons, A., & Gledhill, A. (1997). Effects of neutralizing on intrusive thoughts: An experiment investigating the etiology of obsessive-compulsive disorder. *Behaviour Research and Therapy, 35*(3), 211–219.

Sallee, F., Stiller, R., Perel, J., & Rancurello, M. (1986). Targeting imipramine dose in children with depression. *Clinical Pharmacology and Therapeutics, 40*(1), 8–13.

Sallee, F. R., Richman, H., Beach, K., Sethuraman, G., & Nesbitt, L. (1996). Platelet serotonin transporter in children and adolescents with obsessive-compulsive disorder or Tourette's syndrome. *Journal of the American Academy of Child and Adolescent Psychiatry, 35*(12), 1647.

Salzman, L. (1980). *Treatment of the obsessive personality.* New York, NY: Jason Aronson.

Savage, C. R. (1998). Neuropsychology of obsessive-compulsive disorder: Research findings and treatment implications. In M. A. Jenike, L. Baer, & W. E. Minichiello (Eds.), *Obsessive-compulsive disorders: Practical management* (3rd ed., pp. 254–275). St. Louis, MO: Mosby.

Saxena, S., & Rauch, S.L. (2000) Functional neuroimaging and the neuroanatomy of obsessive-compulsive disorder. *Psychiatric Clinics of North America, 23*(3), 563–586.

Shafran, R. (2005). Cognitive-behavioural models of OCD. In J. S. Abramowitz & A. C. Houts (Eds.), *Concepts and controversies in obsessive-compulsive disorder* (pp. 229–252). New York, NY: Springer.

Shedler, J. (2010). The efficacy of psychodynamic psychotherapy. *American Psychologist, 65*(2), 98–109.

Solomon, R. L., & Wynne, L. C. (1953). Traumatic avoidance learning: Acquisition in normal dogs. *Psychological Monographs: General and Applied, 67*(4), 1–19.

——— (1954). Traumatic avoidance learning: The principles of anxiety conservation and partial irreversibility. *Psychological Review, 61*(6), 353–385.

Stanley, M. A., & Turner, S. M. (1995). Current status of pharmacological and behavioural treatment of obsessive-compulsive disorder. *Behavior Therapy, 26*(1), 163–186.

Stein, D. J., Hollander, E., Chan, S., DeCaria, C. M., Hilal, S., Liebowitz, M. R., & Klein, D. F. (1993). Computed tomography and neurological soft signs in obsessive-compulsive disorder. *Psychiatry Research: Neuroimaging, 50*(3), 143–150.

Stein, D. J., Bouwer, C., Hawkridge, S., & Emsley, R. A. (1997). Risperidone augmentation of serotonin reuptake inhibitors in obsessive-compulsive and related disorders. *The Journal of Clinical Psychiatry, 58*(3), 119–122.

Stone, M. H. (1997). Introduction: The history of obsessive compulsive disorder from the early period to the turn of the twentieth century. In D. J. Stein & M. H. Stone (Eds.), *Essentials papers on obsessive compulsive disorder*. New York, NY: New York University Press.

Stein, D. J., & Stone, M. H. (Eds.). (1997). *Essentials papers on obsessive compulsive disorder*. New York, NY: New York University Press.

Summerfeldt, L. J., Richter, M. A., Antony, M. M., & Swinson, R. P. (1999). Symptom structure in obsessive-compulsive disorder: A confirmatory factor-analytic study. *Behaviour Research and Therapy, 37*(4), 297–311.

Swedo, S. E. (1994). Sydenham's chorea: A model for childhood autoimmune neuropsychiatric disorders. *Journal of the American Medical Association, 272*(22), 1788–1791.

Szeszko, P. R., MacMillan, S., McMeniman, M., Chen, S., Baribault, K., Lim, K. O.,... Rosenberg, D. R. (2004a). Brain structural abnormalities in psychotrophic drug-naive pediatric obsessive compulsive disorder. [Manuscript submitted for publication.]

Szeszko, P. R., MacMillan, S., McMeniman, M., Lorch, E., Madden, R., Ivey, J.,...Rosenberg, D. R. (2004b). Decrease in amygdala volume in pediatric patients with obsessive-compulsive disorder treated with paroxetine. [Manuscript submitted for publication.]

Szeszko, P. R., Robinson, D., Alvir, J. M., Bilder, R. M., Lencz, T., Ashtari, M.,...Bogerts, B. (1999). Orbital frontal and amygdala volume reductions in obsessive-compulsive disorder. *Archives of General Psychiatry, 56*(10), 913–919.

Thoren, P., Asberg, M., Cronholm, B., Jornestedt, L., & Traskman, L. (1980). Clomipramine treatment of obsessive compulsive disorder: I. A controlled clinical trial. *Archives of General Psychiatry, 37*(11), 1281–1285.

Ursu, S., Stenger, V. A., Shear, M. K., Jones, M. R., & Carter, C. S. (2003). Overactive action monitoring in obsessive-compulsive disorder: Evidence from functional magnetic resonance imaging. *Psychological Science, 14*(4), 347–353.

Veale, D. M., Sahakian, B. J., Owen, A. M., & Marks, I. M. (1996). Specific cognitive deficits in tests sensitive to frontal lobe dysfunction in obsessive-compulsive disorder. *Psychological Medicine, 26*(6), 1261–1269.

Watkins, L. H., Sahakian, B. J., Robertson, M. M., Veale, D. M., Rogers, R. D., Pickard, K. M.,...Robbins, T. W. (2005). Executive function in Tourette's syndrome and obsessive-compulsive disorder. *Psychological Medicine, 35*(4), 571–582.

Weizman, A., Carmi, M., Hermesh, H., Shahar, A., Apter, A., Tyano, S., & Rehavi, M. (1986). High-affinity imipramine binding and serotonin uptake in platelets of eight adolescent and ten adult obsessive-compulsive patients. *The American Journal of Psychiatry, 143*(3), 335–339.

Wells, A. (1997). *Cognitive therapy of anxiety disorders: A practice manual and conceptual guide.* Chichester: Wiley.

———. (2000). *Emotional disorders and metacognition: Innovative cognitive therapy.* Chichester: Wiley.

Wells, A., & Matthews, G. (1994). *Attention and emotion: A clinical perspective.* Hove: Lawrence Erlbaum.

Wertz, F. J. (2003). Freud's case of the rat man revisited: An existential phenomenological socio-historical analysis. *Journal of Phenomenological Psychology, 34*(1), 47–78.

Whittal, M. L., & McLean, P. D. (1999). GBT for OGD: The rationale, protocol, and challenges. *Cognitive and Behavioral Practice, 6*(4), 383–396.

Whittal, M. L., Rachman, S., & McLean, P. D. (2002). Psychosocial treatment for OGD: Combining cognitive and behavioural treatment. In G. Simos (Ed.), *Cognitive behaviour therapy: A guide for the practising clinician* (pp. 125–149). Hove: Pacific Press.

2

History Taking, Mental Status Examination and Assessment

Sreemoyee Tarafder and Pritha Mukhopadhyay

Case Study

Priya, a 41-year-old woman, graduate, homemaker, married for 17 years living in a nuclear family presented herself with the complaints of being prone to tension, finicky about cleanliness and hygiene to the extent that she rewashes clothes and utensils after the maid has washed them for the past one year. She feels that she is slow in her everyday activities and has a high need for perfectionism. She has thoughts that she explains as being unwanted, guilt inducing and 'dirty'. For example, she is constantly plagued by thoughts that she will 'kick God', has 'sexual thoughts about God while praying' and thoughts regarding death of her child. She further narrates that she feels so distressed with these thoughts that she tries to substitute them with other thoughts, for instance, she tries to substitute the thought about the death of son with her own death or harm upon herself. Her thoughts induce so much guilt that she is unable to share her distress with her husband. Bottling it up inside her makes her restless, sad and irritable, and she is often impulsively rude and regrets it later on. She even cries often and wishes to die as she feels that she is responsible for her thoughts and is petrified that it will become real. She reports being sensitive to criticism, is by nature an introvert and passive in her communication pattern.

Raghav, a 32-year-old man, walks into the clinic with his parents, late by half an hour. The son, according to his mother, took thirty minutes to groom himself and was checking to see if his shoelaces are in perfect loops. Additionally, his hair is extremely well combed—not even a strand out of place—his shirt is crisp, buttoned up and indeed the shoe laces are in perfect loops. When the problem is narrated by the family members it becomes clear why the gentleman could have spent half an hour over the shoelaces. His mother said that he has met over 50 prospective brides, has not liked even one of them and his inability to take decision is really bothersome for the family. On inquiry, it was found out that the man spent an enormous amount of time even while picking up a shirt. His family members have stopped accompanying him for shopping as they get bored with his nitpicking tendencies. He is looking for the 'perfect bride', as he feels that marriage is a very important decision in his life, and if he hastily takes that decision, just because his parents like the bride, he is liable to ruin his future. He also seeks repeated reassurance from his parents regarding his choices and really wants to do the 'right' thing and marry Ms Right!

Priya presented with the typical symptoms of obsessions in her preoccupation with contamination, blasphemous and aggressive thoughts, and common compulsions of cleaning, washing and covert compulsion of thought substitution. Raghav, on the other hand, did not present with any cleaning and washing obsessions, nor is he a checker in the strictest sense of the word. This does not in any way indicate that he does not have a problem. It is affecting his social and family life and causing him distress too. The clients may always not present with the typical rituals and compulsions that are commonly seen in obsessive compulsive disorder (OCD). OCD is the name given to a set of heterogeneous symptom characteristics with the commonality of the presence of obsessions and compulsions. It is crucial that while assessing a client for OCD, its myriad aspects are taken into account. The assessment chapter starts with the focus on case history taking and specifics to be kept in mind while conducting mental status examination (MSE). This chapter will be especially significant for novices and students who need some help in identifying obsessions, compulsions, obsessive compulsive (OC) traits and symptoms.

Case History Taking

At the outset when case history is elicited from the client, care should be taken to comprehensively rule out generalized anxiety disorder, phobia, panic disorder, psychotic symptoms and organicity, especially where basal ganglia may be involved/affected. It is imperative to look into one's family history, whether positive or not, to even check for obsessive traits such as perfectionism, hoarding and being finicky. Often a pre-morbid personality pattern with a propensity to being pious, 'ultra good' and 'moral' with hypersensitivity towards criticism is found in clients who later on seek help for their OC symptoms. The narratives given by the clients regarding their lives are much detailed and meticulous where they may even be reporting conversations verbatim and feel disturbed if they are unable to recall the exact details. The case history narration may not talk about childhood traumas and/or sexual abuse but more often than not mention strict moral codes of conduct being instilled in them right from childhood; here being an 'ideal girl' or an 'ideal boy' was emphasized by their parents.

MSE is a cross-sectional detailed observational record of an individual by the clinician. The specifics of the MSE are charted in the following table, keeping in mind student readers who may not be well acquainted with OCD symptomatology. These are details pertaining to patients suffering from OCD. There are many books that focus on the MSE with elaborate details and numerous examples from clinical pathologies, but this chapter focuses on what the clinician needs to look at while diagnosing a client with OCD (see Table 2.1).

Table 2.1	Mental Status Examination (MSE)
Domain	**Findings**
General appearance and behaviour	The patients suffering from OCD are mostly constricted in terms of posture; they appear to be somewhat withdrawn keeping their extremities close to their torsos. Often it is a good idea to look out for skin lesions and peeling of skin and rashes owing to over use of water. Women often look tidy, finicky and guarded. Scanning the environment may be observed and they look about suspiciously while talking to the examiner. They also give out details cautiously. Generally appear stiff.
Attitude towards examiner	The clients often feel that their problem is 'unique' in nature and feels that the therapist/clinician may not be able to understand them. Hence, the repetitive presentation of problems. The patients often have a list or case history in written format, so as to not miss out on important details. Presence of reassurance seeking, dependence and checking to understand whether the examiner has indeed comprehended what has been communicated is commonly seen. Not wanting to end the session, or coming back to report something that was apparently left out during session. Clients often write or record the session, lacking in cognitive confidence. Can be guarded towards examiner, but mostly rapport is established with ease.
Psycho-motor activity	Slowness may be marked. They are also fussy, looking out for dust and germs, often hesitate to sit down on chair. May have some repetitive mannerisms especially related to grooming such as settling hair, collar, pleats of saree, neatly folded and pinned dupatta is uniformly seen. Even while seated, they look ill at ease, often sitting at the edge of the chair. One may even observe some ritualistic hand movements or twitching as if to brush off dust or even at times to pray.

(Continued)

Table 2.1	Continued
Domain	**Findings**
Speech	Although a lot can be written about the speech pattern of patients suffering from OCD, what is most commonly observed is speech that is repetitive, definitely circumstantial, at times pedantic and may be seethed in religious and moral content. Feeling unsure in being able to make the examiner fully understand his/her issue, they may often use synonyms or repetitive sentences to explain the same theme over and over again.
Attention	Patients of OCD can mostly attend and sustain their attention, but may feel that he/she is unable to fully concentrate on the session. Lack of cognitive confidence may be noted here. Lapses in attention may be noted especially when examiner tries to challenge or channelize their focus from the long-drawn symptom narration.
Orientation	Mostly intact, may even be a little too particular in terms of reporting. For example, they may say, 'It's 1:34 PM, I think' when asked to estimate whether its morning or afternoon. Meticulous reporting is an obsessive trait and may even be observed in family members.
Memory	Patients may feel that they are forgetting, whereas there may be no lapses noticeable to the examiner. Poor cognitive confidence is a major player in this case too. Less overall confidence in memory is a characteristic finding across studies (Constans, Foa, Franklin, & Mathews, 1995; Foa, Amir, Gershuny, Molnar, & Kozak, 1997; Hermans et al., 2008, MacDonald, Antony, Macleod, & Richter, 1997; McNally & Kohlbeck, 1993; Tolin et al., 2001). Often they may have to recheck as they may not be able to recall whether they have actually done it or not. Poor memory for actions also adds on to their discomfort regarding memory. Clients suffering from OCD mostly perform at par

Domain	Findings
	with others, but doubt prevails. van den Hout and Kindt (2003) have suggested that excessive checking leads to reduced memory confidence.
Intelligence	General intellectual abilities, memory and attention have been found to be adequate in patients with OCD. Although the patients are mostly at par with most, they are often doubtful about their own abilities.
Level of abstraction	Proverb interpretation and unusual uses often yield rigid answers from them. Usually best tested through an uncommon proverb where they mostly provide very concrete linguistic answers, not touching upon the deeper meaning, refusing to read in between the lines. Often it is said for OCD that they cannot see the forest for trees. Category fluency and phonemic fluency too often show a paucity of responses within a time frame, when bounded by certain conditions. For example, they may not be able to report more than two or three words beginning with 'F' when the condition bans proper nouns. In terms of category fluency also, when the restriction is imposed, patients with OCD get thoroughly confused and perform below par. For example, if they are asked to name animals, with the exception of birds and fish, they are at a loss and cannot report it, owing to deficit in response generation.
Decision-making	Decision-making is poor as they fail to monitor all the relevant variables needed to come to a conclusion. Approach avoidance conflict is much noticeable, mostly finding it difficult to decide owing to their ambivalence. They often regret if they are forced to make a choice, feeling guilty that they have not chosen the other alternative as even that option seems equally lucrative. They take a lot of time to consider all alternatives and all parameters.

(Continued)

Table 2.1	*Continued*
Domain	**Findings**
Decision-making	Decision-making needs to be assessed in OCD. Before they come to a decision, they mull over all possible outcomes of the decision. Their inability to quickly decide distresses them as they are unable to work out the valences of each of the poles. This can be understood through their reassurance-seeking behaviour when they insist that someone else should decide on their behalf or sanction the option that they have chosen.
Mood and affect	Mostly anxious affect with visible restlessness and depression is noticeable as common sequelae. Reactivity and congruence is mostly adequate.
Thought	Obsessions are to be considered under the heading of thought possession in MSE. Obsessive themes related to contamination, scrupulosity, blasphemy, sexuality, aggression, perfectionism and doubt are to be looked into. Obsessions are usually unwanted, unavoidable, intrusive, ego-dystonic, occasionally frightening or violent and often impair functioning and quality of life (Eisen, Mancebo, Pinto, Coles, & Rasmussen, 2006). In terms of thought content, presence of endless rumination may be commonly reported by clients, wherein they keep pondering over worst case scenarios and think of (im)possible misfortunes. Metacognitive beliefs of negative worry beliefs regarding harm and danger, beliefs related to thought control and poor cognitive confidence is very common in clients suffering from OCD. Obsessive images that may plague the client may be vivid but are always known by the patient to be products of his own mind. These images have been considered by de Silva (1986) to be one of four types. 1. The 'obsessional image' depicts repetitively the unwanted intrusive cognition—images of blood flowing, injuries and so on.

Domain	Findings
	2. The 'compulsive image' depicts compulsive behaviour by either rectifying an obsessional image—the woman who saw corpses in coffins and had to imagine the same people standing there—or replacing it with an independent compulsive image.
	3. The 'disaster image' affects compulsive checkers who may not only fear that disaster will occur unless they check but also 'see' the disaster happening in fantasy—the house burning down if the gas is not turned off.
	4. The 'disruptive image' may intrude while compulsive rituals are being carried out and necessitate the ritual being recommended.

In terms of beliefs, dysfunctional beliefs have been identified by the Obsessive Compulsive Cognitions Working Group (OCCWG). The OCCWG (1997) originally concluded that six rationally derived belief domains were of central importance in OCD:

• Inflated responsibility
• Over importance of thoughts
• Control of thoughts
• Overestimation of threat
• Intolerance of uncertainty
• Perfectionism

These patterns are commonly observed in patients and can coexist with thought–action fusion. Patients often believe with conviction that thinking about an unpleasant situation makes it more likely to occur in reality. For instance, thinking about an accident involving one's child will invariably increase the probability of it happening in real life. Even having an immoral thought is considered as being morally equivalent to immoral actions. For example, the thought that having a sexual fantasy about a cousin is morally equivalent to incest (Rachman, 1998; Wells, 1997).

(Continued)

Table 2.1	Continued
Domain	**Findings**
Perception	Absence of hallucination or other perceptual dysfunctions is the norm in OCD. One needs to check for pseudo-hallucination and relate it to the level of insight of the sufferer. People with poor insight OCD may experience certain psychotic symptoms.
Judgement	Comprehension skills are apparently adequate, with concreteness in terms of finer personal judgements. Social and test judgement may not be reflective of their inability to decontextualize in accordance with the situation. Judgement based on moral relativism is absent in them. For instance, they may know what is 'right' and 'wrong' much too decisively but may not be able to use tact, and bracket all deviations as 'wrong'.
Insight	Range that varies from intellectual insight to the problem of complete lack of insight. The variation is in terms of severity, co-morbidity, ranging from congruence to incongruence.

Source: Authors.

From the MSE, it can be seen that there are distinct areas that set the patient with OCD apart from the rest of the patient population. These areas need to be probed further to start off with treatment of these patients. Although for major aspects of MSE, assessments are done based on observation, some tools and tests are additionally used to look into the areas of thoughts including belief systems, mood state and executive functions, especially attention, abstraction, planning, memory, decision-making, hypothesis testing, response inhibition. These assessments guide in understanding of the underlying disposition and thus gives us a framework on which to base our treatment, tailor-making the treatment mode to target pinpointed areas of concern.

Assessment

Baseline measures have to be taken as soon as the client comes for therapeutic intervention. Baseline should include Yale Brown Obsessive Compulsive Scale (YBOCS), Leyton Obsessional Inventory (LOI), Beck Depression Inventory (BDI), Metacognition Questionnaire (MCQ) or Obsessive Beliefs Questionnaire (OBQ) in order to determine the status of the clients in terms of severity and spread of symptoms and primary dysfunctional beliefs.

Severity of Obsession and Compulsions

Assessments in OCD essentially should start with the assessment of the nature of the obsessions and compulsions. It can be achieved through the use of symptom checklists. The most useful of the available checklist is YBOCS, which gives information regarding both obsessive symptom severity and the group of obsessions and compulsions that a patient is suffering from; rated on a scale from 0 to 4, in ascending order of severity. It is particularly helpful for students to remember the following acronym DRTIC that stands for the domains assessed on YBOCS.

D: Distress (the amount of distress that the obsession or compulsion causes to the client)

R: Resistance (the degree to which the obsession or compulsion is resisted by the client)

T: Time (the amount of time spent in indulging in obsession or compulsion by the client)

I: Interference (the extent of hindrance that the obsession or compulsion results in)

C: Control (the level to which the client can overcome the obsession or compulsion)

In Priya's case, administration of the YBOCS would give us an overview about the time she spent in obsessions and compulsions, the extent of interference with activities of daily living, the distress the thoughts and rituals cause her, how much effort she puts in to resist them and the actual degree to which she can exercise control over them.

Obsessive Symptoms and Obsessive Personality Traits

We have often found assessment of OC traits and symptoms through the LOI (Cooper, 1970) quite useful as it shows how obsessive personality traits predispose an individual, indicating the level of his/her vulnerability and proneness to develop severe symptoms that hamper global functioning. Most importantly, when the severity is determined at the outset, it provides a benchmark to determine whether a treatment paradigm is effective for the client, be it pharmacotherapy or psychotherapy.

Administration of YBOCS to Raghav, for instance, would not yield much information as his obsessions are such that they cannot be pinpointed, nor are they so severe as to cause dysfunction to an extent that would interfere drastically with his personal, social and occupational life. Here, the administration of LOI would be more beneficial which would give us an indication of obsessional personality traits as well as obsessional symptoms.

Depression

Such thought content adversely influences the overall functioning of the individual affecting the mood of the individual as well. This is simply because clients with adequate insight into their problem are more often than not affected by the negative repetitive thoughts, images or impulses. We find Priya being sad, restless and irritable. Depression is the most common co-morbidity of OCD, existing in about 60% to 80% of the patient population (Pallanti, Grassi, Sarrecchia, Cantisani, & Pellegrini, 2011); it is so imbibed in the symptom structure that it is difficult to tell it apart. Often a subjective index of depression and a clinician rated scale can be given to denote the level of depression. BDI and Hamilton Depression Rating Scale (HDRS) can provide with the information, which too may be monitored throughout the course of the treatment.

Perfectionism

Perfectionism and intolerance for imperfection is one of the central features of OCD thought pattern. It is a reflection of their discomfort with any deviance from their built-in image of perfectionism for a given task. It is quite unique to the OC phenomena, with the individual being driven by a need to correct an inner dissatisfying sense of imperfection—a feeling of 'not just right' (Leckman et al., 1997)—connected with the perception that actions or intentions have been incompletely achieved (Summerfeldt, 1998; Summerfeldt, Antony, & Swinson, 2002).

Metacognition

Thought and belief system is undoubtedly where the problem is supreme when it comes to patients with OCD. Thinking about one's thinking or metacognition and belief structure has to be looked into by any practitioner who wants to effectively deal with OCD. In that pursuit, MCQ yields useful information. The following domains with instances as provided by MCQ are stated as follows:

1. Positive worry beliefs (e.g., 'Worrying helps me to avoid problems in the future')
2. Negative worry beliefs: related to themes of danger (e.g., 'My worrying is dangerous for me')
3. Cognitive confidence (e.g., 'I have difficulty knowing if I have actually done something or just imagined it')
4. Negative worry beliefs: related to themes of need for thought control and responsibility (e.g., 'If I let my

worrying thoughts get out of control, they will end up controlling me')

5. Cognitive self-consciousness (e.g., I am aware of the way my mind works when I am thinking through a problem)

These metacognitive deficits indicate how a patient with OCD misattributes the thoughts that come to him/her. Their attempt is to closely monitor all their thoughts. Metacognitive deficits lead to irrational worrying where obsessions are thought to be helpful and positive, serving a purpose in one's life, yet at the same time regarded as dangerous. Since the obsessions are perceived as dangerous, an individual with OCD tries very hard to overcome these thoughts and banish them altogether. However, they fail in their attempts to do so as in doing so they bring the thoughts back to the focus of their consciousness. The attempt to suppress thoughts, therefore, is counter-intuitive in nature. The concepts related to metacognition will be further dealt with in Chapter 4.

Obsessive Beliefs

To measure such beliefs, the Obsessive Beliefs Questionnaire (OBQ) prepared by the Obsessive Compulsive Cognitions Working Group (OCCWG, 2003) may be very useful. The original instrument contained 87 items to assess the strength of beliefs covering six rational scales:

- Overestimation of threat
- Elevated responsibility
- Importance of thoughts
- Desire to control one's thoughts
- Need for certainty
- Perfectionism

OCCWG in 2005 reported three-factor analytically derived scales (44 items) measuring:

(a) Responsibility/Threat estimation (e.g., 'I often think things around me are unsafe');

(b) importance/control of thoughts (e.g., 'Having nasty thoughts means I am a terrible person'); and

(c) perfectionism/certainty (e.g., 'Things should be perfect according to my own standards'). Although the OBQ has been supported as a useful measure of these beliefs, questions remain with respect to instrument structure and the specificity of OBQ–OCD relations (Wu & Carter, 2008).

Harm Avoidance

A common feature of OCD thought pattern is their preoccupation with danger, threat, estimation of risks and hazards which may be linked to temperamental feature of high harm avoidance (HA) in patients with OCD. Harm avoidance, as assessed on Cloninger's Temperament and Character Inventory (TCI) may be defined as a personality trait characterized by excessive worrying; pessimism; shyness; being fearful and doubtful. It is a temperamental dimension of personality which Cloninger suggested to be linked with high serotonergic activity; further establishing the OCD and serotonin correlation (Cloninger, 1986), HA is posited to be a core dimension in OCD by Summerfeldt (1998) also. Although the domain is present in other anxiety disorders, it is dominated by anxious apprehension and exaggerated avoidance of potential harm. Pietrefesa and Coles (2009) found HA to be linked to 'obsessing' and anxiety or nervousness.

Often while speaking to the OCD group of patients, it is found that they wish to danger-proof their lives. They want to safeguard their family and home from all possible threats from extraneous, at times even invisible, sources. It is like a single-minded pursuit in them to prevent harm and damage of any kind, but it is mostly restricted to a few individuals and just their residence, they may not do it when they are elsewhere. Perhaps this HA makes them hypervigilant of the environment and affects their information processing as well. For example, Priya did not rewash the clothes or utensils when she was visiting her parents. When asked about it, she said that it was not her 'home' and therefore the responsibility of safeguarding it was not hers.

Belief Structure and Cognitive Functions

Dysfunctional belief structure, overactive metacognitive monitoring and exalted regard for safety influence their attention, memory, perception, learning, decision-making, set shifting and other higher order functions. By nature, patients with OCD are hyperattentive (Lavy, van Oppen, & van Den Hout, 1994; Wilson, 1998) and hypervigilant (Wiggs, Martin, Altemus, & Murphy, 1996) which too may be owing to their overemphasis on top-down processing manifested by perfectionism and meticulousness. It is important to understand that top-down processing influences our information processing system and makes us interpret the environment in terms of our belief systems. Individual differences are manifested owing to the meaning one attaches to one's lived experiences and this is the base of cognitive behaviour therapy (CBT). Since interpretations or top-down mechanism determine how we construe reality, if our belief structure is faulty then the information processing system in itself will become deficient. The information acquired from the environment does not remain objective, being subjectively influenced by the psychopathology of the patient. The psychopathology makes one deviate from the normative ways of functioning and coping. It will be cogent to look into how the patients with OCD process information. The following section will deal with attention, perception and memory.

Attention and Working Memory

We have observed that patients with OCD perform at par with others at least up to the point of registration of information and its explicit expression. Attention can be simply assessed through digit forward (DF) task, a test to assess one's capacity for registration and freedom from distractibility. There are a number of reports with digit span and a wide range of findings; researchers have found DF to be at par (Aronowitz et al., 1994), intact (Moritz et al., 2002) and within average range (Milliery, Bouvard, Aupetit, & Cottraux, 2000) and comparable to control group. It is important to note that in test situation one's mental set is directed towards the given task by the clinician. But this performance requires to be matched with their attention efficiency in real-life situation, when their attention is not externally monitored and they are automatically occupied by their obsessive thought as and when it comes. Thus, though their optimal performance on the task suggest their efficiency of information processing system to be intact up to retention point, their vulnerability to open-life situation may hamper their optimal levels of functioning. Clinician's judgement plays a key role to understand the underlying factors as to why one patient with OCD would maximally employ his existing resources to the task and another cannot.

Similarly, for digit backward (DB) tasks there are variations in findings. We have found that patients with moderate to high level of obsessions and compulsions show poor performance on DB task that inherits some working memory load. In DB task, one has to reorganize the number in reverse order of presentation. For example, 'Repeat the numbers backward. So if I say 3–9–4–1 you need to start at the end and come to the beginning like 1-4-9-3'. In this task, one has to retain the presented string of numbers in the storage space of working memory (WM), and then has to reorganize it and retrieve it through the online process. OCD patients mostly face difficulty in performing this task. If in DF task they confirm their intact retention and retrieval capacity, their failure in the DB task may be attributed to their deficit in reorganization capacity. In DB task, this reorganization requires participation of visuo-spatial sketchpad.

Set Shifting

Set shifting is the ability to change a mental set in response to environmental contingencies (Spreen & Strausss, 1998). In order to adapt to one's environment, the individual should be able to regulate or change one's behaviour on the basis of feedback from the environment, which is the primary requirement of set shifting. In patients with OCD, a clinician can typically see a gross rigidity that is reflective of inflexibility and failure to shift sets.

A comprehensive measure of set shifting is the Wisconsin Card Sorting Test (WCST) (Heaton, Chelune, Talley, Kay, & Curtis, 1993), which may be used to gauge the difficulty in set shifting that OCD patients face. Impairment in set shifting is an index of one's difficulty in feedback utilization resulting in problems in making decision regarding response selection. Most typically, the patients with OCD fail to understand that the task focuses on changing response criterion and end up getting stuck in one response-generating style. It results in high percentage of perseverative responses and perseverative error in their protocol, which indicates a failure to shift categories even after receiving a negative feedback. Perseveration occurs when a person keeps on giving a response beyond the point of relevance. In WCST, perseverative response and perseverative error are reflections of rigidity, which is most commonly present in patients with OCD.

Raghav, for example, who did not have a categorical symptom profile, underperformed on the WCST. He showed high levels of perseveration. He could not complete the task demand as he failed to modify his selection by utilizing the feedback provided by the test administrator. Cognitive inflexibility is a major characteristic of OCD. This also indicates a difficulty of OCD in searching relevant information. Keenness of patients with OCD to live in a predefined mode of conducting themselves interferes with their capacity of feedback utilization. This disregard for feedback utilization hampers the processing of divergent information from dynamic environment.

Processing Speed

Time violation, the form of disregarding time limits without any discomfort, suggests their biological clock is attuned to the rhythm of their slow processing speed. Patients with OCD feel a strong sense of dissonance when rapid pace is demanded from them. They take their own sweet time and do things at their own pace without any feeling of discomfort because of time violation. Since their slow pace is in conformity with the image of time perception within them, it causes no guilt in them. It suggests that the

OCD patients feel guilty only when they violate their own norm of behaviour and are not concerned with other-imposed criterion.

Figural Drawing

Draw a Person Test is a useful tool that takes very little time and resource to administer. Yet it can be a rich information provider. OC patients typically show a tendency to overdo details. Thus, shoes may be shown with eyelets, laces, bows, hands and arms with details including fingernails. These persons may pay particular attention to midline emphasis, details of pockets, neckties and clothing in general. There is much erasing in an attempt by the patient to meet his own high standards of performance.

Response Inhibition

Response inhibition is one's ability to resist immediate but inappropriate response tendencies in context to the present environment. Stroop Test (Stroop, 1935) is a test of attention and inhibition. Herein, the subjects are presented a set of colour names printed in different colours and asked to report the printed colours. The interference effect arises owing to the task demand of naming the colour in which the words are printed instead of reading the printed word. A conflict arises as one has to suppress the prepotent response to spontaneously name the word against a weaker but task-relevant process to name the colour. Performance is poorer when the print colour differs from the colour name than when it is the same (it takes longer to say 'blue' to the word 'red' printed in blue than to the word 'blue' printed in blue). Patients with OCD typically take longer and perform poorly on Stroop tasks.

Planning and Problem-solving

Planning is defined as the identification and organization of the steps and elements needed to carry out an intention or achieve a goal (Lezak, 1995). Tower of London (TOL) (Shallice, 1982) can aid to detect deficits in planning. One common use of TOL is for diagnosis of executive impairment. It is observed that patients with OCD show significant planning impairments as compared to control subjects on TOL task (van den Heuvel et al., 2005). Patients with OCD also demonstrate significant slowness related to motor speed (Purcell, Maruff, Kyrios, & Pantelis, 1998) on the TOL task, which makes them violate time limits assigned to the task and rule violation too is common among patients with OCD.

Personality

Basic questionnaires such as Eysenck Personality Questionnaire or NEO Five Factor Inventory (NEO FFI) may be helpful in assessing personality patterns of OCD patients. Projective tests such as Rorschach Inkblot Test and Thematic Apperception Test too may divulge vital information.

Eysenck Personality Questionnaire

Studies have pointed out that people with OC problems and patients with OCD score significantly higher than control groups on the domains of neuroticism and psychoticism. OCD patients scored lower in extraversion than their respective controls, which was not seen in individuals with subclinical OC problems (Fullana et al., 2004).

NEO Five Factor Inventory

A typical big five profile of OCD looks like this—High N, Low E, Low C with at par A and O—indicating that the clients are mostly gloomy, pessimistic by nature with very high expectations of achievement. Their level of goal setting is mostly impractical and that is the reason why they feel that they have not been able to rise up to their set standards.

Thematic Apperception Test

Mostly the Thematic Apperception Test stories provided by the OCD patients are concrete, descriptive and long, but lacking in content. They often take inordinately long to narrate stories, choosing to highlight unimportant details. For example, on the sex card (Card 13MF), they often describe in minutest details the books, lamp and vase and often identify the semi-nude female figure as an ailing mother. The emptiness of their responses and denial of basic instinctual impulses such as sex and aggression is noteworthy. Often in the Indian scenario, the patients with OCD steer clear of any mature conceptualization of sexuality, choosing to see the female lover as the ailing mother on her deathbed with a crying son who is mourning the mother's death. Sexuality and aggression often cause inordinate amount of guilt in them and they attempt to assuage the guilt mostly by using defences such as denial and displacement.

Rorschach Inkblot Test

The OC patient seldom gives a colour dominant response. He/she attempts to be methodical but often has difficulty in separating two adjacent areas appearing on the cards. The OC is the only neurotic who, like the schizophrenic, uses contamination, such as 'green worms seen to be coming out of the rabbit's eyes' (on Card X) (Kahn, Cameron, & Giffen, 1975). Some compulsives feel it is necessary to mention all parts of the blot, even when these are not used in concepts; that is the reason why they have high number of Dd (small detail) responses. The patients are overattentive to details. In the Comprehensive System of Rorschach (Exner, 2003 Obsessive Index/special scores), the number of popular responses are also $Dd > 3$, $Zf > 12$, $Zd = 3$; more than one synthesized form quality responses have been identified as an obsessive style of responding, as they have an eye for details.

On the Kahn Test of Symbols Arrangement, patients with OCD always systematically arrange objects on table before placing them on the strip; they also may have difficulty in sorting or may even refuse to sort one or more objects. Excessive meticulousness in naming objects is seen in the OCD group. They generally get good recall scores and provide higher numerical element on symbol pattern than other types of neurotics. Excessive attempts to straighten objects can be seen. Reason for liking or disliking objects frequently is 'well made' and 'not well made', and 'good' and 'poor workmanship'. Usually there is no variation in direction of arrangements.

Conclusion

Case history taking and conducting MSE are of paramount importance. The specifics highlighted in the chapter in terms of MSE will be helpful guidelines while questioning clients. Case-history taking and MSE are also of vital significance as the interpretation of test results does not depend on cross-sectional performance alone and has to be correlated with clinical/behavioural observations. Understanding the behaviour pattern of the client, providing ease in testing situation and development of rapport are other determining factors which may influence the overall performance on these tests. It is to be noted that test results are not the final conclusion or a fact that is beyond dispute. A clinical acumen is therefore necessary in order to accommodate divergent and contradictory information into a meaningful whole.

References

Aronowitz, B. R., Hollander, E., DeCaria, C., Cohen, L., Saoud, J. B., Stein, D.,...Rosen, W. G. (1994). Neuropsychology of obsessive compulsive disorder: Preliminary findings. *Cognitive and Behavioural Neurology*, 7(2), 81–86.

Constans, J. I., Foa, E. B., Franklin, M. E., & Mathews, A. (1995). Memory for actual and imagined events in OC checkers. *Behaviour Research and Therapy*, 33(6), 665–671.

Cloninger, C. R., (1986). A unified biosocial theory of personality and its role in the development of anxiety states. *Psychiatric Developments*, 4(3), 167–226.

Cooper, J. (1970). The Leyton Obsessional Inventory. *Psychological Medicine*, 1(1), 48–64.

de Silva, P. (1986). Obsessional-compulsive imagery. *Behaviour Research and Therapy, 24*(3), 333–350.

Eisen, J. L., Mancebo, M. A., Pinto, A., Coles, M. E., & Rasmussen, S. A. (2006). Impact of obsessive compulsive disorder on quality of life. *Comprehensive Psychiatry, 47*(4), 270–275.

Exner, J.E, Jr. (2003). *The Rorschach: A comprehensive system. Volume 1: Basic foundations and principles of interpretation* (Vol. 1, 4th ed.). Hoboken, New Jersey: Wiley and Sons.

Foa, E. B., Amir, N., Gershuny, B., Molnar, C., & Kozak, M. J. (1997). Implicit and explicit memory in obsessive-compulsive disorder. *Journal of Anxiety Disorders, 11*(2), 119–129.

Fullana, M. À., Mataix-Cols, D., Trujillo, J. L., Caseras, X., Serrano, F., Alonso, P.,…Torrubia, R. (2004). Personality characteristics in obsessive-compulsive disorder and individuals with subclinical obsessive-compulsive problems. *British Journal of Clinical Psychology, 43*(4), 387–398.

Heaton, R. K., Chelune, G. J., Talley, J. L., Kay, G. C., & Curtiss, G. (1993). Wisconsin Card Sorting Test manual. Odessa, FL: Psychological Assessment Resources.

Hermans, D., Engelen, U., Grouwels, L., Joos, E., Lemmens, J., & Pieters, G. (2008). Cognitive confidence in obsessive-compulsive disorder: Distrusting perception, attention and memory. *Behaviour Research and Therapy, 46*(1), 98–113.

Kahn, T. C., Cameron, J. T., & Giffen, M. B. (1975). *Methods and evaluation in clinical and counselling psychology.* New York, NY: Pergamon Press.

Lavy, E., van Oppen, P., & van Den Hout, M. (1994). Selective processing of emotional information in obsessive compulsive disorder. *Behaviour Research and Therapy, 32*(2), 243–246.

Leckman, J. F., Grice, D. E., Boardman, J., Zhang, H., Vitale, A., Bondi, C.,…Pauls, D. L. (1997). Symptoms of obsessive-compulsive disorder. *The American Journal of Psychiatry, 154*(7), 911–917.

Lezak, M. D. (1995). *Neuropsychological assessment* (3rd ed.). New York, NY: Oxford University Press.

MacDonald, P. A., Antony, M. M., Macleod, C. M., & Richter, M. A. (1997). Memory and confidence in memory judgments among individuals with obsessive compulsive disorder and non-clinical controls. *Behaviour Research and Therapy, 35*(6), 497–505.

McNally, R. J., & Kohlbeck, P. A. (1993). Reality monitoring in obsessive-compulsive disorder. *Behaviour and Research Therapy, 31*(3), 249–253.

Milliery, M., Bouvard, M., Aupetit, J., & Cottraux, (2000). Sustained attention in patients with obsessive-compulsive disorder: A controlled study. *Psychiatry Research, 96*(3), 199–209.

Moritz, S., Birkner, C., Kloss, M., Jahn, H., Hand, I., Haasen, C., & Krausz, M., (2002). Executive functioning in obsessive-compulsive disorder, unipolar depression and schizophrenia. *Archives of Clinical Neuropsychology, 17*(5), 477–483.

Obsessive Compulsive Cognitions Working Group (1997). Cognitive assessment of obsessive-compulsive disorder. *Behaviour Research Therapy, 35*(7), 667–681.

———(2003). Psychometric validation of the obsessive beliefs questionnaire and the interpretation of intrusions inventory. Part I. *Behaviour Research and Therapy, 41*(8), 863–878.

———(2005). Psychometric validation of the obsessive belief questionnaire and interpretation of intrusions inventory. Part 2: Factor analyses and testing of a brief version. *Behaviour Research and Therapy, 43*(11), 1527–1542.

Pallanti, S., Grassi, G., Sarrecchia, E. D., Cantisani, A., & Pellegrini, M. (2011). Obsessive-compulsive disorder comorbidity: Clinical assessment and therapeutic implications. *Frontiers in Psychiatry, 2*, 70. http://doi.org/10.3389/fpsyt.2011.00070

Pietrefesa, Ashley S., and Meredith E., Coles. (2009). Moving beyond an exclusive focus on harm avoidance in obsessive-compulsive disorder: Behavioral validation for the separability of harm avoidance and incompleteness. *Behavior Therapy, 40*(3), 251–259.

Purcell, R., Maruff, P., Kyrios, M., & Pantelis, C. (1998). Cognitive deficits in obsessive-compulsive disorder on tests of frontal–striatal function. *Biological Psychiatry, 43*(5), 348–357.

Rachman, S. (1998). A cognitive theory of obsessions: Elaborations. *Behaviour Research and Therapy, 36*(4), 3–401.

Shallice, T. (1982). Specific impairments of planning. *Philosophical Transactions of the Royal Society of London, 298*(1089), 199–209.

Spreen, O., & Strauss, E. (1998). *A compendium of neuropsychological tests: Administration, norms and commentary* (2nd ed.). New York, NY: Oxford University Press.

Stroop, J. R. (1935). Studies of interference in serial verbal reactions. *Journal of Experimental Psychology, 18*(6), 643–662.

Summerfeldt, L. J. (1998). Cognitive processing in obsessive-compulsive disorder: Alternate models and the role of subtypes. Dissertation Abstracts International, 60, 4288. (Doctoral dissertation, York University, Toronto).

Summerfeldt, L. J., Antony, M. M., & Swinson, R. P. (2002). Reply to Bilsbury and others. More on the phenomenology of perfectionism: 'Incompleteness' [Letter to the editor]. *The Canadian Journal of Psychiatry, 47*(10), 977–978.

Summerfeldt, L. J., Kloosterman, P. H., Antony, M. M., Richter, M. A., & Swinson, R. P. (2004). The relationship between miscellaneous symptoms and major symptom factors in obsessive–compulsive disorder. *Behaviour Research and Therapy, 42*(12), 1453–1467.

Tolin, D. F., Abramowitz, J. S., Brigidi, B. D., Amir, N., Street, G. P., & Foa, E. B. (2001). Memory and memory confidence in obsessive compulsive disorder. *Behaviour Research and Therapy, 39*(8), 913–927.

van den Heuvel, O. A., Veltman, D. J., Groenewegen, H. J., Cath, D. C., van Balkom, A. J., van Hartskamp, J.,...& van Dyck, R. (2005). Frontal-striatal dysfunction during planning in obsessive-compulsive disorder. *Archives of General Psychiatry, 62*(3), 301–309.

van den Hout, M., & Kindt, M. (2003). Repeated checking causes memory distrust. *Behaviour Research and Therapy, 41*(3), 301–316.

Wells, A. (1997). *Cognitive therapy of anxiety disorders: A practice manual and conceptual guide.* Chichester: Wiley.

Wiggs, C. L., Martin, A., Altemus, M., & Murphy, D. L. (1996). Hypervigilance in patients with obsessive-compulsive disorder. *Anxiety, 2*(3), 123–129.

Wilson, K. D. (1998). Issues surrounding the cognitive neuroscience of obsessive-compulsive disorder. *Psychonomic Bulletin & Review, 5*(2), 161–172.

Wu, K. D., & Carter, S. A. (2008). Further investigation of the Obsessive Beliefs Questionnaire: Factor structure and specificity of relations with OCD symptoms. *Journal of Anxiety Disorders, 22*(5), 824–836.

3

Study of Attention in OCD in Comparison with Idiopathic Parkinson's Disease

Sujata Das, Pritha Mukhopadhyay, Shyamal Kumar Das and Suvosree Bhattacharya

Introduction

This chapter highlights the beginning of our journey with obsessive compulsive disorder (OCD) in our neuropsychological laboratory back in 2003. In our laboratory, we had acquired some tools to assess cognitive functions and our interest in OCD was beginning to grow around the same time. There were limited reporting of neuropsychological work being carried out in India focusing specifically on OCD. Studies back then had investigated disorder-specific impairment of cognitive functions in OCD but had not compared it with other clinical groups.

Since the beginning of the twentieth century, investigators have been trying to formulate and conceptualize aetiological factors associated with OCD. These formulations have undergone a sea change from a predominantly psychoanalytical conceptualization to the current understanding of OCD as a neuropsychiatric illness with neurobiological abnormalities. Psychodynamic approach, pioneered by Freud, made an important contribution to the nosology and phenomenology of OCD and has dominated the field since the middle of the last century. Later, each of the major models of psychoanalysis–classical drive theory, ego psychology, interpersonal and object relations theory contributed to enhance our understanding of the phenomenology of OCD. However, with the advances made in the field of neurobiology, especially with the help of sophisticated neuroimaging techniques, the focus has shifted from a purely psychogenic formulation to specific neurobiological abnormalities as significant aetiological factors in the development and maintenance of OCD. Structural and functional neuroimaging studies provide substantial evidence for dysfunction of the ventromedial cortico-subcortical loop and the frontostriatal system (Bolwig, Hansen, Hansen, Merkin, & Prichep, 2007; Velikova, Locatelli, Insacco, Smeraldi, Comi, & Leocani, 2010) in OCD. Furthermore, investigators are currently using the technique of deep brain stimulation (DBS) as a successful mode of treatment for severe and refractory OCD (Aouizerate et al., 2004; Aouizerate et al., 2009; Greenberg et al., 2006) substantiating the role of neurobiology as a major causal factor in OCD symptom manifestation.

Another mode of studying the neurobiological aspects of OCD has been to study it in comparison to other neurological disorders such as Tourette's syndrome, Sydenham's chorea and other disorders with basal ganglia dysfunction such as Parkinson's disease, which exhibit OCD symptoms at least sometimes during the course of the disorder (Rapoport, 1990; Swedo & Rapoport, 1989). OCD and Idiopathic Parkinson's Disease (IPD) share same neural circuits, and there is involvement of dopamine in both the disorders—Parkinson's disease is strongly related to dopamine deficiency, and Koo, Kim, Roh and Kim (2010) have reported preclinical, neuroimaging and neurochemical studies that provide evidence that the dopaminergic system is involved in inducing or aggravating the symptoms that are indicative of OCD. Positive treatment responses to the dopaminergic antagonists in OCD also suggest that dopamine is involved in the pathophysiology of OCD. The basal ganglia structure has been shown to be an important site for associative and limbic information processing and has been implicated to control the ability to stop or inhibit an already initiated response (Aron et al., 2007) which is also a problem in patients with OCD.

Thus, we felt the necessity to study the cognitive aspects of the related disorders with shared neural circuitry, which could be done through neuropsychological investigation. Researchers have hypothesized the presence of neuropsychological deficits which might be associated with clinical phenotype and predict treatment outcomes in OCD (Abramovitch, Abramovitch, & Mittelman, 2013). Since most of the researches revealed abnormal activation of the major sites of the frontostriatal system, the orbitofrontal cortex, the dorsolateral prefrontal cortex, the anterior cingulate cortex and the basal ganglia in OCD, the prevailing hypothesis focuses on studying the neuropsychological functions that are controlled by these systems. Investigators have focused on studying the aspects of attention, executive functions and memory (both verbal and non-verbal). However, the results of these investigations have yielded inconsistent findings across various studies (Abramovitch, Mittelman, Henin, & Geller, 2012; Kuelz, Hohagen, & Voderholzer, 2004). Authors suggest that the major reasons for such inconsistent results are the heterogeneous nature of the disorder, the presence of co-morbid diagnosis and, most importantly, the fact that the comparative groups in all these major studies have been healthy controls and seldom have these functions in OCD group been compared with another similar clinical group (Abramovitch et al., 2013). The scarcity of literature and lack of reliable data make it difficult to make a proper inference about specific impairments in OCD (Abramovitch et al., 2013).

We decided to study attention in these two groups at the outset. Attention is commonly referred to the focusing of mental effort and concentration; a focus that is selective, fluctuating and divisible. Attention underlies most cognitive activities and it is distinct from higher cognitive processes. Unlike higher cognitive processing, tasks of attention generally require significant subjective effort despite their relative simplicity and minimal response output. Attention is not a unitary concept and appreciated to be multifaceted with no single brain area to mediate its function. It is affected in several neuropsychiatric diseases. Various clinical observations and experimental techniques have been used to measure the different aspects of attention in psychiatric patients.

Scientific endeavour to explore varied attentional dimensions in persons suffering from OCD has revealed diverging results (Clayton, Richards, & Edwards, 1999; Milliery, Bouvard, Aupetit, & Cottraux, 2000). Although studies have reported deficient selective attention in OCD patients (Clayton et al., 1999; Okasha et al., 2000), a bulk of documentation on digit forward (DF) task has reported selective attention to be within the normal range (Aronowitz et al., 1994; Cohen et al., 1996; Hollander, Cohen, Richards, Mullen, DeCaria, & Stern, 1993; Milliery et al., 2000; Moritz et al., 2002; Okasha et al., 2000; Savage et al., 1996; Zielinski, Taylor, & Juzwin, 1991). Similarly, some studies have reported sustained attention deficits (Aronowitz et al., 1994; Martinot, 1990; Schmidtke, Schorb, Winkelmann, & Hohagen, 1998), whereas others have reported the contrary (Milliery et al., 2000). Again, it has been stated that one of the major demerits of most of these studies has been the lack of a clinical control group for comparison which would have enhanced the specificity of the results for OCD (Kuelz et al., 2004).

In lieu of the aforementioned context, the present chapter would highlight a study that was designed to assess two important aspects of attentional system—selective attention and sustained attention—on two clinical samples. One sample consists of patients having a diagnosis of OCD and another group consisting of patients diagnosed with IPD and their consecutive matched controls. As has been stated earlier, neuropsychological dysfunction (Hollander et al., 1993) and cognitive deterioration (Lees, 1989) similar to those in OCD have been described in literature on IPD.

It is expected that the similarities and differences in the patho-physiological mechanism of the two conditions would be revealed if we study the cognitive aspects of the patients suffering from OCD and IPD, and this would highlight their respective disorder specific impairment. The present study, therefore, compares these two clinical groups along with their normal control counterparts on measures of selective and sustained attention.

Methodology

Sample and Study Design

This was a cross-sectional study and comprised of two groups of clinical samples—30 patients with a diagnosis of OCD and 33 having IPD in a case-control design. The OCD patients were referred from the psychiatric unit, R. G. Kar Medical College & Hospital, Kolkata. Psychiatrists in the said hospital made the diagnosis of OCD following the DSM-IV (1994) criteria. Both sexes were included in the study with their age ranging from 24 to 50 years with a mean of 36.96 ± 12.92 years. All were right-handed, urban individuals, assessed by the Edinburg Handedness Inventory (Oldfield, 1971), and with an average of 11.40 ± 3.04 years of education.

Thirty-three IPD patients were selected for the study after being diagnosed by a neurologist following a careful history and neurological examination. The patients were referred from the Movement Disorder Clinic, Bangur Institute of Neuroscience & Psychiatry, Kolkata. Their age ranged between 45 and 60 years with a mean of 52.70 ± 6.67 years. Both sexes (M=36; F=27) were included in the study. All were right-handed, urban individuals, assessed by the Edinburg Handedness Inventory (Oldfield, 1971), and with an average of 12.61 ± 2.72 years of education.

The Hamilton Rating Scale for Depression (HRSD) (Hamilton, 1960) was administered to all patients to screen for co-morbid depression. All patients with average or above average intelligence as indicated from the Standard Progressive Matrices Test (Raven, 1938) were chosen for the study. All the patients scored an average of 27 on the Mini-Mental State Examination (MMSE) (Folstein, Folstein, & McHugh, 1975). Care was taken to rule out persons with head injury, co-morbid neurological or psychiatric conditions and patients with substance abuse. Parkinson's plus diseased patients were not included in the IPD group.

Each patient, psychiatric and neurological, was matched with a normal control subject for age ±2 years, gender, education and handedness. All the individuals scored above 27 on the MMSE (Folstein et al., 1975) and scored below the cut-off point on General Health Questionnaire (GHQ) (Goldberg & Hillier, 1979). There was no history of neurological or psychiatric disorders in the CG. They consumed no drugs that were known to affect the functions of the central nervous system. The controls were selected from the families of other patients and also from individuals who volunteered.

Ethical clearance was obtained prior to commencement of the study. All the patients after being screened for inclusion from their respective clinics were sent to the Department of Psychology, University of Calcutta, where neuropsychological assessment was done. A written consent was collected from all the patients before the evaluation started. All the participants were administered the following tests according to standardized procedures to assess selective and sustained attention. The order of presentation was kept constant throughout the administration.

Measures

Screening tools used for evaluation were as follows:

- Edinburg Inventory on Handedness (Oldfield, 1971)
- Hamilton Rating Scale for Depression (Hamilton, 1960)

- Mini-Mental State Examination (Folstein et al., 1975)
- General Health Questionnaire (Goldberg et al., 1979)
- Standard Progressive Matrices (Raven, 1938)

Neuropsychological tools used for assessing selective attention:

- 'A' Random Letter Test (Strub & Black, 1995)
- Digit Forward Test (Pershad & Verma, 1990)

Neuropsychological tools used for assessing sustained attention:

- Digit Backward Test (Pershad & Verma, 1990)
- 20–1 Backward Counting Test (Pershad & Verma, 1990)
- 40–3 Serial Subtraction Test (Pershad & Verma, 1990)

Statistical Analysis

All statistical analyses were carried out using the Statistical Package for the Social Sciences (SPSS version 11.0 for Windows). A p level of 0.05 was used to determine significance. Parametric tests were chosen for the neuropsychological parameters. Means and standard deviations for each of the test parameters for both the patient groups and matched controls were done separately. The t-test was computed to determine group differences, if any, between the patient groups and their respective controls. Analysis of variance was done to compare the attention parameters between the two disease groups, with Tukey's Test done for post-hoc analysis.

Results

Analysis of the demographic data indicated that there was no significant difference between the OCD and the CG on age $(p=0.767)$ and years of education $(p=0.323)$, and also between the IPD group and their CG on age $(p=0.798)$ and years of education $(p=0.15)$ indicating that the groups were very well matched. Spearman's rank correlation coefficient did not show any association between age or years of education with the different measures of attention in the OCD and IPD groups indicating that age or years of education were not associated with their performance on the different tasks of attention.

On HRSD, none of the patients revealed any significant depressive features in this study. The details are provided in Table 3.1.

Table 3.1	Socio-demographic and Clinical Characteristics of the Two Clinical Groups: OCD and IPD	
	OCD (n=30)	IPD (n=33)
Male (n)	10	26
Female (n)	20	7
Age ((Mean ± SD) years)	36.97 ± 12.920	52.70 ± 6.678
Education ((Mean ± SD) years)	11.40 ± 3.047	12.61 ± 2.726
Handedness	Right-handed	Right-handed
Age of onset (Mean ± SD)	36.77 ± 12.734	44.40 ± 7.002
MMSE (Mean ± SD)	28.67 ± 1.373	28.00 ± 1.436
HRSD (Mean ± SD)	2.73 ± 1.704	3.33 ± 2.073

Source: Authors.

Comparison Between OCD Patient Group and Matched Community Controls (CCG1) on Tasks of Sustained Attention

Table 3.2 shows the performance of the OCD group and their matched community controls (CCG1) on measures of selective and sustained attention.

The OCD patient group with lower mean scores on DF Test (5.90 ± 1.047) differed significantly ($p > 0.001$) from the community controls CCG1 (7.10 ± 1.062). On the 'A' Random Letter Test, the OCD group with poor performance differed significantly from CCG1 with respect to both errors of omission ($p > 0.001$) and errors of commission ($p > 0.001$).

Table 3.2	Performance of OCD Group and Their Matched Community Controls (CCG1) on Measures of Selective and Sustained Attention			
Tests	CCG1 (n=30) mean ± SD	OCD group (n=30) mean ± SD	t	P
Counting Backwards 20–1	2.83 ± 0.379	2.27 ± 0.785	3.552	**0.029**
Serial Subtraction (40–3)	2.07 ± 0.980	1.33 ± 0.994	2.919	**0.005**
DF	7.10 ± 1.062	5.90 ± 1.047	4.436	**0.001**
DB	4.57 ± 1.040	4.17 ± 1.167	1.406	0.164
'A' Random Letter Test				
Errors of omission	0.39 ± 1.086 3.386	1.63 ± 1.691	3.386	**0.001**
Errors of commission	0.13 ± 0.428	1.60 ± 1.714	4.572	**0.001**
Perseverative errors	0	0	0	–

Source: Authors.
Notes: SD represents standard deviation.
p values in bold are significant.
None of the participants in either of the groups made any perseverative errors.

On tasks of sustained attention, variability was observed in the performance of the OCD group and the CCG1. On counting backwards from 20 to 1, the performance of the patient group with a lower mean score was found to differ significantly from CCG1 ($t=3.552$; $p=0.029$) indicating that the OCD group could not perform the backward counting task as well as CCG1. The performance of the OCD patients was also found to be significantly poorer than from CCG1 on tasks that required more active and sustained attention ($t=2.919$; $p=0.005$). The OCD patient group (4.17 ± 1.167) compared well ($t=1.406$; $p=0.164$) with CCG1

(4.57 ± 1.040) on Digit Backward (DB) Test. However, group difference was observed on 40–3 Serial Subtraction Test (SST) ($t=2.919$; $p=0.005$), with the OCD subjects performing poorly.

Comparison Between IPD Patient Group and Matched Community Controls (CC) on Tasks of Sustained Attention

Table 3.3 shows the performance of the IPD group and their matched community controls on measures of selective and sustained attention.

Table 3.3	Performance of IPD Group and Their Matched Community Controls on Measures of Selective and Sustained Attention			
Tests	Community Control n=33 Mean ± SD	IPD Group n=33 Mean ± SD	t	P
Counting Backwards 20–1	2.86 ± 0.351	2.76 ± 0.502	0.897	0.373
Serial Subtraction (40–3)	1.69 ± 1.064	1.48 ± 1.149	0.728	0.462
Digit Forward	6.22 ± 1.017	5.55 ± 0.995	**2.594**	**0.011**
Digit Backward	4.33 ± 0.756	3.68 ± 1.045	**2.776**	**0.007**
'A' Random Letter Test				
Errors of omission	0.26 ± 0.561	1.84 ± 2.592	**3.265**	**0.001**
Errors of commission	0.11 ± 0.323	0.38 ± 0.751	1.813	0.074
Perseverative error	0	0	0	—

Source: Authors.
Notes: SD represents standard deviation.
p values in bold are significant.
None of the participants in either of the groups made any perseverative errors.

The mean performance of the IPD patient group on DF Test (5.55 ± 0.995) differed significantly ($p > 0.01$) from their community control group (CCG2) (6.22 ± 1.017). On 'A' Random Letter Test, the patient group was found to differ from CCG2 on errors of omission ($p > 0.001$), with the patient group performing poorly. However, no significant group difference was evident on errors of commission ($p > 0.074$). The IPD group revealed no significant difference from their normal counterparts (CCG2) on counting backwards from 20 to 1 ($t = 0.897$; $p = 0.373$) as well as on tasks which demand more active and sustained attention as evident on 40–3 Serial Subtraction Task ($t = 0.728$; $p = 0.462$). However, significant group difference was observed on DB ($t = 2.776$; $p > 0.007$). The mean performance of the IPD patient group on DB Test was 3.68 ± 1.045 and that of their normal counterparts (CCG2) was 4.33 ± 0.756.

On comparing the OCD and IPD groups on the attention functions, significant group difference was obtained on Tukey Test for post-hoc analysis after ANOVA. It demonstrates that OCD group showed significant deficit in counting backwards 20–1 ($p > 0.010$) in comparison to the IPD group. OCD patients also made significantly more commission errors on the 'A' Random Letter Test indicating higher degree of distractibility in them ($p > 0.001$). The graphical presentation in Figure 3.1 depicts the same.

Discussion

In the present study, two clinical groups—one group consisting of 30 patients suffering from OCD and another group of 33 patients with IPD—were compared with their respective age-, gender- and education-matched community controls on measures of selective and sustained attention.

Results on tasks of attention indicated that both the OCD and the IPD groups had some attentional deficits compared to their community counterpart which is in line with previous literature (Kuelz et al., 2004). These results indicate that dysfunction in the basal ganglia and related circuits, which is accepted as a common

Figure 3.1 *Comparison Between OCD and IPD on Attentional Tasks*

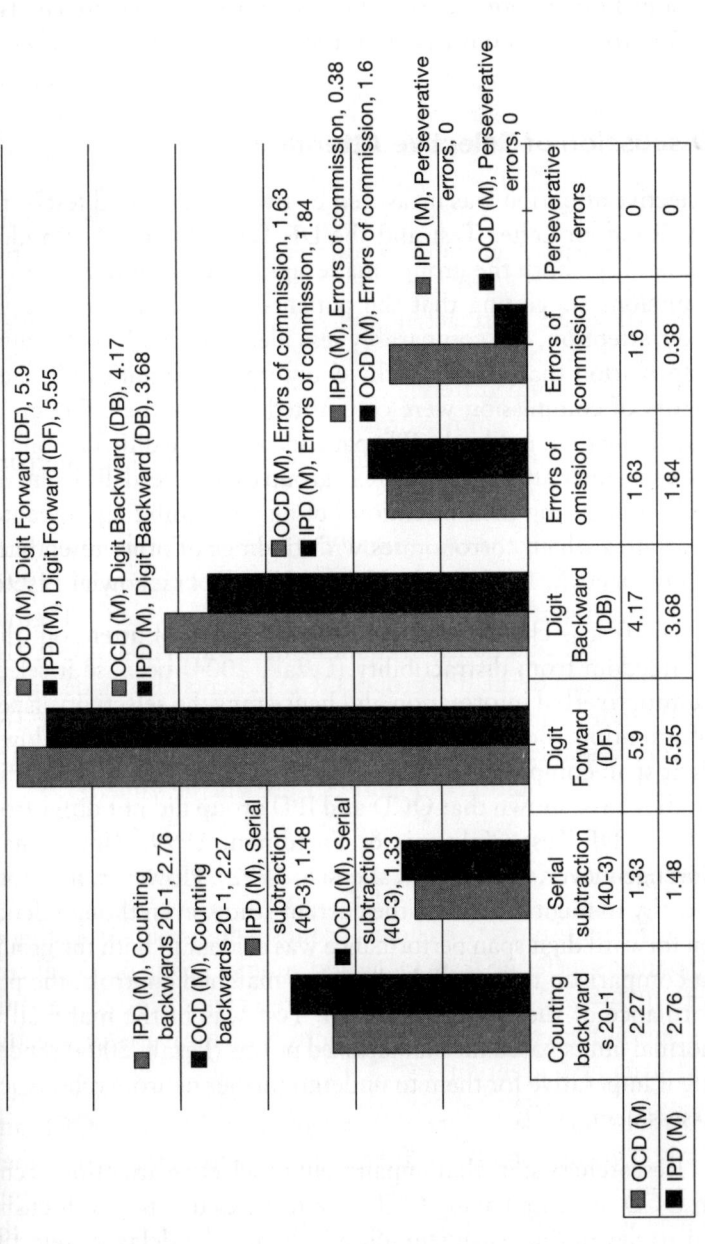

	Counting backwards 20-1	Serial subtraction (40-3)	Digit Forward (DF)	Digit Backward (DB)	Errors of omission	Errors of commission	Perseverative errors
OCD (M)	2.27	1.33	5.9	4.17	1.63	1.6	0
IPD (M)	2.76	1.48	5.55	3.68	1.84	0.38	0

- IPD (M), Counting backwards 20-1, 2.76
- OCD (M), Counting backwards 20-1, 2.27
- IPD (M), Serial subtraction (40-3), 1.48
- OCD (M), Serial subtraction (40-3), 1.33

- OCD (M), Digit Forward (DF), 5.9
- IPD (M), Digit Forward (DF), 5.55
- OCD (M), Digit Backward (DB), 4.17
- IPD (M), Digit Backward (DB), 3.68

- OCD (M), Errors of commission, 1.63
- IPD (M), Errors of commission, 1.84
- IPD (M), Errors of commission, 0.38
- OCD (M), Errors of commission, 1.6
- IPD (M), Perseverative errors, 0
- OCD (M), Perseverative errors, 0

Source: Authors.

dysfunction in both these conditions, may result in compromised ability to select and focus attention.

Discussion of Selective Attention

Selective attention was measured by two standardized tests—the 'A' Random Letter Test and the DF Test. On the 'A' Random Letter Test, both the groups made significantly more number of omissions suggesting that the patients have difficulty focusing their attention, are comparably less alert and tend to lose more information than their healthy counterparts. Significantly more errors of commission were committed only by the OCD group indicating that, unlike the IPD patients who have difficulty only in focusing their attention, the OCD group experienced difficulty not only in focusing their attention but also in inhibiting unwanted responses which corroborates with findings of other researchers (Clayton et al., 1999; Sawle, Hymas, Lees, & Frackowiak, 1991).

DF Test is closely related to the efficiency of attention, that is, freedom from distractibility (Lezak, 2004) because it selects auditory/verbal information and hence taps the selectivity aspect of attention. Both the OCD and the IPD groups had a lower digit span compared to their respective CGs. Most of the earlier studies have shown that OCD and IPD group did not differ from CG on DF Test (Zakzanis & Freedman, 1999; Zimmerman, Sprengelmeyer, Fimm, & Walleesch, 1992). However, it is noteworthy to mention that in the current study, even though deficit on forward digit span performance was evident in both the groups in comparison to age- and education-matched controls, the performance of these patients on DF Test was in the marginal to normal limits based on standardized norms (Lezak, 2004) rendering it imperative for them to undergo further neuropsychological assessment.

Researchers state that impairment in selective attention occurs in OCD or those having OCD-like features due to overfocusing on irrelevant/intrusive stimuli, and hence the delay in selective attention to relevant task (Clayton et al., 1999; Okasha et al., 2000). Surprisingly, it was noted that the OCD group made substantially more number of errors of commission in 'A' Random Letter Test compared to IPD group indicating that this group had problem also in response inhibition. Impairment of response inhibition is a cardinal feature of OCD patients (Aycicegi, Dinn, Harris, & Erkmen, 2003; Hymas et al., 1991). However, this feature has also been seen in IPD patients in previous studies (Cronin-Golomb, Corkin, & Growdon, 1994; Pollux & Robertson, 2002). In this group of IPD patients, however, such a feature was not evident. It may be suspected that the similarity in the pathophysiological mechanism of the two groups (OCD and IPD), that is, dysfunction in the basal ganglia and related circuitry may be having an effect on the process of selective attention.

Discussion of Result of Sustained Attention Task

Sustained attention was measured by two tasks—DB and serial subtraction with increasing level of difficulty (20–1, 40–3). In case of DB task, the performance of the two groups was found to differ. The performance of the OCD group did not differ significantly from their respective controls; however, it was seen that the scores of the IPD group on DB task was significantly below that of their respective controls. DB measures a more effortful mental activity requiring holding the numbers online briefly which is clearly an attentional function, rehearsing the digits in order to prevent the decay from the storage and simultaneously reversing the numbers backward and in the process calling upon the 'central executive' component of the working memory. For such a complex task like DB, it is important to consciously detect events and to exercise executive attentional control over voluntary behaviour and thought process (Lezak, 1995; Mirsky, Anthony, Duncan & Ahearn, 1991). Most of the previous studies on the cognitive aspect of OCD have yielded variable results (Kuelz et al., 2004). This group of OCD patients has performed poorly on tasks of selective attention such as 'A' Random Letter and DF; however, on a relatively more complex task like DB which requires more effortful engagement on the part of the participants, the OCD group did not differ significantly from the control indicating that they were not impaired in this regard. It can be inferred that the cardinal OCD features, that is, intrusive/self-emanating thoughts and overfocusing on irrelevant stimuli and subsequent reduction of alertness to environmental events may be one of the significant factors for such a variable performance on cognitive tasks. When the task demand is greater which commands more attention, the OCD group is able to focus and occupy themselves on the presented stimuli; they can perform at par with normal on complex attentional tasks like DB.

On the other hand, in case of the IPD group, it was found that their performance on DB was significantly impaired compared to the CG. This is in corroboration with previous literature which states that complex attentional tasks, especially those requiring sustained mental effort and working memory functions are disturbed in the advanced stages of Parkinson's disease (Cooper & Sagar, 1993; Downes et al., 1989; Maruyama, 2000). Researchers attribute its cause to a disturbed frontal regulation of attentional processes in the advanced stages of IPD (Stam et al., 1993).

In case of counting backward and serial subtraction tasks, the two groups were again found to have a variable performance. The OCD group had a significantly lower mean score compared to controls, whereas the IPD group did not differ significantly from their respective controls on these tasks. In both the counting backward task (20–1) and the serial subtraction task (40–3), the processes involved numerical processing where both resort to semantic representation (Zhou et al., 2006) and magnitude manipulation (Dehaene & Cohen, 1997). Backward serial recitation (20–1) relies on some visual processing such as imagery of number sequences (Zago et al., 2001). In addition, both the tasks involve working memory, even though the load differs. 20–1 backward counting simply relies on the visuospatial sketchpad (Zhou et al., 2006); serial subtraction (40–3) on the other hand involves holding an arithmetic problem in working memory while using an arithmetic rule, that is, subtraction (Cowell, Egan, Code, Harasty, & Watson, 2000). During the calculation procedure, digits and operations may also be visualized using the visuospatial sketchpad (Baddeley & Wilson, 1986). Most importantly, in case of both the tasks, active and sustained attention has to be maintained for a substantial amount of time to complete the tasks. It is evident from the study that both OCD and IPD groups had some disturbance of attention due to their condition. Both the groups had problems of focusing attention as was evident from their performance in selective attention tasks. In case of tasks of sustained attention, patients with OCD showed greater deficits than patients with IPD. The finding strongly suggests the involvement of the prefrontoparietal and prefrontotemporal network (Knight, 1991) in the OCD and IPD patients.

However, there were limitations to the study with respect to the sample size, inclusion of a homogeneous OCD group based on symptom clusters and of not employing structural and functional imaging techniques which could further substantiate the findings on a stronger foothold.

Conclusion

The present study revealed that the two groups—OCD and IPD—both had deficits in certain areas of selective and sustained attention as was measured by the tests in the study in comparison to their control counterparts. In case of selective attention, deficits were found to be greater in people with OCD compared to IPD. When the OCD and IPD were compared on their performance on tasks of sustained attention, a more variable picture was revealed with the OCD group performing better compared to controls on complex tests (such as DB) and not on those requiring sustained attention to stimuli for a longer duration such as counting backward and serial subtraction.

102 / Sujata Das et al.

Acknowledgements

The first author would like to acknowledge the immense contributions of Dr Avijit Hazra and Dr Aparna Dutta, without whom the study would have been difficult.

References

Abramovitch, A., Abramovitch, J. S., & Mittelman, A. (2013). The neuropsychology of adult obsessive-compulsive disorder: A meta-analysis. *Clinical Psychology Review, 33*(8), 1163–1171.

Abramovitch, A., Mittelman, A., Henin, A., & Geller, D. A. (2012). Neuroimaging and neuropsychological findings in pediatric obsessive-compulsive disorder: A review and developmental considerations. *Neuropsychiatry, 2*(4), 17.

Aouizerate, B., Cuny, E., Martin-Guehl, C., Guehl, D., Amieva, H., Benazzouz, A.,...Burbaud, P. (2004). Deep brain stimulation of the ventral caudate nucleus in the treatment of obsessive-compulsive disorder and major depression: Case report. *Journal of Neurosurgery, 101*(4), 682–686.

Aouizerate, B., Cuny, E., Bardinet, E., Yelnik, J., Martin-Guehl, C., Rotge, J.Y.,...Guehl, D. (2009). Distinct striatal targets in treating obsessive-compulsive disorder and major depression. *Journal of Neurosurgery, 111*(4), 775–779.

Aron, A. R., Durston, S., Eagle, D. M., Logan, G. D., Stinear, C. M., & Stuphorn, V. (2007). Converging evidence for a fronto-basal-ganglia network for inhibitory control of action and cognition. *Journal of Neuroscience, 27*(44), 11860–11864.

Aronowitz, B. R., Hollander, E., DeCaria, C., Cohen, L., Saoud, J. B., Stein, D.,...Wilma, R. G. (1994). Neuropsychology of obsessive-compulsive disorder: Preliminary findings. *Neuropsychiatry, Neuropsychology and Behavioural Neurology, 7*(8), 81–86.

Aycicegi, A., Dinn, W. M., Harris, C. L., & Erkmen, H. (2003). Neuropsychological function in obsessive-compulsive disorder: Effects of comorbid conditions on task performance. *European Psychiatry, 18*(5), 241–248.

Baddeley, A., & Wilson, B. (1986). Amnesia, Autobiographical memory and confabulation. In D. C. Rubin (Ed.), *Autobiographical memory* (pp. 225–252). Cambridge, MA: Cambridge University Press.

Bergman, H., & Deuschl, G. (2002). Pathophysiology of Parkinson's disease: From clinical neurology to basic neuroscience and back. *Movement Disorders, 17*(3), S28–40.

Bolwig, T. G., Hansen, E. S., Hansen, A., Merkin, H., & Prichep, L. S. (2007). Toward a better understanding of the pathophysiology of OCD SSRI responders: QEEG source localization. *Acta Psychiatrica Scandinavica, 115*, 237–242. doi: 10.1111/j.1600-0447.2006.00889.x

Clayton, I. C., Richards, J. C., & Edwards, C. J. (1999). Selective attention in obsessive-compulsive disorder. *Journal of Abnormal Psychology, 108*(1), 171–175.

Cohen, J. (1977). *Statistical power analysis for the behavioural sciences* (2nd ed.). New York, NY: Academic Press.

Cohen, L. J., Hollander, E., DeCaria, C. M., Stein, D. J., Simeon, D., Liebowitz, M. R., & Aronowitz, B. R. (1996). Specificity of neuropsychological impairment in obsessive-compulsive disorder: A comparison with social phobic and normal control subjects. *Journal of Neuropsychiatry and Clinical Neurosciences, 8*(1), 82–85.

Cooper, J. A., & Sagar, H. J. (1993). Incidental and intentional recall in Parkinson's disease: An account based on diminished attentional resources. *Journal of Clinical and Experimental Neuropsychology, 15*(5), 713–731.

Cowell, S. F., Egan, G. F., Code, C., Harasty, J., & Watson, J. D. G. (2000). The functional neuroanatomy of simple calculation and number Repetition: A parametric PET activation study. *NeuroImage, 12*(5), 565–573.

Cronin-Golomb, A., Corkin, S., & Growdon, J. H. (1994). Impaired problem-solving in Parkinson's disease: Impact of a set-shifting deficit. *Neuropsychologia, 32*(5), 579–593.

Cummings, J. L. (1995). Anatomic and behavioural aspects of frontal-subcortical circuits. *Annals of the New York Academy of Sciences, 769*, 1–13.

De Rammelaere, S., Stuyven, E., & Vandierendonk, A. (1999). The contribution of working memory resources in the verification of simple arithmetic sums. *Psychological Research, 62*(1), 72–77.

Dehaene, S., & Cohen, L. (1997). Cerebral pathways for calculation: Double dissociation between rote verbal and quantitative knowledge of arithmetic. *Cortex, 33*(2), 219–250.

Denys, D., Zohar, J., & Westenberg, H. G. M. (2004). The role of dopamine in obsessive-compulsive disorder: Preclinical and clinical evidence. *The Journal of Clinical Psychiatry, 65*(Suppl.), 11–17.

Downes, J. J., Roberts, A. C., Sahakian, B. J., Evenden, J. L., Morris, R. G., & Robbins, T. W. (1989). Impaired extra-dimensional shift performance in medicated and unmedicated Parkinson's disease: Evidence for a specific attentional dysfunction. *Neuropsychologia, 27*(11–12), 1329–1343.

Eapen, V., Yakeley, J. W., & Robertson, M. M. (2003). Gilles de la Tourette syndrome and obsessive-compulsive disorder. In Randolph B. Schiffer,

104 / Sujata Das et al.

Stephen M. Rao, & B. S. Fogel (Eds.), *Neuropsychiatry* (2nd ed., pp. 947–990). Philadelphia, PA: Lippincott Williams and Wilkins.

Fahn, S., Elto, R., & Members of the UPDRS Development Committee. (1987). Unified Parkinson's disease rating scale. In S. Fahn, C. D. Marsden, D. Calne, & M. Goldstein (Eds.), *Recent developments in Parkinson's disease* (Vol. 2, pp. 153–163, 293–304). Florham Park, NJ: Macmillan Health Care Information.

Folstein, M. F., Folstein, S. E., & McHugh, P. R. (1975). Mini mental state: A practical method for grading the cognitive state of patients for the clinician. *Journal of Psychiatric Research, 12*(3), 189–198.

Fontaine, D., Mattei, V., Borg, M., von Langsdorff, D., Magnie, M. N., Chanalet, S.,...Paquis, P. (2004). Effect of subthalamic nucleus stimulation on obsessive-compulsive disorder in a patient with Parkinson disease: Case report. *Journal of Neurosurgery, 100*(6), 1084–1086.

Eko, F., & Randolph, N. (2014). The impact of individual depressive symptoms on impairment of psycho-social functioning. *PLOS One, 9*(2), e90311.

Goldberg, D. P., & Hillier, V. E. (1979). A scaled version of the General Health Questionnaire. *Psychological Medicine, 9*(1), 139–145.

Goodman, W. K., Lawrence, H. P., Rasmussen, A., Mazure, C., Delgado, P., Heninger, G. R., & Charney, D. S. (1989). The Yale-Brown Obsessive Compulsive Scale (Y-BOCS). Part I: Development, use and reliability. *Archives of General Psychiatry, 46*(11), 1006–1011.

Grabli, D., McCairn, K., Hirsch, E. C., Agid, Y., Feger, J., Francois, C., & Tremblay, L. (2004). Behavioural disorders induced by external globus pallidus dysfunction in primates: I. Behavioural study. *Brain, 127*(9), 2039–2054.

Greenberg, B. D., Malone, D. A., Friehs, G. M., Rezai, A. R., Kubu, C. S., Malloy, P. F.,...Rasmussen, S. A. (2006). Three-year outcomes in deep brain stimulation for highly resistant obsessive-compulsive disorder. *Neuro-Psychopharmacology, 31*(11), 2384–2393.

Hamilton, M. (1960). A rating scale for depression. *Journal of Neurology, Neurosurgery & Psychiatry, 23*(1), 56–62.

Hirsch, C. R., Mathews, A., Lequertiera, B., Permana, G., & Hayesa, S. (2013). Characteristics of worry in GAD. *Journal of Behavior Therapy and Experimental Psychiatry, 44*(4), 388–395.

Hoehn, M. M., & Yahr, M. D. (1967). Parkinsonism: Onset, progression and mortality. *Neurology, 17*(5), 427–442.

Hollander, E., Cohen, L., Richards, M., Mullen, L., DeCaria, C., & Stern, Y. (1993). A pilot study of the neuropsychology of obsessive-compulsive disorder and Parkinson's disease: Basal ganglia disorders. *The Journal of Neuropsychiatry and Clinical Neurosciences, 5*(1), 104–107.

Hymas, N., Less, A., Bolton, D., Epps, K., & Head, D. (1991). The neurology of obsessional slowness. *Brain, 114*(5), 2203–2233.

Kish, S.J., Tong, J., Hornykiewicx, O., Rajput, A., Chang, L., Guttman, M., & Furukawa, Y. (2008). Preferential loss of serotonin markers in caudate versus putamen in Parkinson's disease. *Brain, 131*(1), 120–131.

Knight, R. T. (1991). Evoked potential studies of attention capacity in human frontal lobe. In H. S. Levin, H. M. Eisenberg, & A. L. Benton (Eds.), *Frontal lobe function and dysfunction* (pp. 139–153). New York, NY: Oxford University Press.

Koo, M. S., Kim, E. J., Roh, D., & Kim, C. H. (2010). Role of dopamine in the pathophysiology and treatment of obsessive-compulsive disorder. *Expert Review of Neurotherapeutics, 10*(2), 275–290.

Kuelz, A. K., Hohagen, F., & Voderholzer, U. (2004). Neuropsychological performance in obsessive-compulsive disorder: A critical review. *Biological Psychology, 65*(3), 185–236.

Lees, A. J. (1989). Neuropsychological disorders in Parkinson disorders. Relations to psychomotor inhibition and obsessive-compulsive disease. *Nervenarzt, 60*(2), 71–79.

Lezak, M. (1995). *Neuropsychological assessment* (3rd ed.) New York, NY: Oxford University Press.

Lezak, M. D., Howieson, D. B., & Loring, D. W. (2004). *Neuropsychological assessment* (4th ed.). New York, NY: Oxford University Press.

Mallet, L., Mesnage, V., Houeto, J. L., Pelissolo, A., Yelnik, J., Behar, C.,…Agid, Y. (2002). Compulsions, Parkinson's disease, and stimulation. *Lancet, 360*(9342), 1302–1304.

Mallet, L., Polosan, M., Jaafari, N., Baup, N., Welter, M. L., Fontaine, D.,…Pelissolo, A. (2008). Subthalamic nucleus stimulation in severe obsessive-compulsive disorder. *New England Journal of Medicine, 359*(20), 2121–2134.

Mallet, L., Schupbach, M., N'Diaye, K., Remy, P., Bardinet, E., Czernecki, V.…Yelnik, J. (2007). Stimulation of subterritories of the subthalamic nucleus reveals its role in the integration of the emotional and motor aspects of behaviour. *Proceedings of the National Academy of Sciences of the United States of America, 104*(25), 10661–10666.

Martinot, J. L., Allilaire, J. F., Mazoyer, B. M., Hantouche, E., Huret, J. D., & Legaut-Demare, F. (1990). Obsessive compulsive disorder: A clinical neuropsychological and positron emission tomography study. *Acta Psychiatrica Scandinavica, 82*(3), 233–242.

Maruyama, T. (2000). *Cognitive dysfunction in Parkinson's disease. Nippon Rinsho, 58*(10), 2007–2015.

Milliery, M., Bouvard, M., Aupetit, J., & Cottraux, (2000). Sustained attention in patients with obsessive-compulsive disorder: A controlled study. *Psychiatry Research, 96*(3), 199–209.

Mirsky, A. F., Anthony, B. J., Duncan, C. C., & Ahearn, M. B. (1991). Analysis of the elements of attention: A neuropsychological approach. *Neuropsychology Review, 2*(2), 109–145.

Moritz, S., Birkner, C., Kloss, M., Jahn, H., Hand, I., Haasen, C., & Krausz, M. (2002). Executive functioning in obsessive-compulsive disorder, unipolar depression and schizophrenia. *Archives of Clinical Neuropsychology, 17*(5), 477–483.

Okasha, A., Rafaat, M., Mahallawy, N., El Nahas, G., Seif El Dawla, A., Sayed, M., & El Kholi, S. (2000). Cognitive dysfunction in obsessive-compulsive disorder. *Acta Psychiatrica Scandinavica, 101*(4), 281–285.

Oldfield, R. C. (1971). The assessment and analysis of handedness: The Edinburgh inventory. *Neuropsychologia, 9*(1), 97–113.

Pershad, D., & Verma, S. K. (1990). *Handbook of PGI battery of brain dysfunction.* Agra: National Psychological Corporation.

Pollux, P. M., & Robertson, C. (2002). Reduced task-set inertia in Parkinson's disease. *Journal of Clinical and Experimental Neuropsychology, 24*(8), 1046–1056.

Raven, J. C. (1938). *Progressive matrices: A perceptual test of intelligence.* London: H.K. Lewis.

Rapoport, J. (1990). Obsessive compulsive disorder and basal ganglia dysfunction. *Psychological Medicine, 20*(3), 465–469.

Savage, C. R., Keuthen, N. J., & Jenike, M. A. (1996). Recall and recognition memory in obsessive-compulsive disorder. *The Journal of Neuropsychiatry and Clinical Neurosciences, 8*(1), 99–103.

Sawle, G. V., Hymas, N. F., Lees, A. J., & Frackowiak, R. S. J. (1991). Obsessional slowness: Functional studies with positron emission tomography. *Brain, 114*(5), 2191–2202.

Schmidtke, K., Schorb, A., Winkelmann, G., & Hohagen, F. (1998). Cognitive frontal dysfunction in obsessive compulsive disorder. *Biological Psychiatry, 43*(9), 666–673.

Stam, C. J., Visser, S. L., Op de Coul, A. W., De Sonneville, L. M. J., Schellens, R. L. L. A., Brunia, C. H. M.,...Gielen, G. (1993). Disturbed regulation of attention in Parkinson's disease. *Brain, 116*(5), 1139–1158.

Stengler-Wenzke, K., Muller, U., Angermeyer, M. C., Sabri, O., & Hesse, S. (2004). Reduced serotonin transfer-availability in OCD. *European Archives of Psychiatry and Clinical Neuroscience, 254*(4), 252–255.

Strub, R. L., & Black, F. W. (1995). *The mental status examination in neurology* (3rd ed.). New Delhi: Jaypee.

Swedo, S. E., & Rapoport, J. L. (1989). Phenomenology and differential diagnosis of obsessive-compulsive disorder in children and adolescents. In J. L. Rapoport (Ed.), *Obsessive-compulsive disorder in children and adolescent* (pp. 355). Washington, DC: American Psychiatric Press.

Vander Wee, N. J., Stevens, H., Hardeman, J., Mandl, R. C., Denys, D., van Megan, H. J.,...Westenberg, H. M. (2004). Enhanced dopamine transporter density in psychotropic naïve patients with OCD shown by β-CIT SPECT. *The American Journal of Psychiatry, 161*(12), 2201–2206.

Velikova, S., Locatelli, M., Insacco, C., Smeraldi, E., Comi, G., & Leocani, L. (2010). Dysfunctional brain circuitry in obsessive-compulsive disorder: Source and coherence analysis of EEG rhythms. *Neuro Image*, 49(1), 977–983.

Zago, L., Pesenti, M., Mellet, E., Crivello, F., Mazoyer, B., & Tzourio-Mazoyer, N. (2001). Neural correlates of simple and complex mental calculation. *NeuroImage*, 13(2), 314–327.

Zakzanis, K. K., & Freedman, M. (1999). A neuropsychological comparison of demented and non-demented patients with Parkinson's disease. *Applied Neuropsychology*, 6(3), 129–146.

Zalewski, C., Johnson-Selfridge, M. T., Ohriner, S., Zarella, K., & Seltzer, J. C. (1998). A review of neuropsychological differences between paranoid and nonparanoid schizophrenia patients. *Schizophrenia Bulletin*, 24(1), 127–145.

Zhou, X., Chen, C., Zhang, H., Xue, G., Dong, Q., Jin, Z.,...Chena, C. (2006). Neural Substrates for forward and backward recitation of numbers and the alphabet: A close examination of the role of intraparietal sulcus and perisylvian areas. *Brain Research*, 1099(2006), 109–120.

Zielinski, C. M., Taylor, M. A., & Juzwin, K. R. (1991). Neuropsychological deficits in obsessive-compulsive disorder. *Neuropsychiatry, Neuropsychology and Behavioral Neurology*, 4(2), 110–116.

Zimmermann, P., Sprengelmeyer, R., Fimm, B., & Wallesch, C. W. (1992). Cognitive slowing in decision tasks in early and advanced Parkinson's disease. *Brain and Cognition*, 18(1), 60–69.

4

Obsessive Personality Traits, Metacognitive Beliefs and Executive Functions in Patients with OCD

Sreemoyee Tarafder and Pritha Mukhopadhyay

Introduction

The patients of OCD often take a lot of time in going about their work, in taking decisions, completing chores and activities of daily living that causes marked distress and impairment in terms of socio-occupational functioning (DSM-IV; American Psychiatric Association, 1994). The incapacitating nature of OCD can be understood when one takes into account that OCD was named by the World Health Organization as one of the leading causes worldwide of 'years lived with illness-related disability' (Murray & Lopez, 1996) and identified as the fourth most common psychiatric disorder (Karno, Golding, Sorenson, & Burnam, 1988), indicating its serious impact on quality of life. From the neurophysiological perspective, OCD is addressed exclusively as resulting from dysfunction of the corticostriatal circuitry, with particular emphasis on the orbitofronto-striato-thalamic circuits (Graybiel & Rauch, 2000; Saxena, Bota, & Brody, 2001; Saxena, Brody, Schwartz, & Baxter, 1998), and with a disregard of growing evidence base of psychotherapy research outcomes which have found metacognitive factors to be of crucial significance in this disorder (Rees & van Koesveld, 2008; Solem, Håland, Vogel, Hansen, & Wells, 2009). It is yet to be confirmed whether the (a) OCD symptoms are initiated by their idiosyncratic metacognitive disposition, (b) OCD trait is being mediated by the neurophysiological mechanism resulting in symptoms or (c) the psychological disposition is the outcome of the neurophysiological predisposition. Need was therefore felt for parallel investigations to address these unresolved queries. Given that relatively little is known about the neurobiological basis and aetiological origins of OCD (Chamberlain, Blackwell, Fineberg, Robbins, & Sahakian, 2005), due consideration of each of the perspectives is necessary to develop a comprehensive account of the symptomatology of OCD.

Neuroimaging studies suggest that OCD is fundamentally a disorder affecting the function of, and interaction between, several frontal–subcortical circuits, including the lateral orbitofrotal–subcortical circuit and the dorsolateral prefrontal–subcortical circuit (DLPFC). The symptoms, according to Arciniegas and Beresford (2001), appear to be related to over-activity of the orbitofrontal–subcortical circuit and is found to be reduced by either reduction in activity of this circuit (being modulated by selective serotonin reuptake inhibitors or SSRIs) or increased activity in the dorsolateral prefrontal–subcortical circuit (as happens in cognitive behaviour therapy or CBT), which increases the ability to inhibit, or more effectively modulate the activity in OFC. Both pharmacotherapy and psychotherapy work by altering the activities of the frontal–subcortical circuits via different channels in OCD. SSRIs work by attenuating activity of the striatum to facilitate behavioural inhibition; whereas CBT works by inhibiting the dorsolateral–prefrontal cortex which appears to attenuate the drive in the OFC. The reports of positive outcome of CBT in

110 / Sreemoyee Tarafder and Pritha Mukhopadhyay

symptom reduction (O'Kearney, Anstey, & von Sanden, 2006) point out the importance of the common ground between psychological disposition and neurobiological functioning. Alteration in personality traits may lead to subsequent reduction in executive dysfunction; modifications may lead to symptom reduction and bring about a change in the neural network operative in the disorder. This necessitated an investigation to cover a wider gamut of variables considering both personality trait and myriad aspects of executive functions to help understand this complex disorder more comprehensively. Previous research has implicated the importance of studying obsessive personality traits, neuroticism, metacognitive beliefs and executive dysfunction in OCD. The relationship between obsessive personality traits and OCD symptomatology, between executive functions and obsessive symptoms and traits and that between beliefs and OC symptoms and OC traits will be examined in the present chapter.

Most patients who suffer from obsessions readily admit that their thoughts/images/impulses are irrational, excessive and unwanted. They also admit that they are a product of their own mind and not imposed from without (Khanna & Reddy, 2004). In this chapter, we will highlight what is meant by executive functions and metacognition in the specific context of OCD.

Executive Functions

Executive functions (EFs) can be defined as the ability to perform complex tasks, such as planning and carrying out a problem-solving task. It requires the ability to develop and maintain an appropriate problem-solving strategy across changing stimulus conditions in order to achieve a future goal (Luria, 1973). Attentional set shifting, verbal fluency, planning, decision-making and WM are integral parts of executive functions. EF are higher-order cognitive skills requiring the ability to develop and maintain an appropriate problem-solving strategy across changing conditions of stimuli in order to achieve a future goal (Luria, 1973). Perry and Hodges (1999) refer to EF as 'those higher-order cognitive capabilities that are called upon in order to formulate new plans of action and to select, schedule, and monitor appropriate sequences of action'. The broader term 'executive functions' refers to so-called higher-order cognitive functions such as volition, intended action, planning and self-monitoring of behaviour. These higher-order functions coordinate and integrate basic cognitive functions and depend upon frontal cortex integrity (Lezak, 1995). According to Lezak (1995), EF is necessary for appropriate, socially responsible and effectively self-serving adult conduct. In other words, these definitions point out the nature of EF which incorporates engagement in independent, goal-directed behaviour that monitors our self-regulatory behaviour. Based on the assumption that OCD is associated with a frontal–striatal loop metabolic dysfunction, executive functions have been extensively examined in OCD patients (Kuelz, Hohagen, & Voderholzer, 2004).

Studies of neuropsychological functions in OCD have documented deficits in several cognitive domains, particularly with regard to visuospatial abilities, executive functioning, and motor speed (Tükel et al., 2011), wherein EF deficit seems to be the more consistent neuropsychological deficit in OCD (Martínez-González & Piqueras-Rodríguez, 2008). Examinations of neuropsychological functioning in OCD have been conducted extensively all over the world and the present study concentrates on the areas of set shifting, fluency, processing speed, working memory and planning, justified by a variety of clinical observations and evidence base suggesting the relevance of its inclusion in further investigation.

Metacognition

Metacognition is defined as 'cognition about one's own cognition' and was first used in the context of developmental psychology to describe the cognitive processes and structures that monitor and control aspects of cognition (Flavell, 1979; Moses & Baird, 1999). In a broader context, metacognition has been conceptualized as general purpose and plans that guide information processing and maintain maladaptive processing configurations responsible for emotional vulnerability, such as those typified by rumination and threat monitoring (Wells & Matthews, 1994, 1996). Metacognition refers to any knowledge or cognitive process that monitors or controls cognition. Metacognition is a broad term, encompassing both knowledge and regulation of cognitive activity. The schema in Table 4.1 is based on the work of Moses and Baird (1999).

From the definition, we can see that metacognition may be closely related to EF, which involves the ability to monitor and control the information processing necessary to produce voluntary action (Fernandez-Duque, Baird, & Posner, 2000). Metacognitive regulation refers to a number of EF tasks such as planning, resource allocation (i.e., selective attention), monitoring, checking and error detection and correction, which in turn reflects either monitoring or control processes. The monitoring process keeps track of ongoing cognition, whereas the control process modifies ongoing cognitive activities (e.g., by shifting attentional focus). The control and monitoring processes interact with a metacognitive knowledge to provide holistic understanding of a cognitive task.

Table 4.1	Metacognition Schema	
Metacognitive Knowledge	**Metacognitive Regulation**
Metacognitive knowledge consists primarily of knowledge or beliefs about the factors that affect the course and outcome of cognitive enterprises. This knowledge may be accurate or inaccurate and, like other types of information stored in memory, can be triggered unintentionally by retrieval cues. Once activated, metacognitive knowledge is likely to influence the course of thought processes.	Metacognitive regulation refers to a number of EFs, such as planning, resource allocation (i.e., selective attention), monitoring, checking, and error detection and correction, which in turn reflect either monitoring or control processes. The monitoring process keeps track of ongoing cognitions whereas the control process modifies ongoing cognition (e.g., by shifting attentional focus). The control and monitoring processes interact with metacognitive knowledge.

Source: Authors.

One of the features of OCD is a tendency to focus attention on their thought process. This heightened cognitive self-consciousness increases the detection of unwanted target thoughts and may trigger further intrusions. Self-regulatory Executive Function (S-REF) model proposed by Wells and Matthews (1994) suggests that obsessionals have a tendency to assign priority to internally generated events rather than external events. Thus, even when sensory input confirms the execution of behaviour, individuals attentively focus upon the penalty of not performing the action. This tendency to focus on doubts reduces confidence in memory for actions/events and may contribute to checking behaviour even more. Maladaptive self-processing tendencies are also manifested in the internal signals that patients with OCD use to signal the cessation or maintenance of overt and covert rituals. In particular, there is a tendency to rely on internal cognitive criteria, such as 'perfect' uninterrupted memories of events or 'feelings of certainty' as stop signals for rituals. Unfortunately, such signals are difficult to accomplish and are prone to disruption by a range of factors.

Researchers studying the relationship between metacognition and OC symptoms report that metacognitive factors that are measured by MCQ are positively related to OC factors (Gwilliam, Wells, & Cartwright-Hatton, 2004; Hermans, Martens, De Cort, Pieters, & Eelen, 2003; Janeck, Calamari, Riemann, & Heffelfinger, 2003; Wells & Papageorgiou, 1998). A number of studies have highlighted the role of metacognition in OCD (Fisher & Wells, 2005; Myers & Wells, 2005; Wells & Papageorgiou, 1998). Solem, Myers, Fisher, Vogel and Wells (2010) point out that treatment data consisting of a case-series study of meta-cognitive therapy (Fisher & Wells, 2008) and group treatment studies (e.g., Rees & van Koesveld, 2008) show that change in metacognitions predict treatment outcome following exposure and response-prevention treatment (Solem et al., 2009). Wells (2000) reports significant relationship between OC symptoms and metacognitions, and the metacognitive measures differentiated between the OCD group and the CG adding to the validity of the metacognitions assessed as discriminatory factors.

This study was an attempt to understand metacognition and EFs in OCD from the same platform, investigating how each influences the other and adds to the symptom repertoire of patients suffering from OCD.

Methods

Sample

The study was a cross-sectional comparative study based on purposive sampling. There were two groups of participants in the study—the patients with OCD (n=75) and their age-, sex-, education-matched CG (n=75) consisting of 44 males and 33 females in each group. Exclusion criteria kept common for all the groups were serious head injury, substance abuse and epilepsy.

The clinical sample (age mean=27.63 years, standard deviation [SD]=9.63 years, right-handed, urban, with at least standard VIII education) of patients with a diagnosis of OCD without co-morbidity as per *International Classification of Disorders* (ICD-10) criteria (F42) and with onset of illness at 17 years or later, was selected from psychiatric services of R. G. Kar Medical College & Hospital, Kolkata, India. Age of onset earlier than 12 years, patients above 45 years, patients with history of other psychiatric illnesses, hoarders were excluded to minimize the heterogeneity of the OCD sample. Patients with diagnosis of OCD with comorbid conditions other than depression were excluded. The community sample was selected through snowballing technique and screened on the GHQ.

Measures

To determine the nature of obsessional symptoms and traits, metacognitive beliefs and overall executive functioning of the patients with OCD, their first-degree relatives (FDR) and normal controls, the following tools were used:

1. Semi-structured socio-demographic and clinical data sheet
2. Yale Brown Obsessive Compulsive Scale (Goodman et al., 1989): to measure severity of obsessions and compulsions (OCD group)

3. Leyton Obsessional Inventory (Cooper, 1970): to assess obsessive symptoms and anankastic traits
4. Metacognition Questionnaire (Cartwright-Hatton & Wells, 1997): to determine metacognitive beliefs in terms of positive worry beliefs, negative worry beliefs, cognitive consciousness and cognitive confidence
5. Beck Depression Inventory (Beck, Ward, Menderson, Mock, & Erbaugh, 1961): to measure subjective level of distress
6. General Health Questionnaire (Goldberg & Hillier, 1979): to rule out psychiatric morbidity (in CG)
7. Edinburgh Handedness Inventory (Oldfield, 1971): to determine handedness of the participants
8. Wisconsin Card Sorting Test (Heaton, Chelune, Talley, Kay, & Curtiss, 1993): to assess perseveration and set shifting ability
9. Controlled Oral Word Association Test (Rao, Subbakrishna, & Gopukumar, 2004): to test phonemic fluency
10. Animals Names Test (Lezak, 1995): to test categorical fluency
11. Processing Speed Index (PSI) from WAIS-III (Wechsler, Wycherley, & Benjamin, 1997): subtests to measure processing speed
12. Working Memory Index from WAIS-III (Wechsler et al., 1997): subtests to measure WM
13. N-Back (Verbal) Test (Rao et al., 2004) (Verbal): to determine verbal WM
14. Tower of London Test—Drexel University Test (Culbertson & Zillmer, 2001): to assess planning

Procedure

Subjects were selected on the basis of the inclusion/exclusion criteria mentioned earlier, after getting their consent. A semi-structured socio-demographic and clinical data sheet was filled by the subjects. YBOCS was administered to the OCD group and GHQ to the community controls. Edinburgh Handedness Inventory (EHI) followed. After the screening, LOI, MCQ,

NEO-FFI, BDI, COWAT, Animals Names Test, the WAIS-III subtests, N-Back (Verbal) Test, WCST and TOL Test were administered, but not in any particular order so as to nullify order effect. The study period was from July 2007 to August 2010. Testing was completed in seven hours distributed over two or three sessions, owing to time constraints or to ensure sustained attention. Efforts were made to make the testing conditions constant for the different subjects as far as practicable. The participants were tested at the Department of Psychology, University of Calcutta.

Analysis of Data

Statistical analysis of the data was done with the help of SPSS 17. The obtained data was checked for normal distribution using Levene's Test for equality of variances. As the data followed normal distribution, parametric statistics were considered. Independent sample t-test was used for OCD and CG comparisons. To find out the nature of relationship between the different neuropsychological measures taken and OC symptoms, OC traits and aspects of metacognition, the Pearson's coefficient correlation was computed for the patient group. When the correlations were found to be significant, Stepwise Multiple Regression Analysis (SMRA) was computed to determine the relative contribution of different variables upon OC symptoms and symptom severity. For analysis, 0.05 and 0.01 level of significance was accepted as critical level.

Results

Section A: Socio-demographic Details of the Sample

Before going into the narration of the results obtained from the study, it is imperative to consider the socio-demographic details of the sample.

Socio-demographic description of the sample shows that study group was comparable with their community counterparts in terms of age, sex (44 males and 33 females in each group), and years of education, ranging from standard VIII to postgraduation.

The symptom severity in the clinical group, as assessed on YBOCS, ranged from 10 to 40, with the mean being 22 that falls within moderate range. Duration of illness ranged from 2 to 10 years. The socio-demographic details of the two groups are provided in Table 4.2.

Table 4.2	Socio-demographic Details of OCD and their Control Group		
Variable	**Statistic**	**OCD**	**CG**
Age	Range	17–49	17–47
	Mean	27.63	26.64
	SD	9.03	5.75
	t	0.798;	
Education	Range	10–20	10–20
(In years)	Mean	13.14	13.38
	SD	2.86	3.5
	t	0.496; $p=0.62$	
Sex	Male	44	44
	Female	33	33
Handedness		Right-handed	Right-handed

Source: Authors.

Section B.1: Comparison of Distress, Obsessional Traits, Obsessional Symptoms and Metacognitive Beliefs Among OCD and the CG

Table 4.3 indicates that the two groups—OCD and CG—showed significant difference in experience of subjective depression, obsessive symptom and obsessive personality trait, with greater impairment being shown in the OCD. The OCD group also scores higher than the peers on all domains of MCQ, namely, positive beliefs about worry, negative beliefs about worry focusing

118 / Sreemoyee Tarafder and Pritha Mukhopadhyay

Table 4.3	Comparison Between OCD and the Peer CG on BDI, LOI and MCQ by Unpaired t-test with Mean (M), SD, t-test Values and Corresponding Level of Significance				
	OCD		CG		Mean Difference
Variables	M	SD	M	SD	t
Depression (BDI)	26.64	12.27	8.76	6.30	11.22**
Obsessive symptoms	24.93	9.26	12.48	6.51	9.53**
Obsessive personality trait	12.45	4.48	7.85	4.09	6.57**
Positive beliefs about worry	36.68	11.08	32.79	10.98	2.16*
Negative worry beliefs (Uncontrollability)	50.33	9.62	30.91	8.68	12.98**
Low cognitive confidence	23.85	7.29	17.67	5.70	5.78**
Negative worry beliefs (Punishment, responsibility)	35.40	5.54	24.51	6.04	11.52**
Cognitive Self-consciousness	20.81	7.12	17.36	4.84	3.47**

Note: * $p < 0.05$ level, ** $p < 0.01$, df = 148
Source: Authors.

on uncontrollability and danger, low cognitive confidence, negative beliefs about thoughts including themes of superstition, punishments, responsibility and need for control and cognitive self-consciousness, which indicates a difficulty in metacognitive processing in them.

Figure 4.1 shows the comparative performance of the two groups on BDI and LOI indicated by mean obtained by the OCD and CG.

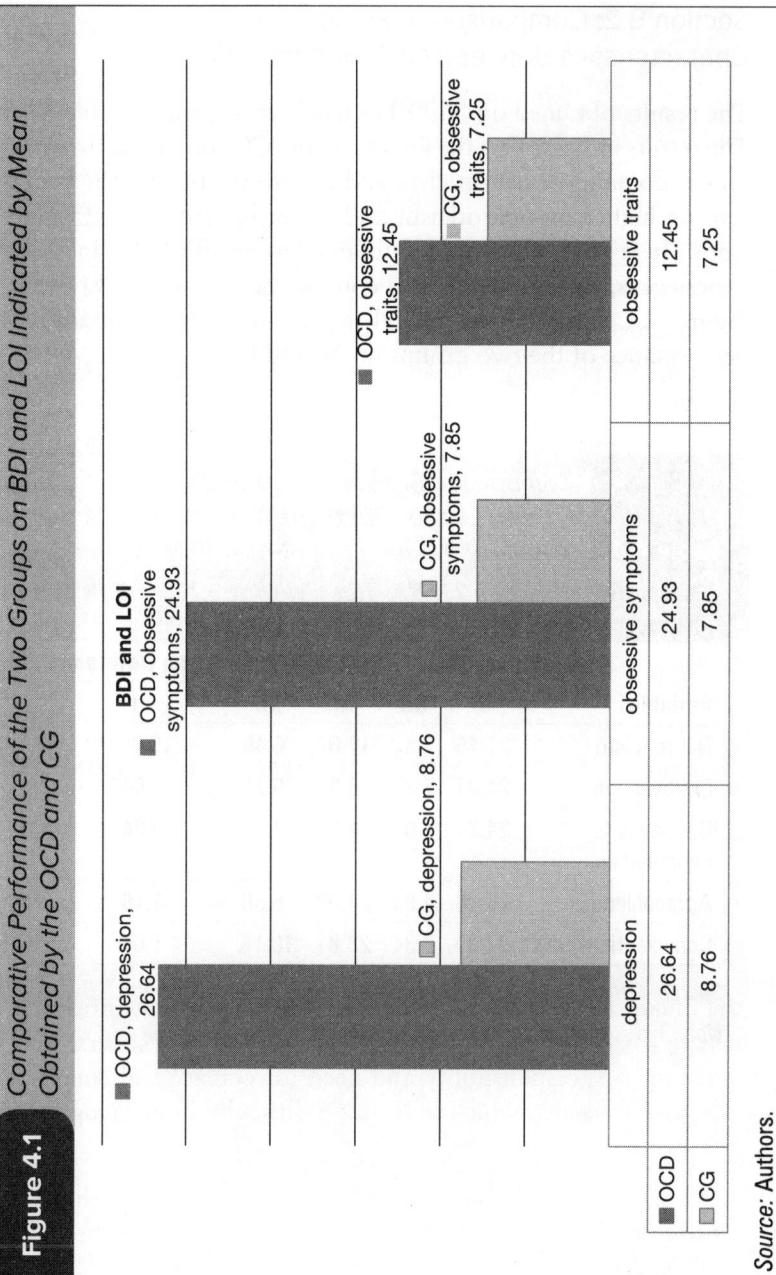

Figure 4.1 *Comparative Performance of the Two Groups on BDI and LOI Indicated by Mean Obtained by the OCD and CG*

	depression	obsessive symptoms	obsessive traits
OCD	26.64	24.93	12.45
CG	8.76	7.85	7.25

Source: Authors.

Section B.2: Comparison of Personality Characteristics Between OCD and the CG

The results obtained on NEO-FFI has been shown in Table 4.4. The results indicate that the OCD and the CGs differ significantly on the domains of neuroticism and extroversion, with the OCD scoring higher on neuroticism and lower in terms of extroversion. There are no differences obtained in terms of Openness to experiences, Agreeableness and conscientiousness on NEO-FFI. Figure 4.2 shows the graphical depiction of the comparative performance of the two groups on NEO-FFI.

Table 4.4	Comparison Between OCD and the Control Group (CG) on NEO-Five Factor Inventory by Unpaired t-test with Mean (M), Standard Deviations (SD), t-test Values and Corresponding Level of Significance

	OCD		CG		Mean Difference
Variables	M	SD	M	SD	t
Neuroticism	31.48	7.5	17.02	6.45	13.09**
Extroversion	24.27	7.32	26.97	9.21	1.99*
Openness to Experiences	24.21	4.67	24.25	7.19	0.04
Agreeableness	25.16	4.84	24.09	6.36	1.16
Conscientiousness	27.31	7.34	28.81	10.16	1.04

Source: Authors.
Note: * $p < 0.05$ level, ** $p < 0.01$.

Figure 4.2 *Comparative Performance of the Two Groups on NEO Five Factor Inventory*

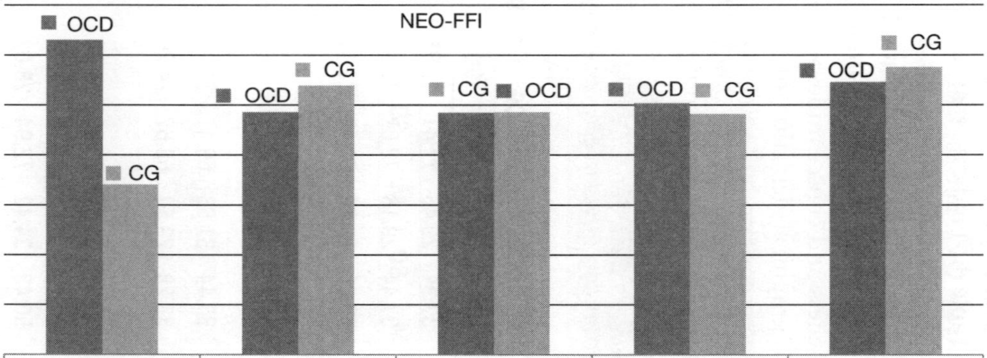

NEO-FFI

	N	E	O	A	C
OCD	31.48	24.27	24.21	25.16	27.31
CG	17.02	26.97	24.25	24.09	28.81

Source: Authors.

Section B.3: Comparison of Executive Functions Among OCD and the CG

WCST was used to assess set-shifting in both the groups. The findings (provided in Table 4.5) indicate that the OCD and CG differ significantly in terms of set shifting as assessed on the WCST with the OCD group showing deficit in all domains of set shifting with the exception of failure to maintain set as compared to CG.

Table 4.5	Comparison Between OCD and the Peer Control Group (CG) on Wisconsin Card Sorting Test by Unpaired t-test with Mean (M), Standard Deviations (SD), t-test Values and Corresponding Level of Significance

	OCD		CG		Mean Difference
Variables	M	SD	M	SD	t
Error	37.94	29.46	77.41	22.31	9.25**
Percentage of error	37.44	29.18	72.62	22.93	8.21**
Perseverative response	30.25	29.04	61.40	23.13	7.26**
Percentage of perseverative response	28.25	27.36	58.80	22.49	7.47**
Perseverative error	33.44	31.03	69.41	24.45	7.89**
Percentage of perseverative error	33.28	29.89	68.52	24.20	7.93**
Nonperseverative Error	48.96	34.87	73.30	26.90	4.79**
Percentage of non-perseverative error	50.43	34.42	72.94	28.02	4.39**
Conceptual-level response	40.12	27.35	65.86	20.01	6.58**
Percentage of conceptual-level response	36.33	29.73	69.16	24.67	7.36**

| Variables | OCD | | CG | | Mean Difference |
	M	SD	M	SD	t
Number of categories completed	46.43	36.95	81.92	29.02	6.54**
Trials to complete first category	41.40	35.81	67.25	31.97	4.66**
Failure to maintain set	64.15	35.27	74.88	37.11	1.82

Note: df = 148F

Source: Authors.

Fluency

Results obtained on tests assessing phonemic and lexical fluency have been depicted in Table 4.6. It indicates significant difference between the OCD and CG on the domains of COWAT of words starting with 'F', 'A' and 'S'. The CG has performed better on COWAT and has been able to generate more options within the specified lexical category.

Table 4.6 *Comparison Between OCD and the CG on COWAT and Animal Naming Test by Unpaired t-test with M, SD, t-test Values and Corresponding Level of Significance*

| Variables | OCD | | CG | | Mean Difference |
	M	SD	M	SD	t
COWA—F	10.86	4.71	14.05	4.43	4.26**
COWA—A	10.77	4.64	12.22	4.30	1.99*
COWA—S	10.76	4.72	14.50	4.93	4.75**
Fluency—Animals	14.16	3.29	14.61	4.09	0.75
Fluency—Fruits	13.57	4.24	13.69	4.55	0.17

Note: * $p < 0.05$ level, ** $p < 0.01$ level, df = 148.

Source: Authors.

Working Memory

Table 4.7 indicates that in terms of WM the OCD and CG differs significantly. On all the domains of WMI, the OCD group did poorly revealing deficit in WM functions in them. They, however, performed better in terms of N-Back (Verbal) Tests.

Table 4.7	Comparison Between OCD and the CG on Arithmetic, Letter Number Sequencing (LNS) and Digit Span That Provides the Working Memory Index (WAIS-III), the N-Back (Verbal) Test by Unpaired t-test with M, SD, t-test Values and Corresponding Level of Significance

	OCD		CG		Mean Difference
Variables	M	SD	M	SD	T
Arithmetic	9.32	3.369	13.06	3.35	6.82**
LNS	8.08	3.46	10.80	2.57	5.45**
DF	9.12	2.48	11.01	2.68	4.47**
DB	6.44	2.33	8.05	2.71	3.89**
Digit span	8.70	2.69	11.29	3.70	4.89**
WMI	92.01	16.80	110.16	15.95	6.48**
WMI percentile	37.50	30.08	67.75	27.20	6.46**
N-Back 1 Hit	78.73	28.58	63.30	37.04	2.85**
N-Back 1 Error	80.54	30.43	62.17	40.48	3.14**
N-Back 2 Hit	45.56	30.23	46.08	28.18	0.11
N-Back 2 Error	56.58	29.65	39.29	30.65	3.51**

Note: $p < 0.05$ level, **$p < 0.01$ level, df = 148.

Source: Authors.

Processing Speed

Processing Speed has been assessed using subtests from WAIS and the findings have been shown in Table 4.8. It reveals that the OCD and CG groups differ significantly on all the sub-tests determining processing speed, with CG performing significantly better in all them.

| Table 4.8 | Comparison Between OCD and the Control Group (CG) on Symbol Search and Coding That Provides the Processing Speed Index (WAIS-III) by Unpaired t-test with Mean (M), Standard Deviations (SD), t-test Values and Corresponding Level of Significance |

	OCD		CG		Mean Difference
Variables	M	SD	M	SD	T
Symbol search	6.09	2.75	9.02	1.867	7.63**
Error on symbol search	1.53	1.54	2.77	2.66	3.48**
Coding	5.93	2.71	8.42	2.51	5.83**
PSI	78.45	12.31	92.77	10.36	7.70**
PSI percentile	13.38	18.02	34.64	22.35	6.41**

Note: * $p < 0.05$ level, ** $p < 0.01$ level, df = 148.

Source: Authors.

Planning

Planning has been assessed using TOL-DX and it indicates that the OCD and CG differ significantly on all the domains of planning and goal-directed behaviour except on initiation time, with the OCD group performing poorly on the measures of this test. The findings have been shown in Table 4.9.

Table 4.9	Comparison Between OCD and the Control Group (CG) on Various Measures of Tower of London Test by Unpaired t-test with Mean (M), Standard Deviations (SD), t-test Values and Corresponding Level of Significance

	OCD		CG		Mean Difference
Variables	M	SD	M	SD	t
Correct Score	40.97	24.43	57.82	22.88	4.36**
Move score	26.46	24.34	36.86	26.52	2.50**
Initiation time	65.44	22.36	61.32	25.05	1.06
Execution time	15.12	16.96	28.32	22.314	4.07**
Total time	16.10	18.10	31.74	21.49	4.82**
Time violations	42.37	38.10	74.18	34.91	5.33**
Rule violations	68.38	42.74	91.09	19.80	4.18**

Note: * $p < 0.05$ level, ** $p < 0.01$, level df = 148.
Source: Authors.

Section C: Correlation of Variables

From Pearson's product moment coefficient of correlation, it can be seen that in OCD group, obsessive symptom and trait ($r = 0.801$) are highly correlated with each other, thereby showing positive relationship between the two. With respect to metacognition and obsessive symptoms and obsessive traits, it can be seen that there is a positive correlation between symptom severity and MCQ 1 ($r = 0.315$) and MCQ 3 ($r = 0.266$), that is, positive belief about worry and low cognitive confidence among the OCD, indicating that with rise in worry and deficit in cognitive confidence, severity of symptom increases. Obsessive symptoms showed a positive correlation with low cognitive confidence (MCQ 3) ($r = 0.435$) and negative worry beliefs about uncontrollability (MCQ 2) ($r = 0.275$) in the OCD group indicating these metacognitive deficits to be directly correlated with obsessive symptoms.

It can also be seen that when obsessive symptoms, trait and metacognition variables were correlated with the five factors of personality it showed that neuroticism was positively correlated with metacognitive deficits in OCD (r=0.271). Agreeableness (r=−0.34) and openness (r=−0.266) were found to be negatively correlated with metacognitive deficits indicating that the rise in the latter led to the decrease in the former attributes.

When obsessive symptoms, trait and metacognition variables were correlated with set shifting variables, a negative correlation was found to exist between obsessive symptoms and traits with different domains of set shifting, namely, error (rsymptom = −0.266, p=0.05; rtrait=−0.346, p=0.01); perseverative error (rsymptom=−0.326, p=0.01; rtrait=−0.405, p=0.01); perseverative response (rsymptom=−0.306, p=0.01; rtrait=−0.408, p=0.01); conceptual level responses (rsymptom=−0.334, p=0.01; rtrait=−0.389, p=0.01) and number of categories completed (NOCC) (rsymptom=−0.429, p=0.01; rtrait=−0.406, p=0.01) on WCST in the OCD group. The direction of the relationship suggests that with rise in obsessive symptom, flexibility gets hampered. Certain domains of metacognition (MCQ 1, MCQ 2 and MCQ 3) were found to be indirectly correlated with domains of set shifting in OCD suggesting that rise in metacognitive deficits leads to poor performance on tasks assessing flexibility.

Obsessive symptom, trait and metacognition correlated with almost all the variables of fluency test studied. Obsessive traits were found to be negatively correlated with aspects of phonemic fluency (r=−0.258) among the OCD and category naming was negatively correlated with aspects of metacognition (r=−0.311). The findings indicate that metacognitive deficits and obsessive traits hamper fluid generation of alternatives.

In terms of WM, variables were found to be correlated with obsessive symptoms, trait and metacognitive beliefs in OCD group. The performance on tasks pertaining to WM, namely, arithmetic (r=−0.264), digit span (r=−0.338) and LNS (r=−0.271) were negatively correlated with symptoms and trait in the OCD. Positive belief about worry (MCQ 1) were negatively correlated with performance on WM tasks (r=−0.272) emphasizing how defunct metacognition affects performance on WM tasks. A negative relationship between low cognitive confidence (MCQ 3) and WMI (r=−0.313) was observed in the OCD group. When correlation of obsessive symptoms, trait and metacognition was done with variables of processing speed it emerged as significant in the OCD group. Symptom severity and Processing Speed Index (r=−0.274) were negatively correlated with each other indicating an inverse relationship between severity and prompt manipulation of information. Symptoms (r=−0.401) and trait (r=−0.428) both also showed significant negative correlation with processing speed indicating that rise in obsessive trait and symptom brings about reduction in processing speed. Obsessive symptom, trait and metacognition were found to be correlated with planning variables assessed on TOL Test. Obsessive traits showed significant inverse relationships with move score (r=−0.228), execution time (r=−0.347) and total time (r=−0.315) along with rule violation (r=−0.318) in the OCD. The findings indicate rise in obsessive traits and metacognitive dysfunctions negatively affect planning.

Section D: Regression Analysis of Variables

In order to assess the impact of the aforesaid variables on symptom manifestation, and on the severity of the symptoms a series of regression analysis were computed. Results of SMRA showed that positive beliefs about worry (MCQ 1) in combination with the domain of neuroticism contributed significantly to severity of OC symptoms (as assessed on YBOCS). The model predicted symptom severity to the extent of 13% and reiterates the significance of metacognitive deficits in this disorder.

Predictors of obsessive symptoms in OCD: Results of SMRA (Table 4.10) show that obsessive trait in combination with the variables, namely, negative worry beliefs regarding responsibility

Table 4.10	Results of SMRA Showing the Variables Contributing Significantly to OC Symptoms (as Assessed on LOI) in OCD Group		
Model	DV: Obsessive Symptoms	Adjusted R^2	Significance
1	Obsessive personality traits	0.636	0.001
2	Traits + Metacognition (Negative worry beliefs of responsibility/control [MCQ 2])	0.673	0.001
3	Trait + MCQ 2 + Total time (on TOL)	0.695	0.001
4	Trait + MCQ 2 + Total time + NOCC on WCST	0.713	0.001
5	Trait + MCQ 2 + Total time + NOCC + Neuroticism (on NEO-FFI)	0.735	0.001

Source: Authors.

and need for control (MCQ 2), total problem-solving time (on TOL), NOCC—the index of cognitive inflexibility (NOCC on WCST)—and neuroticism (assessed on NEO-FFI) contributed significantly to OC symptoms (as assessed on LOI). The model predicted OCD symptoms to the extent of 73.5% with obsessive personality traits emerging as the highest contributor (adjusted $R^2 = 0.735$; $p = 0.001$).

In sum, the results show the following:

1. The OCD and controls were found to significantly differ in terms of depression, obsessive symptoms and obsessive personality traits with OCD scoring higher on the measures.
2. On all domains of metacognition, the OCD groups scored significantly higher than the community controls.
3. On NEO-FFI, OCD group significantly differed from controls, being more neurotic and less extroverted than the CG.

4. With respect to set shifting, the OCD and the CG significantly differed from each other in terms of trials to complete first category, error, perseverative response, perseverative error, nonperseverative error and conceptual-level response percentage, with the OCD group showing deficits in all the domains.

5. There was a significant difference between the OCD and CG on the domains of COWAT of words starting with 'F', 'A' and 'S', but in terms of category fluency no significant difference was found between the OCD and the controls.

6. With respect to WM, the OCD and CG differed significantly on arithmetic, LNS, DF, DB, digit span, and N-Back 2 Error.

7. In terms of processing speed, the OCD and CG differed significantly on symbol search, errors committed on the symbol search and coding along with Processing Speed Index.

8. With respect to TOL, OCD and CG varied in terms of correct score, move score, execution time, total time, time violation and rule violation.

Discussion

Discussion of the obtained results will help in understanding the findings and come to some clearer understanding of the OCD symptomatology and aetiology.

Depression: Patients with OCD and their CG differed with respect to subjective level of **depression** as assessed on BDI. It is to be expected as OCD is a chronic, disabling disorder which results in marked distress and impairment of social and occupational functioning. Although no subject was suffering primarily from major depressive disorder at the time of assessment, the symptomatology of OCD is often found to lead to subjective distress among sufferers of OCD. The rate of psychiatric co-morbidity in patients with OCD is high, with the most common co-morbid diagnosis being major depressive disorder, which affects two-thirds of persons with OCD at some point in life (Pinto, Mancebo, Eisen, Pagano, & Rasmussen, 2006). The presence of depression has been found to be associated with symptom severity in past research with greater chronicity of OC symptoms in clinical samples (Steketee, Chambless, & Tran, 2001; Welnereich, Reich, Robbins, Fishman, & Van Doren, 1976) and with elevated OC symptoms among non-patient participants as well (Scarrabelotti, Duck, & Dickerson, 1995). Mineka, Watson and Clark (1998) posited that people with OCD (or any other anxiety disorder) may feel depressed because of perceived uncontrollability inherently present in the aetiology of anxiety. These symptoms are perceived as uncontrollable and over prolonged periods a state of certain helplessness would be expected to emerge, which would then lead to depression. Fenske and Schwenk (2009) cite studies that have shown that depression among those with OCD is particularly high, with 50% of patients reporting suicidal ideation and 15% having attempted suicide. Kamath, Reddy and Kandavel (2007) have also reported alarming rates of suicidal ideation among Indian patients, worst ever and current, being 59% and 28%, respectively. History of suicide attempt was reported in 27% of the subjects. The study which was carried out in NIMHANS on 100 patients suffering from OCD revealed that depression and hopelessness were the major correlates of suicidal behaviour. Present finding of significant correlation between depression and obsessive symptoms, obsessive traits along with symptom severity confirms the aforementioned association that exists between subjective distress and obsessionality in the patient group.

Obsessive compulsive symptoms and obsessive compulsive personality traits: As individuals with OCD suffer from recurrent, unwanted and intrusive thoughts (obsessions), and/or engage in repetitive, ritualistic behaviours (compulsions), the present finding that the OCD group differed from the normal controls in terms of obsessive symptom and obsessive personality trait was an expected outcome. Their elevated score on the symptom domain on LOI justifies their selection as the pathological group.

Regarding obsessive personality traits, significantly higher scores obtained by the OCD group on LOI indicate the presence of personality traits such as perfectionism, rigidity, doubt, cautiousness and drive for order and symmetry in patients suffering from OCD. Obsessive compulsive personality traits (OCPTs) have been defined by Aycicegi-Dinn, Dinn and Caldwell-Harris (2009) as a 'preoccupation' with rules, organization and perfection. The present findings corroborate with Frost and colleagues' (1994) assertion that obsessive compulsives are more risk-aversive, perfectionistic and guilt-ridden than non-obsessive compulsives, and that these characteristic traits are central features of the disorder. Rasmussen and Tsuang (1986) found that most of their OCD patients were perfectionistic, while Rasmussen and Eisen (1989) found perfectionism common among the childhood traits of adult OCD patients; Steketee and Frost (1992) found OCD patients scored lower on a measure of everyday risk-taking than non-patients. The present findings go hand in hand with these reports where a significant elevation in terms of obsessive traits was seen among the patient population as compared to control counterparts.

Big five factors of personality: The overall analysis of the big five characteristics of personality reveal higher neuroticism and lower extroversion in the OCD group on the NEO-FFI, which is in keeping with previous reports. Rector, Cassin, Richter and Burroughs (2009) mention previous research (e.g., Rector, Hood, Richter, & Bagby, 2002; Samuels et al., 2000) on personality factors, which have demonstrated that relative to control subjects, OCD probands score higher on facets of neuroticism (i.e., anxiety, angry hostility, depression, self-consciousness, impulsiveness and vulnerability to stress). Extraversion was observed more in CG as compared to the OCD group. The OCD may therefore be defined as being reserved, even-paced individuals who prefer to remain alone, being introspective and serious (Costa & McCrae, 1992). The present findings tally with reports of very low extraversion in OCD by Rector et al., (2002) and Fullana et al., (2004), with the former researchers using NEO Personality Inventory (NEO-PI) and the latter using Eysenck Personality Questionnaire (EPQ) as a tool for assessing extroversion. Fullana and associates (2004) even found that OCD patients, with the exception of individuals with subclinical OC problems, scored lower in extraversion than their respective controls. Moreover, the findings strengthen the hypothesis that obsessional symptoms are associated with an introverted personality style (Rachman & Hodgson, 1980).

Metacognitive beliefs: The MCQ consists of five factor-derived subscales: positive worry beliefs (subscale 1; e.g., 'Worrying helps me cope'); negative beliefs about worry focusing on uncontrollability and danger (subscale 2; e.g., 'When I start worrying, I cannot stop'); **cognitive** confidence (subscale 3; e.g., 'I have a poor memory'); negative beliefs about thoughts including themes of superstition, punishment, responsibility and need for control (subscale 4; e.g., 'Not being able to control my thoughts is a sign of weakness') and cognitive self-consciousness (subscale 5; e.g., 'I pay close attention to the way my mind works'). OCD group scored higher than the normal on all domains of MCQ, namely, positive beliefs about worry (MCQ 1); negative beliefs about worry focusing on uncontrollability and danger (MCQ 2); low cognitive confidence (MCQ 3); negative beliefs about thoughts including themes of superstition, punishments, responsibility and need for control (MCQ 4) and cognitive self-consciousness (MCQ 5) which indicates a difficulty in metacognitive processing in the OCD. This finding is in conformity with previous research reports of dysfunctional metacognitive beliefs and importance of intrusions fundamental to the development and maintenance of OCD in the metacognitive model proposed by Adrian Wells in 1997. The result of significantly greater distortion in all the domains of metacognition in the OCD as compared to the CG signifies the tendency of the OCD to put greater importance to their thoughts, attaching meaning to intrusions, being unable to disregard them as unimportant (Rachman & de Silva, 1978), which signifies their deficit in verifying the debilitating thought through reality testing. It facilitates intrusion of thoughts as opposed to the consideration of the relevant stimuli coming from extrapersonal space that contributes to the development and maintenance of pathology. This proposition may be further substantiated from the cognitive models of OCD proposed by Salkovskis (1985, 1989), Rachman (1997, 1998), Purdon and Clark (1999) or Wells' (Wells, 1997; Wells & Matthews, 1994)—all of which emphasize negative appraisals of intrusive thoughts. Janeck et al. (2003) concluded that the OCD group revealed a tendency to reflect excessively on their cognitive processes, thereby increasing opportunities for negative appraisal of intrusive thoughts and foster overimportance of thought beliefs. In contrast the normal controls can distribute attention in a balanced manner to both intra- and extrapersonal spaces and effectively integrate information in terms of assimilation and accommodation, in order to adapt to the dynamic environment.

Executive Functions

Set Shifting, Fluency, Working Memory, Processing Speed and Planning

The results revealed that the patients with OCD had significant deficits in all the domains of EFs measured in the study. Neither did they have adequate set shifting ability or flexibility, nor could they finish the tasks on time. Marked inability of the patient group was seen in terms of allocating attention, online processing of memory, generating alternatives and planning. The OCD group, with their propensity to be guided by their internal stimuli, neglect feedback from extrapersonal space, and thereby demonstrate a marked deficit in terms of trial and error learning. Their failure to pick up environmental cues makes them inept at tasks demanding cognitive flexibility, feedback utilization and an inability to assimilate bottom-up information.

The patients with OCD perform poorly on WCST, making greater number of errors, perseverative responses, perseverative errors, nonperseverative errors, conceptual responses and attaining lesser categories in comparison to CG. The findings are in line with numerous prior reports (Boone, Ananth, & Philpott, 1991;

Christensen et al., 1992; Harvey, 1987; Head, Bolton, & Hyman, 1989; Lucey et al., 1997; Moritz et al., 2009; Mukhopadhyay, Tarafder, Bilimoria, Paul, & Bandyopadhyay, 2010; Tarafder, Bhattacharya, Paul, Bandyopadhyay, & Mukhopadhyay, 2006; see review: Olley, Malhi, & Sachdev, 2007). The failure of the OCD group to attain category completion is an indication of their difficulty in concept attainment, hypothesis testing and cognitive flexibility.

It has been suggested that OCD is associated with cognitive dysfunction wherein disturbances of WM seem to be particularly important (Boldrini et al., 2005; Nakao et al., 2009; Purcell, Maruff, Kyrios, & Pantelis, 1998a; Purcell, Maruff, Kyrios, & Pantelis, 1998b; Singh, Mukundan, & Khanna, 2003). The three subscales of WAIS-III require WM processes applied to the manipulation of orally presented verbal sequences. It assesses the ability one has to temporarily retain information in memory, by performing some operation or manipulation with it, and produce a result. It involves attention, concentration, mental control along with reasoning ability—essential components of other cognitive higher-order processes (Wechsler et al., 1997). A similar pattern of impairment has been observed in the OCD group in the present study. Moreover, inverse correlation was observed between MCQ 1 (positive beliefs about worry) with LNS and WMI and MCQ 4 (negative worry beliefs) with digit span subtests among the pathological group. The observation reveals that WM is adversely influenced by metacognitive beliefs, which presumably clog the WM space, limiting its executive functioning.

The OCD group showed deficit in lexical fluency when compared with their age-matched controls. Present findings on COWA corroborates with reports of Hwang and colleagues (2007) who have shown that the patients with late-onset OCD exhibit impaired performance on COWA, compared to normal controls. The observation of inverse association between low cognitive confidence (MCQ 3) and categorical fluency in the OCD highlights the role of metacognitive deficits in fluency.

The OCD group displayed deficit in terms of processing speed with significantly worse performances on symbol search and coding but better performance in terms of error scores on symbol search as compared to the CGs. The OCD group is found to be impaired in the domains of visuo-motor speed and the findings are in agreement with Rampacher et al. (2010). The slowness of the OCD group observed on speed tests along with significantly lesser number of errors on symbol search could be attributed to their quest for perfectionism (Rhéaume, Freeston, Dugas, Letarte, & Ladouceur, 1995). A closer analysis of the results reveal that the OCD group performed more accurately than the controls, with lesser errors, prioritizing accuracy over speed, taking greater time for task execution. Metacognitive deficits (positive worry beliefs—MCQ 1, negative worry beliefs related to uncontrollability—MCQ 2 and low cognitive confidence—MCQ 3) show an indirect relationship with subtests of processing speed, yet again establishing the crucial role played by metacognitive factors in adversely affecting performance on cognitive tasks. Metacognition is found to be highly correlated to performance on tasks assessing executive functions, suggesting that both work in synchrony with each other and manifests itself through marked slowness in information processing.

The present findings reveal that on the TOL Test the OCD showed a deficit on the time aspects of the test, taking greater time in execution, problem solving and making greater time violations, compared to CG. The OCD group differed from their cohort controls in terms of total correct score, move score and rule violation. The findings also highlight the deficit in consideration of the time factor in OCD. Greater execution time reflects delayed processing speed in the pathological group and goes with the findings on processing speed index, mentioned earlier. The finding of greater time violations, which reflects poor response inhibition, is in agreement with numerous research reports (e.g., Aycicegi, Dinn, Harris, & Erkmen, 2003; Bannon, Gonsalvez, Croft, & Boyce, 2002; Morein-Zamir, Fineberg, Robbins, &

Sahakian, 2010; Rao et al., 2008; Rosenberg, Dick, O' Hearn, & Sweeney, 1997).

Correlation of Variables in Patients with OCD

Considering the overall pattern of findings, the observation of the significant correlation of metacognitive beliefs, OCD trait and symptoms with all the parameters of executive function in OCD indicates how a pathological constellation is operative in the clinical group. Associations between obsessive symptoms and almost all domains of WCST in the OCD group point out the debilitating impact of cognitive rigidity on obsessive symptoms. Each aspect of higher-order cognitive functioning in the patient group is influenced by the dysexecution and metacognitive deficits.

Predictors of Obsessive Symptoms

In order to assess the impact of the aforesaid variables on symptom manifestation and on the severity of the symptoms, a series of regression analyses were computed. Results of SMRA showed that obsessive trait in combination with the variables, namely, negative worry beliefs regarding responsibility and need for control (MCQ 2), total problem-solving time (on TOL), NOCC—the index of cognitive inflexibility on WCST—and neuroticism (assessed on NEO-FFI), contributed significantly to OC symptoms (assessed on LOI). The model predicted OCD symptoms to the extent of 73.5% with obsessive personality traits emerging as the highest contributor.

Conclusion

In conclusion, it may be stated that OCD is the function of metacognitive deficits as well as executive dysfunction which work in synchrony with each other leading to symptom formation. Metacognitive deficits influence the execution of cognitive functions in the patients who are suffering from OCD.

References

American Psychiatric Association (1994). *Diagnostic and statistical manual of mental disorders* (DSM-IV) (revised 4th ed.). Washington, DC: American Psychiatric Association.

Arciniegas, D., & Beresford, T. (2001). *Neuropsychiatry: An introductory approach*. Cambridge, MA: Cambridge University Press.

Aycicegi-Dinn, A., Dinn, W. M., & Caldwell-Harris, C. L. (2009). Obsessive-compulsive personality traits: Compensatory response to executive function deficit? *International Journal of Neuroscience, 119*(4), 600–608.

Aycicegi, A., Dinn, W. M., Harris, C. L., & Erkmen, H. (2003). Neuropsychological function in obsessive-compulsive disorder: Effects of comorbid conditions on task performance. *European Psychiatry, 18*(5), 241–248.

Bannon, S., Gonsalvez, C., Croft, R., & Boyce, P. (2002). Response inhibition deficits in obsessive-compulsive disorder. *Psychiatry Research, 110*(2), 165–174.

Beck, A. T., Ward, C. H., Menderson, M., Mock, J. E., & Erbaugh, J. K. (1961). An inventory for measuring depression. *Archives of General Psychiatry, 4*(6), 561–571.

Boone, K. B., Ananth, J., & Philpott, L. (1991). Neuropsychological characteristics of nondepressed adults with obsessive-compulsive disorder. *Neuropsychiatry, Neuropsychology, and Behavioral Neurology, 4*(2), 96–109.

Boldrini, M., Del Pace, L., Placidi, G. P. A., Keilp, J., Ellis, S. P., Signori, S.,…Cappa, S. F. (2005). Selective cognitive deficits in obsessive-compulsive disorder compared to panic disorder with agoraphobia. *Acta Psychiatrica Scandinavica, 111*(2), 150–158.

Cartwright-Hatton, S., & Wells, A. (1997). Beliefs about worry and intrusions: The metacognitions questionnaire and its correlates. *Journal of Anxiety Disorders, 11*(3), 279–296.

Chamberlain, S. R., Blackwell, A. D., Fineberg, N. A., Robbins, T. W., & Sahakian, B. J. (2005). The neuropsychology of obsessive compulsive disorder: The importance of failures in cognitive and behavioural inhibition as candidate endophenotypic markers. *Neuroscience & Biobehavioral Reviews, 29*(3), 399–419.

Christensen, K. J., Kim, S. W., Dysken, M. W., & Hoover, K. M. (1992). Neuropsychological performance in obsessive-compulsive disorder. *Biological Psychiatry, 31*(1), 4–18.

Culberston, W. C., & Zilmer, E. A. (2001). *Tower of London* – Drexel University. Chicago, IL: Multi-Health Systems.

Cooper, J. (1970). The Leyton Obsessional Inventory. *Psychological Medicine, 1*(1), 48–64.

Costa, P. T., & McCrae, R. R. (1992). *Revised NEO Personality Inventory (NEO-PI-R) and NEO Five-Factor Inventory (NEO-FFI): Professional manual.* Odessa, FL: Psychological Assessment Resources.

Fenske, J., & Schwenk, T. (2009). Obsessive-compulsive disorder: Diagnosis and management. *American Family Physician, 80*(3), 239–245.

Fernandez-Duque, D., Baird, J. A., & Posner, M. I. (2000). Executive attention and metacognitive regulation. *Consciousness and Cognition, 9*(2), 288–307.

Fisher, P. L., & Wells, A. (2005). Experimental modification of beliefs in obsessive–compulsive disorder: A test of the metacognitive model. *Behaviour Research and Therapy, 43*(6), 821–829.

———— (2008). Metacognitive therapy for obsessive-compulsive disorder: A case series. *Journal of Behavior Therapy and Experimental Psychiatry, 39*(2), 117–132.

Flavell, J. H. (1979). Metacognition and cognitive monitoring: A new area of cognitive development inquiry. *American Psychologist, 34*(10), 906–911.

Frost, R. O., Steketee, G., Cohn, L., & Griess, K. (1994). Personality traits in subclinical and non-obsessive-compulsive volunteers and their parents. *Behaviour Research and Therapy, 32*(1), 47–56.

Fullana, M. A., Mataix-Cols, D., Trujillo, J. L., Caseras, X., Serrano, F., Alonso, P.,…Torrubia, R. (2004). Personality characteristics in obsessive-compulsive disorder and individuals with subclinical obsessive-compulsive problems. *British Journal of Clinical Psychology, 43*(4), 387–398.

Goldberg, D. P., & Hillier, V. F. (1979). A scaled version of the General Health Questionnaire. *Psychological Medicine, 9*(1), 139–145.

Goodman, W. K., Lawrence, H. P., Rasmussen, A., Mazure, C., Delgado, P., Heninger, G. R., & Charney, D. S. (1989). The Yale-Brown obsessive compulsive scale: Validity. *Archives of General Psychiatry, 46*(11), 1012–1016.

Graybiel, A. M., & Rauch, S. L. (2000). Toward a neurobiology of obsessive compulsive disorder. *Neuron, 28*(2), 343–347.

Gwilliam, P., Wells, A., & Cartwright-Hatton, S. (2004). Does meta-cognition or responsibility predict obsessive-compulsive symptoms: A test of the metacognitive model. *Clinical Psychology & Psychotherapy, 11*(2), 137–144.

Harvey, N. S. (1987). Neurological factors in obsessive-compulsive disorder. *British Journal of Psychiatry, 150*(4), 567–568.

Head, D., Bolton, D., & Hymas, N. (1989). Deficit in cognitive shifting ability in patients with obsessive-compulsive disorders. *Biological Psychiatry, 25*(7), 929–937.

Heaton, R. K., Chelune, G. J., Talley, J. L., Kay, G. C., & Curtiss, G. (1993). *Wisconsin Card Sorting Test Manual*. Odessa, FL: Psychological Assessment Resources.

Hermans, D., Martens, K., De Cort, K., Pieters, G., & Eelen, P. (2003). Reality monitoring and metacognitive beliefs related to cognitive confidence in obsessive-compulsive disorder. *Behaviour and Research Therapy, 41*(4), 383–401.

Hwang, S. H., Kwon, J. S., Shin, Y. W., Lee, K. J., Kim, Y. Y., & Kim, M. S. (2007). Neuropsychological profiles of patients with obsessive-compulsive disorder: Early onset versus late onset. *Journal of the International Neuropsychological Society, 13*(1), 30–37.

Janeck, A. S., Calamari, J. E., Riemann, B. C., & Heffelfinger, S. K. (2003). Too much thinking about thinking? Metacognitive differences in obsessive compulsive disorder. *Journal of Anxiety Disorders, 17*(2), 181–195.

Kamath, P., Reddy, Y. C., & Kandavel, T. (2007). Suicidal behaviour in obsessive-compulsive disorder. *Journal of Clinical Psychiatry, 68*(11), 1741–1750.

Karno, M., Golding, J. M., Sorenson, S. B., & Burnam, M. A. (1988). The epidemiology of obsessive compulsive disorder in five US communities. *Archives of General Psychiatry, 45*(12), 1094–1099.

Khanna, S., & Reddy, Y. J. (2004). *Obsessive compulsive disorder: An Indian perspective*. Mumbai: Abbott India Ltd.

Kuelz, A. K., Hohagen, F., & Voderholzer, U. (2004). Neuropsychological performance in obsessive-compulsive disorder: A critical review. *Biological Psychology, 65*(3), 185–236.

Lezak, M. D. (1995). *Neuropsychological assessment*. Oxfordshire: Oxford University Press.

Lucey, J. V., Burness, C. E., Costa, D. C., Gacinovic, S., Pilowsky, L. S., Ell, P. J.,...Kerwin, R. W. (1997). Wisconsin Card Sorting Task (WCST) errors and cerebral blood flow in obsessive-compulsive disorder. *British Journal of Medical Psychology, 70*(4), 403–411.

Luria, A. R. (1973). The working brain. New York: Basic Books.

Martínez-González, A. E., & Piqueras-Rodríguez, J. A. (2008). Neuropsychological update on obsessive-compulsive disorder. *Revista de Neurologia, 46*(10), 618–625.

Mineka, S., Watson, D., & Clark, L. A. (1998). Comorbidity of anxiety and unipolar mood disorders. *Annual Review of Psychology, 49*(1), 377–412.

Moritz, S., Hottenrott, B., Randjbar, S., Klinge, R., Von Eckstaedt, F. V., Lincoln, T. M., & Jelinek, L. (2009). Perseveration and not strategic deficits underlie delayed alternation impairment in obsessive-compulsive disorder (OCD). *Psychiatry Research, 170*(1), 66–69.

Morein-Zamir, S., Fineberg, N. A., Robbins, T. W., & Sahakian, B. J. (2010). Inhibition of thoughts and actions in obsessive-compulsive disorder: Extending the endophenotype? *Psychological Medicine, 40*(2), 1–10. doi: 10.1017/S003329170999033X

Moses, L. J., & Baird, J. A. (1999). Metacognition. In R. Wilson (Ed.), *Encyclopedia of cognitive neuroscience.* Cambridge, MA: MIT Press.

Mukhopadhyay, P., Tarafder, S., Bilimoria, D. D., Paul, D., & Bandyopadhyay, G. (2010). Instinctual impulses in obsessive compulsive disorder: A neuropsychological and psychoanalytic interface. *Asian Journal of Psychiatry, 3*(4), 177–185.

Murray, C. J. L., & Lopez, A. D. (Eds.) (1996). *The global burden of disease: A comprehensive assessment of mortality and disability from diseases, injuries and risk factors in 1990 and projected to 2020.* Cambridge, Harvard School of Public Health on behalf of the World Health Organization and the World Bank.

Myers, S. G., & Wells, A. (2005). Obsessive-compulsive symptoms: The contribution of metacognitions and responsibility. *Journal of Anxiety Disorders, 19*(7), 806–817.

Nakao, T., Nakagawa, A., Nakatani, E., Nabeyama, M., Sanematsu, H., Yoshiura, T.,…Kanba, S. (2009). Working memory dysfunction in obsessive-compulsive disorder: A neuropsychological and functional MRI study. *Journal of Psychiatric Research, 43*(8), 784–791.

O'Kearney, R. T., Anstey, K. J., & von Sanden, C. (2006). Behavioural and cognitive behavioural therapy for obsessive compulsive disorder in children and adolescents. *Cochrane Database of Systematic Reviews* (4). Art. No.: CD004856.

Oldfield, R. C. (1971). The assessment and analysis of handedness: The Edinburgh inventory. *Neuropsychologia, 9*(1), 97–113.

Olley, A., Malhi, G., & Sachdev, P. (2007). Memory and executive functioning in obsessive compulsive disorder: A selective review. *Journal of Affective Disorders, 104*(1–3), 15–23.

Perry, R. J., & Hodges, J. R. (1999). Attention and executive deficits in Alzheimer's disease: A critical review. *Brain, 122*(Pt 3), 383–404.

Pinto, A., Mancebo, M. C., Eisen, J. L., Pagano, M. E., & Rasmussen, S. A. (2006). The Brown longitudinal obsessive compulsive study: Clinical features and symptoms of the sample at intake. *The Journal of Clinical Psychiatry, 67*(5), 703–711.

Purcell, R., Maruff, P., Kyrios, M., & Pantelis, C. (1998a). Cognitive deficits in obsessive- compulsive disorder on tests of frontal-striatal function. *Biological Psychiatry, 43*(5), 348–357.

Purcell, R., Maruff, P., Kyrios, M., & Pantelis, C. (1998b). Neuropsychological deficits in obsessive-compulsive disorder: A comparison with unipolar depression, panic disorder, and normal controls. *Archives of General Psychiatry, 55*(5), 415–423.

Purdon, C., & Clark, D. A. (1999). Metacognition and obsessions. *Clinical Psychology & Psychotherapy, 6*(2), 102–110.

Rachman, S., & de Silva, P. (1978). Abnormal and normal obsessions. *Behaviour Research and Therapy, 16*(4), 233–248.

Rachman, S. J. (1997). A cognitive theory of obsessions. *Behaviour Research and Therapy, 35*(9), 793–802.

———(1998). A cognitive theory of obsessions: Elaborations. *Behaviour Research and Therapy, 36*(4), 385–401.

Rachman, S. J., & Hodgson, R. J. (1980). *Obsessions and compulsions.* New Jersey, NJ: Prentice-Hall.

Rao, S. L., Subbakrishna, D. K., & Gopukumar, K. (2004). *NIMHANS Adult Neuropsychological Battery manual.* Bangalore: NIMHANS.

Rampacher, F., Lennertz, L., Vogeley, A., Schulze-Rauschenbach, S., Kathmann, N., Falkai, P., & Wagner, M. (2010). Evidence for specific cognitive deficits in visual information processing in patients with OCD compared to patients with unipolar depression. *Progress in Neuro-Psychopharmacology & Biological Psychiatry, 34*(6), 984–991.

Rasmussen, S., & Tsuang, M. (1986). Clinical characteristics and family history in DSM-III obsessive-compulsive disorder. *The American Journal of Psychiatry, 143*(3), 317–322.

Rasmussen, S., & Eisen, J. (1989). Clinical features and phenomenology of obsessive compulsive disorder. *Psychiatric Annals, 19*(2), 67–72.

Rector, N. A., Cassin, S. E., Richter, M. A., & Burroughs, E. (2009). Obsessive beliefs in first-degree relatives of patients with OCD: A test of the cognitive vulnerability model. *Journal of Anxiety Disorders, 23*(1), 145–149.

Rector, N. A., Hood, K., Richter, M. A., & Bagby, R. M. (2002). Obsessive-compulsive disorder and the five-factor model of personality: Distinction and overlap with major depressive disorder. *Behaviour Research and Therapy, 40*(10), 1205–1219.

Rees, C. S., & van Koesveld, K. E. (2008). An open trial of group metacognitive therapy for obsessive-compulsive disorder. *Journal of Behavior Therapy and Experimental Psychiatry, 39*(4), 451–458.

Rhéaume, J., Freeston, M. H., Dugas, M. J., Letarte, M. H., & Ladouceur, H. (1995). Perfectionism, responsibility and obsessive-compulsive symptoms. *Behaviour and Research Therapy, 33*(7), 785–794.

Rosenberg, D., Dick, E., O'Hearn, K., & Sweeney, J. (1997). Response-inhibition deficits in obsessive-compulsive disorder: An indicator of dysfunction in frontostriatal circuits. *Journal of Psychiatry & Neuroscience, 22*(1), 29–38.

Salkovskis, P. M. (1985). Obsessive compulsive problems: A cognitive-behavioural analysis. *Behaviour Research and Therapy, 23*(5), 571–584.
———(1989). Cognitive-behavioural factors and the persistence of intrusive thoughts in obsessional problems. *Behaviour Research and Therapy, 27*(6), 677–682.

Samuels, J., Nestadt, G., Bienvenu, O. J., Costa, P. T., Riddle, M. A., Liang, K.Y.,...Cullen, B. A. M. (2000). Personality disorders and normal personality dimensions in obsessive-compulsive disorder. *The British Journal of Psychiatry, 177*(November), 457–462.

Saxena, S., Bota, R. G., & Brody, A. L. (2001). Brain-behaviour relationships in obsessive-compulsive disorder. *Seminars in Clinical Neuropsychiatry, 6*(2), 82–101.

Saxena, S., Brody, A. L., Schwartz, J. M., & Baxter, L. R. (1998). Neuroimaging and frontal-subcortical circuitry in obsessive-compulsive disorder. *British Journal of Psychiatry, 173*(35), 26–37.

Scarrabelotti, M. B., Duck, J. M., & Dickerson, M. M. (1995). Individual differences in obsessive compulsive behaviour: The role of the Eysenckian dimensions and appraisals of responsibility. *Personality and Individual Differences, 18*(3), 413–421.

Singh, S., Mukundan, C. R., & Khanna, S. (2003). Working memory deficits in obsessive-compulsive disorder. *Psychological Studies* (Mysore), *48*(2), 69–73.

Solem, S., Myers, S. G., Fisher, P. L., Vogel, P. A., & Wells, A. (2010). An empirical test of the metacognitive model of obsessive-compulsive symptoms: Replication and extension. *Journal of Anxiety Disorders, 24*(1), 79–86.

Solem, S., Håland, Å. T., Vogel, P. A., Hansen, B., & Wells, A. (2009). Change in metacognitions predicts outcome in obsessive-compulsive disorder patients undergoing treatment with exposure and response prevention. *Behaviour Research and Therapy, 47*(4), 301–307.

Steketee, G., Chambless, D. L., & Tran, G. Q. (2001). Effects of axis I and II comorbidity on behaviour therapy outcome for obsessive-compulsive disorder and agoraphobia. *Comprehensive Psychiatry, 42*(1), 76–86.

Steketee, G., & Frost, R. (1992). Measurement of risk-taking in obsessive-compulsive disorder. [Unpublished manuscript. Cited in R. O. Frost, G. Steketee, L. Cohn, & K. Griess, Personality traits in subclinical and non-obsessive-compulsive volunteers and their parents (1994). *Behaviour and Research Therapy, 32*(1), 47–56].

Tarafder, S., Bhattacharya, P., Paul, D., Bandyopadhyay, G., & Mukhopadhyay, P. (2006). Neuropsychological disposition and its impact on the executive functions and cognitive style in patients with obsessive-compulsive disorder. *Indian Journal of Psychiatry, 48*(2), 102–106.

Tükel, R., Gürvit, H., Ertekin, B. A., Oflaz, S., Ertekin, E., Baran, B.,...
Atalay, F. (2011). Neuropsychological function in obsessive-compulsive
disorder. *Comprehensive Psychiatry, 53*(2), 167–175.

Wechsler, D., Wycherley, J. R., & Benjamin, L. (1997). *Wechsler Adult
Intelligence Scale* (3rd ed.). San Antonio, TX: The Psychological
Corporation.

Wells, A. (1997). Cognitive therapy of anxiety disorders: A practice manual
and conceptual guide. Chichester, UK: Wiley.

——— (2000). *Emotional disorders and metacognition: Innovative cognitive
therapy*. Chichester: Wiley.

Wells, A., & Matthews, G. (1994). *Attention and emotion: A clinical perspective*. Hove: Lawrence Erlbaum.

———(1996). Modelling cognition in emotional disorder: The SREF model.
Behaviour Research and Therapy, 34(11–12), 881–888.

Wells, A., & Papageorgiou, C. (1998). Relationships between worry,
obsessive-compulsive symptoms and meta-cognitive beliefs. *Behaviour
Research and Therapy, 36*(9), 899–913.

Welner, A., Reich, T., Robbins, E., Fishman, R., & Van Doren, T. (1976).
Obsessive compulsive neurosis: Record, follow up and family studies.
Comprehensive Psychiatry, 17(4), 527–539.

5

Search for an Endophenotypic Model of Obsessive Compulsive Disorder

Sreemoyee Tarafder and Pritha Mukhopadhyay

Introduction

I would like to start the chapter with a little story. I was working as an MPhil intern at the University of Calcutta at that time and had been asked to assess a young adult for diagnostic purposes. While interviewing the 18-year-old male, I also spoke to his parent, who had come in as his informant. I asked the young man his age to which he replied that he was 18 years old, and promptly his father added, 'And seven months, 12 days'! I was quite tickled by the incident. Perhaps it was the first time that I was hearing an adult man's age being reported in months and days! It was much later, when I started reflecting about my day, did I understand the import of the parent's need for providing me with precise details regarding his son—the indexed client. By then I also knew that the young man referred to me was suffering from obsessive compulsive disorder (OCD), about his time-consuming rituals, cleaning and washing compulsions, obsessions pertaining to perfection and contamination. My thoughts kept going back to the parent, his insistence that I take notes while he mentioned about when his son had chicken pox, when he first walked, when he started his middle school—narrating the details minutely and making sure I had it all written down. He was precise, carefully organized, yet somewhat nagging and repetitive. He had many anal traits—untoward perfectionism, his preoccupation with orderliness and detail and his covert need to control the clinician. There was no reporting of any compromise in his socio-occupational functioning owing to his overconcern with organization and rigid precision though. When I started thinking about the father, I realized that none of his anal traits qualified for diagnosis. That is when the research idea started germinating in my head. I realized that there could be some traits that the parents of individuals with OCD possess that are similar to the ones suffering from OCD. But I realized that these traits and their behaviour pattern were not manifested as symptoms of OCD in a debilitating or even dysfunctional manner. My rudimentary hypothesis was that there may be a possibility that the parents too had some neuropsychological soft signs, which were more prominent and dominant in their children, who were being diagnosed as having OCD. It is known that a disease process could be influenced by heredity and genetic history, and even the environment, but we needed to know how the neuropsychological mechanism worked through which only the proband (one who showed the disorder) showed the disorder but the first-degree relatives (FDRs) did not. Also, I needed to see that whether what I had observed could be empirically corroborated with the proband and relative dyad. While doing my literature review for the study, I was introduced to the concept of endophenotypic studies being conducted with OCD involving the proband and their FDRs.

Endophenotypes are intermediate phenotypes or biomarkers that are objective, heritable, quantitative traits hypothesized to represent genetic risk for polygenic disorders at more biologically tractable levels than distal behavioural and clinical phenotypes

(Menzies et al., 2007). An endophenotype was originally defined in the 1960s as a 'measurable component unseen by the unaided eye on the pathway between disease (phenotype) and distal genotype' (Gottesman & Shields, 1973; John & Lewis, 1966). It is a heritable quantitative trait associated with greater genetic risk for a disorder and therefore found to be present in both patients and their clinically unaffected relatives (Bearden & Freimer, 2006; Gottesman & Gould, 2003). Interest in endophenotypes (or intermediate phenotypes) has been stirred by the difficulties faced in ascertaining specific genetic causes for complex disorders. It is theorized that endophenotypic models of disease will help to clarify both diagnostic classification and aetiological understanding of complex brain disorders such as OCD. An endophenotype may be neuropsychological, neuroanatomical, neurophysiological or even biochemical in nature (Ganesan, 2007). National Library of Medicine provides a comprehensive definition of endophenotype that includes behavioural (psychometric pattern) or cognitive markers that are found more often in individuals with a disease than in the general population. Because many endophenotypes are present before the disease onset and in individuals with heritable risk for disease such as unaffected family members, they can be used to help diagnose and search for causative genes. Chamberlain et al. (2007) opined that by establishing endophenotypic models of diseases, we could clarify the aetiological understanding of disorders that are as complex as OCD. Such biomarkers could be important for detecting people who may be vulnerable to the condition; it would help in clarifying aetiological factors and targeting novel treatments as it helps to understand the genesis of a given disorder by identifying the vulnerability marker tracing it through their FDRs who do not manifest the disease clinically.

In our book, we have highlighted how OCD is a highly heritable disease that has a debilitating impact on the sufferer's life owing to its onset in adolescence with a life-time prognosis of 2% to 3% (Alsobrook & Pauls, 1998; Karno, Golding, Sorenson, & Burnam, 1988; Weissman et al., 1994). In the previous chapter, we have dealt with executive functions (EFs) and metacognitive beliefs in OCD and community samples. In this chapter, we will be exploring the executive functions and metacognition and their correlates in the OCD probands and their FDRs. Metacognition refers to the understanding that we have about our own cognitions and can be held responsible for maintaining maladaptive processing configurations that may be responsible for emotional vulnerability (Wells & Matthews, 1994, 1996). EFs is the basic cognitive mechanic that is involved in higher-order cognitive functions such as planning, organizing, problem solving, sequencing, self-monitoring and controlling behaviour. Deficit in executive functioning seems to be a consistent neuropsychological deficit in OCD (refer to Chapter 4), and therefore it was taken up for further investigation in this study involving probands and their relatives.

Genetic Component in OCD

Last decade has seen a rapid progress in our understanding of the genetic mechanisms involved in OCD, and according to the collective knowledge till date, it is evident that OCD has a significant genetic component (Eapen et al., 2003; Grados, Walkup, & Walford, 2003; Kim & Kim, 2006). OCD and heritability links may be understood from twin studies where a concordance rate of around 50% to 60% (Rasmussen & Tsuang, 1986) has been reported. Using the Maudsley Twin Register, Carey and Gottesman (1981) reported the rate among 15 monozygotic (MZ) twin pairs for OC features to be 87% as compared to 47% in 15 dizygotic (DZ) twin pairs. In a study of 419 pairs of twins using the Leyton Obsessional Inventory (LOI), heritability of 44% for OC traits and 47% for OC symptoms were reported (Clifford, Murray, & Rulker, 1984). In another study, McGuffin and Mawson (1980) reported that identical twin pairs reared apart had similar onset age for OC symptoms and it followed a similar course in both pairs. In a comprehensive review of twin researches by van Grootheest, Cath, Beekman and Boomsma (2005), they mention that studies have conclusively shown that OC symptoms are heritable in children, with genetic factors accounting for 45% to 65% of symptom formation when the data was analysed through structural equation modelling (SEM). On a similar vein, Jonnal, Gardner, Prescott and Kendler (2000) in a study of 527 twin pairs, using the self-report Padua Inventory of OC symptoms, found heritability of 33% and 26% for obsessions and compulsions, respectively. Thus, while the data from twin studies support a genetic basis for OCD, it should be noted that in all twin data reported, the concordance for MZ twins was less than 1.0, and heritability estimates were consistently less than 1.0 suggesting that while genetic factors are important, these behaviours are also influenced by environmental factors. Analysis of OC traits by Cox (1975) showed a strong interaction between genetic and environmental factors.

A review of family studies in OCD suggest significantly higher rates in parents and siblings of OCD probands with an age-corrected morbid risk of around 35% in FDRs (Eapen & Robertson, 2002). In the 1930s, Lewis (1935) reported a rate of 32.7% OC traits in a sample of 306 FDRs. Several family studies since then have reported significantly higher rates of OCD in parents and siblings of OCD probands, with rates among parents being 5 to 10 times higher, when compared to population prevalence estimates (Pauls, 1992). Rasmussen and Tsuang (1986) found that 4.5% of parents of OCD patients met the full criteria for OCD as per DSM-III, while an additional 11.4% had probable OCD or OC traits. Lenane et al. (1990) in a study of 145 FDRs of 46 children and adolescents with OCD found an age-corrected morbid risk of 35% in FDRs for OCD and subclinical OCD. Riddle et al. (1990) in a clinically referred sample of children with OCD observed that 71% had a parent with either OCD or OC symptoms. In this regard, Black, Noyes, Goldstein and Blum (1992) studied FDRs of 32 adult probands and 33 psychiatrically normal controls. Risk for a broadly defined OCD was increased among the parents of OCD probands but not among the parents of controls (16% vs. 3%). Bellodi, Sciuto, Diaferia, Ronchi and Smeraldi (1992), using 21 OCD patients with an age at onset of less than 14 years, observed the morbidity risk to be 8.8% among FDRs of these probands, as compared to 3.45%

among the relatives of 71 later-onset probands. Similarly, Pauls, Alsobrook, Goodman, Rasumussen and Leckman (1995) found the rates among FDRs of OCD probands to be 10.3% for OCD and 7.9% for sub-threshold OCD as compared to 1.9% and 2.0%, respectively, for control subjects. Nestadt et al. (2000) also reported similar rates of 11.7% among FDRs of patients with OCD as compared to 2.7% for control subjects. A study by Fyer, Lipstiz, Mannuzza, Arnowitz and Chapman (2005) noted a significantly higher risk for OCD but not for other anxiety disorders, and a subsequent study by the same group (Lipstiz, Mannuzza, Chapman, Foa, Franklin, Goodwin, & Fyer, 2005) found evidence of familial OCD only when the diagnostic threshold was lowered to include cases with probable OCD or OCD symptoms. In a family study of OCD, Pauls et al. (1995) reported that the rates of OCD and sub-threshold OCD were significantly greater among the relatives of the probands with OCD (10.3% and 7.9%, respectively) than among the comparison subjects (1.9% and 2.0%, respectively).

Endophenotypes in OCD

Analysis of twin and family studies suggest that the familial transmission of OCD is genetic in origin though the exact mode of transmission is still unclear. In their path-breaking work, published in *Brain*, Menzies et al. (2007) investigated endophenotypes in OCD by measuring brain structure using magnetic resonance imaging (MRI) and behavioural performance on a response-inhibition task (stop signal) in 31 OCD probands, their unaffected FDRs and 31 unrelated matched controls. Both patients and relatives displayed delayed response inhibition on the stop-signal task compared with healthy controls. Structural variation in large-scale brain systems related to motor inhibitory control was proposed by them to be a genetic risk factor for OCD, representing a neurocognitive endophenotype of OCD. The same group of researchers (Chamberlain et al., 2007) also studied inhibitory control processes in unaffected FDRs of OCD patients, using intradimensional/extradimensional shift, stop-signal and

Cambridge Gamble tasks. It was found that unaffected FDRs and OCD patient probands showed cognitive inflexibility (in extradimensional set shifting tasks) and motor impulsivity (in stop-signal reaction times), but their decision-making (assessed on Cambridge Gamble Task) was found to be intact. They suggested that the deficits in cognitive flexibility and motor inhibition may be regarded as cognitive endophenotypes for OCD.

Alongside the publication of these two research reports, there were a number of studies being conducted all over the world that started studying proband and FDR dyads and the search was aimed to identify more endophenotypic markers for a complex disorder like OCD. The salient features of the other research conducted in the field, in order to establish endophenotypes, have been charted further (refer to Table 5.1). In India, some researchers from NIMHANS (Rao, Reddy, Kumar, Kandavel, & Chandrashekar, 2008) published reports that identified neuropsychological endophenotype markers for OCD. They assessed patients with OCD who manifested significant deficits on tests of set shifting ability, response inhibition, alternation and non-verbal memory—despite being assessed in the recovered phase of the iliness—suggesting these to be trait like factors. Empirical research with FDR with asymptomatic siblings of OCD probands, carried out by Viswanath, Reddy, Kumar, Kandavel and Chandrashekar (2009), showed significant deficits on tests of decision-making and behavioural reversal on the Iowa Gambling Task (IGT) and the Delayed Alternation Test, respectively, suggesting the involvement of the orbitofrontal cortex among FDRs. In 2011, Rajender and team assessed FDR and probands with OCD on domains of attention, verbal memory, visual memory, set shifting, response inhibition, planning and visuo-constructive abilities. Their results revealed that there were no statistically significant differences between patients with OCD and their FDRs on the domains of delayed verbal recall, set shifting, response inhibition and visuo-constructive abilities, which helped them to identify set shifting, inhibitory control, visuo-constructive abilities and delayed verbal recall as potential endophenotypes for OCD.

Table 5.1 Brief Summary of Impairments in Executive Functions Reported Among the FDRs by Earlier Researchers

Researchers	Neuropsychological Deficits Reported in FDRs
Chamberlain et al. (2007)	Reported cognitive inflexibility (extradimensional set shifting) and motor Impulsivity (stop-signal reaction times) in both the patients with OCD and their FDRs.
Delorme et al. (2007)	Found deficient planning and working memory processes in unaffected FDRs of probands with OCD.
Menzies et al. (2007)	Noted delayed response inhibition on the stop-signal task compared with healthy controls among the FDRs of individuals with OCD.
Rao et al. (2008)	Identified neuropsychological deficits to be possible candidate endophenotype markers for OCD by assessing patients with OCD in the recovered phase of the illness that showed considerable deficits on tests of set shifting ability, response inhibition, alternation and non-verbal memory.
Viswanath et al. (2009)	Deficits in decision-making and behavioural reversal were postulated as potential endophenotypes in OCD.
Cavedini, Zorzi, Piccinni, Cavallini and Bellodi (2010)	Found high concordance rates in decision-making and planning deficits suggesting it to be heritable components of OCD.

Rajender, Bhatia, Kanwal, Malhotra, Singh and Chaudhary (2011)	Opined that set shifting, inhibitory control and visuo-constructive abilities, delayed verbal recall are endophenotypes for OCD, based on their study.
Hou et al. (2014)	The researchers used resting-state fMRI, and their findings confirmed that patients with OCD have abnormal resting-state functional connectivity that is not limited to cortico–striatal–thalamic–cortical (CSTC) circuits and involves abnormalities in the limbic system as well. Similar abnormalities in functional connectivity were also seen in their healthy FDRs, suggesting it to be a brain-based neuroimaging endophenotype.
Albert et al. (2015)	In order to determine the specificity of obsessive beliefs in the FDR of probands with OCD, they were compared to non-affected FDRs of patients with bipolar bisorder. FDRs of subjects with OCD scored significantly higher than controls on domains of inflated responsibility and overestimation of threat on Obsessive Beliefs Questionnaire (OBQ) 44. This study provides proof that a specific cognitive vulnerability for OCD exists in the FDRs of probands with OCD.
Vaghi et al. (2017)	Hypoactivation of the right dorsolateral prefrontal cortex (DLPFC) during goal-directed planning coupled with reduced functional connectivity between DLPFC region and the putamen was reported in patients with OCD and their clinically unaffected relatives.

Source: Authors.

The endophenotypic studies over the years have strengthened the familial claim by studying the unaffected and asymptomatic FDR of the proband with OCD. It is to be understood that for the neuropsychological deficits to be considered as endophenotypes, they should be demonstrable in unaffected family members. A brief summary of the impairments in EFs reported among the FDRs by earlier researchers have been summarized in Table 5.1.

The findings so far have highlighted certain similarities in the profiles of the patients with OCD and their FDR, but the earlier studies have not identified the factors that work as buffers for the FDRs. The answer needs to be sought by analysing not just the neuropsychological factors but also their belief system or meta-cognitive belief structure as metacognition is closely related to executive functioning, which involves the ability to monitor and control the information processing necessary to produce voluntary action (Peña, Kayashima, Mizoguchi, & Dominguez, 2011).

The present study is an endeavour to investigate the domain of executive functioning and metacognition in OCD, their FDRs and healthy controls from the community. The present chapter also looks into obsessive personality traits and obsessive symptoms since cognitive contents and processes are aetiologically important in understanding OCD.

Methodology

Sample

A total of 250 participants were selected, dividing them into four groups, seventy-five were diagnosed with OCD, and 75 normal individuals selected as the control group (CG) of the OCD. However, only 50 FDR could be included in the study and their control counterparts (FCG) were drawn from the community matched on the basis of age, sex, educational level and handedness. The patient group was recruited from psychiatric outpatient services of Kolkata after agreement upon diagnosis following ICD

10 diagnostic criteria for research with age ranging from 16 to 45 years, of both genders, with minimum of standard X education, right-handed and willing. Exclusion criteria for OCD group were history of co-morbid psychological disorders, except depression. Depression was not excluded as there is a high co-morbidity of OCD with depression with one-third of OCD patients having concurrent major depressive disorder (MDD) (Rasmussen & Eisen, 1992). Serious/acute/chronic medical illness/disability/neurological condition/developmental disorders were excluded. The other study group comprised of the FDR where 50 nonclinical FDRs of patients with OCD were selected after acquiring their consent. Minimum of standard X education, right-handed participants who consented were included. They were excluded if subjects were currently suffering from any psychiatric disorder, older than 60 years of age, without a history of serious/acute/chronic medical illness/disability/neurological/developmental disorders. Community control groups (CCGs), namely, CG and FCG-control participants (control group=CG and FDR control group=FCG) were drawn from the community. Subjects were considered eligible if there was no history of any psychological disorder and screened for psychiatric morbidity on General Health Questionnaire (GHQ), being right-handed with voluntary participation. Serious medical illness was the exclusion criterion for the community controls.

Measures

1. Semi-structured socio-demographic and clinical data sheet
2. Yale Brown Obsessive Compulsive Scale (YBOCS) (Goodman, Price, & Rasmussen, 1989)
3. Leyton Obsessional Inventory (LOI) (Cooper, 1970)
4. Metacognition Questionnaire (MCQ) (Cartwright-Hatton & Wells, 1997)
5. General Health Questionnaire (GHQ) (Goldberg & Hillier, 1979)
6. Edinburgh Handedness Inventory (EHI) (Oldfield, 1971)

7. Wisconsin Card Sorting Test (WCST) (Heaton, Chelune, Talley, Kay, & Curtiss, 1993)
8. Tower of London Drexel University (TOL – DX) (Culbertson & Zillmer, 2001)
9. Subtests of WAIS-III that comprise the Processing Speed Index (PSI): Symbol search and coding (Wechsler, Wycherley, & Benjamin, 1997)
10. Subtests of WAIS-III constituting the Working Memory Index (Wechsler et al., 1997): Digit span, arithmetic and Letter Number Sequencing (LNS)

Procedure

Subjects were selected on the basis of the inclusion/exclusion criteria mentioned earlier, after getting their consent. A semi-structured socio-demographic and clinical data sheet was filled by the subjects. Severity was assessed using the YBOCS for the OCD group after which EHI, LOI, MCQ, WCST, TOL—DX and the selected subtests of WAIS-III were administered. The subjects were tested at the Department of Psychology, University of Calcutta following the same procedure for all the groups.

Statistical Analysis

Parametric statistics were considered. Although independent sample t-test was used for OCD and CG, FDR and FCG, OCD-FCG comparisons, paired sample t-test was used to obtain differences of means between the OCD and FDR groups, as they were a related pair. To find out the nature of relationship between the different neuropsychological measures taken and OC symptoms, OC traits and aspects of metacognition, the Pearson's coefficient correlation was computed for the study groups. Stepwise Multiple Regression Analysis (SMRA) was computed to determine the relative contribution of different variables upon OC symptoms and symptom severity. For analysis, 0.05 and 0.01 level of significance were accepted as critical levels.

Results

Socio-demographic Description of the Sample

The two study groups were comparable with their community counterparts in terms of age, sex and years of education. The symptom severity in the clinical group, as assessed on YBOCS, ranged from 10 to 40, with the mean being 22, which falls within moderate range. Duration of illness ranged from 2 to 10 years. The socio-demographic details of the four groups are provided in Table 5.2.

Table 5.2	Socio-demographic Details of the Participants				
Variable	**Statistics**	**OCD**	**CG**	**FDR**	**FCG**
Age (in years)	Range	17–49	17–47	19–59	16–58
	Mean	27.63	26.64	44.5	42.81
	SD	9.03	5.75	11.59	11.49
	T	0.789; $p=0.43$		1.108; $p=0.27$	
Education (in years)	Range	10–20	10–20	10-20	10–20
	Mean	13.14	13.38	13.21	13.21
	SD	2.86	3.5	4.02	3.20
	T	0.496; $p=0.62$		0.141; $p=0.791$	
Sex	Male	44	44	25	25
	Female	33	33	25	25
Handedness	Right-handed	Only Right-handed			

Source: Authors.

Findings Obtained by OCD, CG, FDR and FCG on tests of Obsessive Symptoms, Traits, Metacognition and Executive Functions

The finding, as shown in Table 5.3, of equal status of OCD and FDR in terms of obsessive personality traits on LOI, in spite of greater reporting of obsessive symptoms by the OCD group

Table 5.3 Mean (M), Standard Deviations (SD), t-test Values with Corresponding Level of Significance of the Findings Obtained by OCD, Control Group (CG), FDR and FCG on Beck Depression Inventory, Leyton Obsession Inventory, Metacognition Questionnaire, Wisconsin Card Sorting Test, Processing Speed Index, Working Memory Index (on WAIS-III) and Tower of London Test

Study Groups >	OCD		CG		t	FDR		FCG		T	OCD		FDR		Paired t	OCD		FCG		t
Variables	M	SD	M	SD		M	SD	M	SD		M	SD	M	SD		M	SD	M	SD	
Depression BDI	26.64	12.27	8.76	6.30	11.22**	10.28	6.67	7.05	5.97	2.01*	28.26	10.06	10.28	6.67	10.293**	28.26	10.06	7.05	5.97	10.53**
Obsessive symptoms	24.93	9.26	12.48	6.51	9.53**	14.63	9.27	10.70	6.85	1.79	23.92	10.42	14.63	9.27	4.195**	23.92	10.42	10.70	6.85	6.05**
Obsessive traits	12.45	4.48	7.85	4.09	6.57**	10.68	4.18	6.35	4.17	4.12**	11.95	5.00	10.68	4.18	1.199	11.95	5.00	6.35	4.17	4.86**
MCQ 1—Positive beliefs about worry	36.68	11.08	32.79	10.98	2.16*	33.71	11.21	30.27	7.81	1.46	38.05	11.85	33.71	11.21	1.753	38.05	11.85	30.27	7.81	3.21**
MCQ 2—Negative worry beliefs (Uncontrollability)	50.33	9.62	30.91	8.68	12.98**	36.05	11.14	29.62	8.66	2.59**	50.74	10.04	36.05	11.14	7.125**	50.74	10.04	29.62	8.66	9.37**
MCQ 3—Low cognitive confidence	23.85	7.29	17.67	5.70	5.78**	17.05	5.56	19.29	9.32	1.27	25.39	7.37	17.05	5.56	5.313**	25.39	7.37	19.29	9.32	3.024**
MCQ 4—Negative beliefs (Punishment, responsibility)	35.40	5.54	24.51	6.04	11.52**	27.97	6.57	22.37	5.83	3.49**	36.32	5.59	27.97	6.57	6.617**	36.32	5.59	22.37	5.83	10.08**
MCQ 5—Cognitive self-consciousness	20.81	7.12	17.36	4.84	3.47**	18.23	4.33	15.97	4.01	1.93	21.13	8.94	18.23	4.33	1.603	21.13	8.94	15.97	4.01	2.87**

Percentage of error	37.44	29.18	72.62	22.93	8.21**	53.23	32.16	72.29	27.10	2.537*	45.84	33.22	53.23	32.16	1.380	45.84	33.22	72.29	27.10	3.50**
Percentage of perseverative response	28.25	27.36	58.80	22.49	7.47**	40.44	29.07	62.35	26.01	3.329*	35.71	30.59	40.44	29.07	0.835	35.71	30.59	62.35	26.01	3.93**
Percentage of perseverative error	33.28	29.89	68.52	24.20	7.93**	48.13	32.01	68.35	25.07	2.836**	41.79	32.21	48.13	32.01	1.038	41.79	32.21	68.35	25.07	3.74**
Percentage of nonperseverative error	50.43	34.42	72.94	28.02	4.39**	64.10	30.09	65.78	30.34	0.051	51.24	33.72	64.10	30.09	1.487	51.24	33.72	65.78	30.34	1.72
WMI	92.01	16.80	110.16	15.95	6.48**	87.34	15.27	107.70	17.77	5.339**	96.16	15.00	87.34	15.27	2.716**	96.16	15.00	107.70	17.77	3.13**
PSI	78.45	12.31	92.77	10.36	7.70**	77.13	14.98	87.83	24.01	3.168**	77.87	10.93	77.13	14.98	0.247	77.87	10.93	87.83	24.01	3.29**
Move score	26.46	24.34	36.86	26.52	2.50**	44.15	25.09	35.32	28.20	1.55	29.29	27.38	44.15	25.09	2.685**	29.29	27.38	35.32	28.20	0.76
Initiation time	65.44	22.36	61.32	25.05	1.06	69.15	23.85	53.02	27.19	2.408*	66.05	24.19	69.15	23.85	0.611	66.05	24.19	53.02	27.19	1.87
Execution time	15.12	16.96	28.32	22.314	4.07**	26.34	18.69	29.00	24.34	0.544	18.05	20.19	26.34	18.69	2.089*	18.05	20.19	29.00	24.34	2.08*
Total time	16.10	18.10	31.74	21.49	4.82**	25.34	16.50	31.97	24.53	1.286	17.37	20.97	25.34	16.50	2.014*	17.37	20.97	31.97	24.53	2.64**
Time violations	42.37	38.10	74.18	34.91	5.33**	58.57	36.38	75.97	33.48	1.839	47.26	39.40	58.57	36.38	1.243	47.26	39.40	75.97	33.48	3.05**
Rule violations	68.38	42.74	91.09	19.80	4.18*	82.73	31.91	91.02	24.15	1.112	75.82	40.25	82.73	31.91	0.830	75.82	40.25	91.02	24.15	1.80
	* $p < 0.05$ level, ** $p < 0.01$ level					* $p < 0.05$ level, ** $p < 0.01$ level					* $p < 0.05$ level, ** $p < 0.01$ level					* $p < 0.05$ level, ** $p < 0.01$ level				
	df = 148					df = 98					df = 98					df = 49				
																df = 98				

Source: Authors.

again highlights OCD–FDR similarities, thereby strengthening the endophenotypic understanding of the disorder, not just in terms of obsessive personality traits but also in terms of positive worry beliefs and cognitive self-consciousness (on MCQ), set shifting deficits (on WCST), processing speed deficits (on WAIS-III), working memory deficits (on WAIS-III) and time violations (on TOL Test). But the proband–relative comparison also revealed that the OCD group portrayed greater negative worry beliefs, lower cognitive confidence (on MCQ), deficits in working memory (LNS on WAIS-III) and deficits in planning (on TOL Test). The dissimilarities that appeared in the OCD–FDR comparisons may arguably be then looked at as protective factors for the FDR.

The point may be raised that the findings may have come about owing to the significant age difference between the patient probands and their FDRs. Age is indeed an aspect that may be considered as a contributory factor which may have nullified the differences between the proband and relative performances. Could the findings then not be attributed to age? Since this is a very valid concern, the OCD group needed to be compared against both the CGs, namely, CG (of comparable age) and FCG (with age comparable to their parents/siblings). Since the OCD group significantly differed from their FDR in terms of age, need was felt to specifically address the factor of age. Therefore, we included the FCG, who were unrelated to the OCD group, yet as old as the FDR, thereby ruling out the age-related effects, if any.

Closer analysis of the patient group (OCD) displayed deficits in terms of metacognitive beliefs (on MCQ), trials to complete first category, error, perseverative response, perseverative error, nonperseverative error (on WCST), working memory and processing speed (on WAIS-III) and move score, time violation, rule violation (on TOL Test) as compared to both the control groups; but they performed better than them in terms of N-Back 2 Error and symbol search error score.

FDR–FCG comparisons revealed deficits in obsessive compulsive personality traits (OCPTs) (on LOI), negative worry beliefs (on MCQ), error, perseverative response, perseverative error, categories completed (on WCST), initiation time (on TOL Test), working memory and processing speed (on WAIS-III) in FDR; but the FDR group performed better in terms of N-Back 2 Error and symbol search error scores as compared to FCG, like OCD.

In the OCD group, significant correlations were found between symptom dimensions and obsessive traits and domains of EFs, but the FDR showed no significant correspondence between obsessive symptoms or traits with any of the measures of EFs, as is shown in Table 5.4.

Table 5.4	Criterion Measures and Test Variables and Correlated Variables for OCD and FDR		
Criterion Measures & Test Variables	Correlated Variables	OCD	FDR
Obsessive symptom + Trait + MCQ and Set shifting	Obsessive symptom & % Error	−0.266*	NS
	Obsessive symptom & % PR	−0.306**	NS
	Obsessive symptom & % PE	−0.326**	NS
	Obsessive symptom & % CLR	−0.334**	NS
	Obsessive symptom & NOCC	−0.429**	NS
	Obsessive symptom & TCFC	−0.416**	NS
	Obsessive trait & % Error	−0.346**	NS
	Obsessive trait & % PR	−0.408**	NS
	Obsessive trait & % PE	−0.405**	NS
	Obsessive trait & % CLR	−0.389**	NS
	Obsessive trait & NOCC	−0.406**	NS
	Obsessive trait & TCFC	−0.360**	NS
	MCQ 1 & Error	NS	−0.321**
	MCQ 2 & TCFC	−0.292*	NS
	MCQ 3 & FTMS	−0.244*	NS

Source: Authors.
Note: * p < 0.05 level, ** p < 0.01, NS = not significant.

SMRA showed that obsessive trait in combination with the variables, namely, negative worry beliefs regarding uncontrollability and danger (MCQ 2) and NOCC (the index of cognitive inflexibility on WCST) contributed significantly to OC symptoms (on LOI). The model predicted OCD symptoms to the extent of 73.5% (adjusted $R^2=0.735$; $p=0.001$) with obsessive personality traits emerging as the highest contributor. Positive beliefs about worry (MCQ 1) contributed significantly to severity of OC symptoms (as assessed on YBOCS).

Discussion

OCD-CG and OCD-FCG comparisons reveal that although the patients with OCD are able to perceive the task demand of EF with changing contingencies, they perseverate, failing to manipulate existing information and generate multiple alternatives. This perhaps happens owing to their cognitive rigidity. Cognitive rigidity is an outcome of their inability to assimilate top-down processes with bottom-up mechanism and the provided feedback is unheeded by them. Their top-down bias may be an outcome of remaining cued to prepotent thought processes, which is perhaps an index of their metacognitive deficit.

OCD–FDR comparison findings uphold executive dysfunction to be a cognitive endophenotype, with OCD-proband and relative being on the same plane in terms of EFs. Like previous researchers, we too found that the FDRs were as deficient as the probands on almost all parameters of WCST, TOL Test and subtests assessing working memory and processing speed. Metacognitive beliefs emerged as factors that differentiated the OCD from their FDR.

In OCD, negative worry beliefs about controllability and danger (MCQ 2) maximally preoccupied them, to the extent that it disconnected them from any other information coming from extrapersonal space. The OCD patients perhaps worry that if they give free rein to their thoughts they will be overwhelmed by their obsessions and impulses. They regard these impulses as threatening stimuli that would engulf them and overestimate the severity of the consequences of having these thoughts. Maintenance of the obsessive thought disallows the entry of other inputs from the environment. The environmental feedback is, therefore, regarded as noise that interferes with the thoughts which have been attributed to be important for their survival, which in reality is detrimental for their existence.

Although an integrity between bottom-up information and top-down processing is a necessary condition for dynamicity of brain to cope with changing environmental contingencies, the OCD cannot distribute attention in a balanced manner to both intra- and extrapersonal spaces resulting in a failure to effectively integrate information in terms of assimilation and accommodation essential to adapt to the dynamic environment. Effective metacognition precludes that when one utilizes the feedback, he uses explicit consciousness-controlled processes to modify implicitly generated automatic processes. Here a spontaneous interplay between metacognitive knowledge and monitoring takes place wherein fluid flexibility is retained. This process continues with the encounters with reality as assimilation and accommodation are continuous processes. Metacognition too is not static but dynamic in nature. Metacognitive belief structure of FDR that is less plagued by negative worry beliefs regarding uncontrollability and danger, responsibility, need for control and having better levels of cognitive confidence work as buffers that ward off the manifestation of pathology in FDR.

Positive belief about worry (MCQ 1) that is characterized by attributing advantages to worrying have been found to be significantly endorsed by OCD group and emerges as a major predictor of symptom severity. The observation of positive beliefs about worry being directly correlated with symptom severity suggests the significance of positive belief about worry on maintenance of obsessions. The finding also corroborates with Anand (2005) where he found positive worry beliefs to be directly correlated with obsessions and that of Wells and Papageorgiou's (1998) study that reported the same to be associated with pathological worrying. This finding might seem surprising in view of the knowledge that obsessions are primarily ego-dystonic and therefore are not regarded positively by the OCD patients. But closer analysis of the items shows that herein the emphasis is on reflecting about the advantage of worrying, that is, how worrying helps one to avoid dangers in the future and cope with the environment. For example, 'worrying helps me avoid problems in the future', 'worrying helps me cope', 'I will lose out on life if I do not worry', 'I need to worry in order to get things done'. This is perhaps best understood in view of existing psychodynamic notion of the use of reaction formation as a defence against impulses by patients with OCD to establish to themselves that worrying works for them as a controllability factor. As if their worry has a positive impact on the action outcome. It may be added that the recurrent thoughts/images related to their symptoms are ego-dystonic to the OCD patients, but the belief about their thought structure, that is, their thinking about their own thinking process remains ego-syntonic, which makes them feel that worrying helps them to cope. Presumably, the OCD group feels that if they stop worrying, their thought might have the propensity to wreak havoc with the semblance of order that they work so hard to establish.

Solem, Haland, Vogela, Hansen and Wells (2009) undertook a research to assess whether change in metacognitions predicts outcome in OCD patients undergoing treatment with exposure and response prevention. Assessing 83 outpatients with a diagnosis of OCD who completed exposure and response prevention (ERP) treatment, they found significant changes in symptoms and metacognition scores at post-treatment and follow-up. As a matter of fact, only changes in metacognition were significant on regression analysis using post-treatment YBOCS as the dependent variable (Solem et al., 2009). Furthermore, regression revealed that need to control thoughts (MCQ 4) and positive beliefs about worry (MCQ 1) made independent contributions to symptom severity. Patients who achieved clinically significant change had lower scores on the MCQ 30 compared to patients who could not change. Their finding not only offers further support for the importance of metacognitions in treating OCD, but also highlights the importance of positive beliefs about the need to worry in the maintenance of symptoms.

The patients with OCD perform poorly on WCST, making greater number of errors, perseverative responses, perseverative errors, nonperseverative errors, conceptual responses and attaining lesser categories in comparison to both CG and FCG—an indication of their difficulty in concept attainment, hypothesis testing and cognitive flexibility, and in taking decision regarding response selection (as proposed by Aycicegi et al., 2003). Associations between obsessive symptoms and almost all domains of WCST in the OCD group point out the debilitating impact of cognitive rigidity on obsessive symptoms. The FDR too performed poorly on WCST as compared to their control counterparts, with significant difference in terms of error, perseverative response, perseverative error and NOCCs. But the FDRs were at par with their corresponding CG in terms of nonperseverative error, unlike the OCD group. This finding implies that the pathological group has a potent inclination to be guided by internal stimuli, at the cost of neglecting feedback from external space. This demonstrates a marked deficit in strategy based on trial and error method that is measured through nonperseverative error. The OCD group, especially in contrast to controls, fails to use a searching technique and cannot figure out a way to shift between sets utilizing the provided feedback. More nonperseverative error in the OCD indicates their restricted response selection which perhaps blocks their selection of an appropriate response to identify a new response category. This inference may be drawn on the basis of the evidence that execution of a novel response as well as improvement of ongoing performance is a result of utilization of feedback to one's response when the stimulus–response task is based on trial and error mechanism (McDonald & White, 1994). Poorer NPE percentile in the OCD, therefore, could also be explained as the error in feedback utilization, resulting in poor response selection, culminating in poor conceptual-level response and category completion on WCST. Poor conceptual-level response in OCD further signifies that their psychopathology is most likely to prevent them from developing an effective strategy to deal with the task, which seems to be the function of the DLPFC (Goldstein et al., 2004; Haut et al., 1996; Stuss et al., 2000) in conjunction with other cortical, subcortical and cerebellar regions (Mukhopadhyay et al., 2008) of the brain.

Although the OCD group showed significant correlations between symptom dimensions, obsessive traits and set shifting, the FDR showed no significant correspondence between obsessive symptoms or traits with any of the set shifting measures which may throw light upon why they do not manifest the pathology. This also indicates how a pathological constellation is operative in the OCD probands, where each aspect of higher-order cognitive functioning, specifically set shifting, is influenced by the disorder, whereas the symptoms presumably remain as a discrete feature in FDR, who do not manifest the pathology even with comparable set shifting difficulty in them.

The uniqueness of this study lies in the fact that although other researchers have concentrated on establishing the similarity in neuropsychological profiles of the proband–relative dyad, we have additionally tried to look into the buffers that prevent them from manifesting the disorder. The dissimilarities in their neuropsychological and metacognitive profiles, however subtle, offer important clues into the aetiological understanding of the disorder. The earlier studies conducted do not provide any explanation as to why the relative of the proband, with an equally defunct executive functioning system, remains asymptomatic. In our study, we have been able to establish why the FDR has the problems that they have, yet remain right outside the circumference of the identified disordered position. An endophenotypic model of OCD may thus be proposed as depicted in Figure 5.1.

Conclusion

The heritable nature of the disease has been highlighted by emphasizing the shared deficit in EFs, metacognitions and obsessive personality traits among the FDRs of the patients, which points

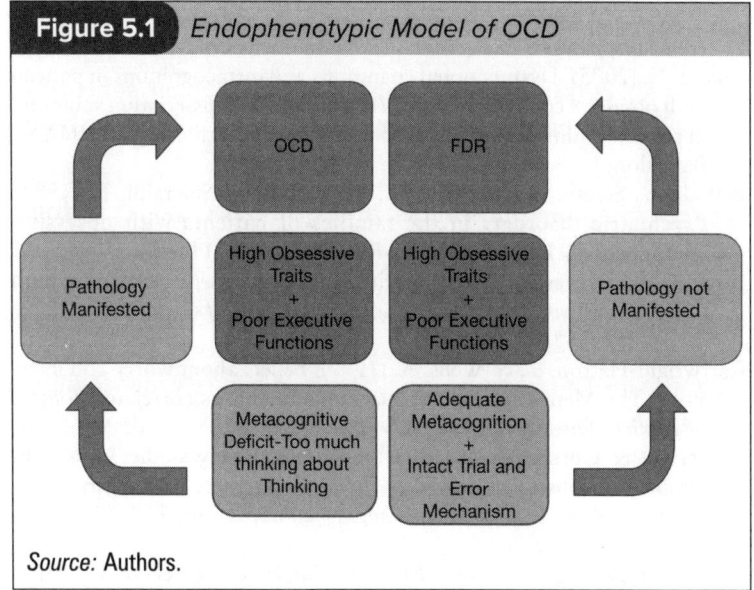

Figure 5.1 *Endophenotypic Model of OCD*

Source: Authors.

towards highlighting the dispositional loading of the disorder. The present chapter upholds the endophenotypic model of OCD and identifies metacognitive beliefs and an intact trial and error mechanism as protective factors for unaffected FDRs of OCD probands, which prevent in manifestation of pathology in them.

References

Aycicegi, A., Dinn, W. M., Harris, C. L., & Erkmen, H. (2003). Neuropsychological function in obsessive-compulsive disorder: Effects of comorbid conditions on task performance. *European Psychiatry, 18*(5), 241–248.

Albert, U., Barcaccia, B., Aguglia, A., Barbaro, F., De Cori, D., Brunatto, C.,...Maina, G. (2015). Obsessive beliefs in first-degree relatives of probands with obsessive-compulsive disorder: Is the cognitive vulnerability in relatives specific to OCD? *Personality and Individual Differences, 87*, 141–146.

Alsobrook, J. P., & Pauls, D. L. (1998). The genetics of obsessive compulsive disorder. In M. A. Jenike, L. Baer, & W. E. Minichiello (Eds.),

Obsessive-compulsive disorders: Theory and management: A guide for clinicians, patients and families (3rd ed.). Littleton, MA: Year Book.

Anand, N. (2005). Dysfunctional cognitions and metacognitions in patients with obsessive compulsive disorder. [Unpublished dissertation submitted in partial fulfilment for the M. Phil. in Clinical Psychology, NIMHANS, Bangalore.]

Bellodi, L., Sciuto, G., Diaferia, G., Ronchi, P., & Smeraldi, E. (1992). Psychiatric disorders in the families of patients with obsessive-compulsive disorder. *Psychiatry Research, 42*(2), 111–120.

Black, D. W., Noyes, R., Jr., Goldstein, R. B., & Blum, N. (1992). A family study of obsessive compulsive disorder. *Archives of General Psychiatry, 49*(5), 362–368.

Cartwright-Hatton, S., & Wells, A. (1997). Beliefs about worry and intrusions: The Meta-Cognitions Questionnaire and its correlates. *Journal of Anxiety Disorders, 11*(3), 279–296.

Carey, G., & Gottesman, I. (1981). Twin and family studies of anxiety phobic and obsessive disorders. In D. F. Klein & J. Rabkin (Eds.), *Anxiety: New research and changing concepts* (pp. 117–136). New York, NY: Raven Press.

Cavedini, P., Zorzi, C., Piccinni, M., Cavallini, M. C., & Bellodi, L. (2010). Executive dysfunctions in obsessive-compulsive patients and unaffected relatives: Searching for a new intermediate phenotype. *Biological Psychiatry, 67*(12), 1178–1184.

Chamberlain, S. R., Fineberg, N. A., Menzies, L. A., Blackwell, A. D., Bullmore, E. T., Robbins, T. W., & Sahakian, B. J. (2007). Impaired cognitive flexibility and motor inhibition in unaffected first-degree relatives of patients with obsessive-compulsive disorder. *The American Journal of Psychiatry, 164*(2), 335–338.

Clifford, C. A., Murray, R. M., & Fulker, D. W. (1984). Genetic and environmental influences on obsessional traits and symptoms. *Psychological Medicine, 14*(4), 791–800.

Cooper, J. (1970). The Leyton Obsessional Inventory. *Psychological Medicine, 1*(1), 48–64.

Cox, D. R. (1975). Partial likelihood. *Biometrika, 62*(2), 269–276.

Culberston, W. C., & Zilmer, E. A. (2001). *Tower of London – Drexel University*. Chicago, IL: Multi-Health Systems.

Delorme, R., Gousse, V., Roy, I., Trandafir, A., Mathieu, F., Mouren-Simeoni, M. C.,...Leboyer, M. (2007). Shared executive dysfunctions in unaffected relatives of patients with autism and obsessive compulsive disorder. *European Psychiatry, 22*(1), 32–38.

Eapen, V., & Robertson, M. M. (2002). Tourette syndrome and obsessive compulsive disorder. In *Encyclopaedia of the Human Brain* (pp. 615–622). San Diego, CA: Academic Press.

Eapen, V., Yakely, M., & Robertson, M. M. (2003). Gilles de la Tourette syndrome and obsessive compulsive disorder. In B. S. Fogel, R. B. Schiffer, & M. Rao (Eds.), *Neuropsychiatry* (2nd ed., pp. 947–990). Baltimore, MD: Lippincott Williams and Wilkins.

Eapen, V., Pauls, D. L., & Robertson, M. M. (2006). The role of clinical phenotypes in understanding the genetics of obsessive-compulsive disorder. *Journal of Psychosomatic Research, 61*(3), 359–364.

Fyer, A. J., Lipstiz, J. D., Mannuzza, S., Arnowitz, B., & Chapman, T. F. (2005). A direct interview family study of obsessive-compulsive disorder I. *Psychological Medicine, 35*(11), 1611–1621.

Ganesan, V. (2007). Neurobiology of OCD. In Y. C. Reddy & S. Srinath (Eds.), *Obsessive compulsive disorder: Current understandings and future directions.* Bangalore: NIMHANS.

Goldberg, D. P., & Hillier, V. F. (1979). *A scaled version of the General Health Questionnaire. Psychological Medicine, 9*(1), 139–146.

Goldstein, B., Obrzut, J. E., John, C., Ledakis, G., & Armstrong, C. L. (2004). The impact of frontal and nonfrontal brain tumor on Wisconsin Card Sorting Test performance. *Brain and Cognition, 54*(2), 110–116.

Goodman, W. K., Price, L. H., & Rasmussen, S. A. (1989). Yale-Brown Obsessive Compulsive Scale: I. Development, use and reliability. *Archives of General Psychiatry, 46*(11), 1006–1010.

Gottesman, I. I., & Gould, T. D. (2003). The endophenotype concept in psychiatry: Etymology and strategic intentions. *The American Journal of Psychiatry, 160*(4), 636–645.

Gottesman, I. I., & Shields, J. (1973). Genetic theorizing and schizophrenia. *The British Journal of Psychiatry, 122*(566), 15–30.

Grados, M. A., Walkup, J., & Walford, S. (2003). Genetics of obsessive compulsive disorders: New findings and challenges. *Brain & Development, 25*(Suppl. 1), 55–61.

Haut, M. W., Cahill, J., Cutlip, W. D., Stevenson, J. M., Makela, E. H., & Bloomfield, S. M. (1996). On the nature of Wisconsin Card Sorting Test performance in schizophrenia. *Psychiatry Research, 65*(1), 15–22.

Heaton, R. K., Chelune, G. J., Talley, J. L., Kay, G. C., & Curtiss, G. (1993). *Wisconsin Card Sorting Test Manual.* Odessa, FL: Psychological Assessment Resources.

Hou, J. M., Zhao, M., Zhang, W., Song, L. H., Wu, W. J., Wang, J.,...Qu, W. (2014). Resting-state functional connectivity abnormalities in patients with obsessive–compulsive disorder and their healthy first-degree relatives. *Journal of Psychiatry & Neuroscience, 39*(5), 304–311.

John, B., & Lewis, K. R. (1966). Chromosome variability and geographic distribution in insects. *Science 152*(3723), 711–721.

Jonnal, A. H., Gardner, C. O., Prescott, C. A., & Kendler, K. S. (2000). Obsessive and compulsive symptoms in a general population sample of female twins. *American Journal of Medical Genetics, 96*(6), 791–796.

Karno, M., Golding, J. M., Sorenson, S. B., & Burnam, M. A. (1988). The epidemiology of obsessive-compulsive disorder in five US communities. *Archives of General Psychiatry, 45*(12), 1094–1099.

Kim, S. J., & Kim, C. H. (2006). The genetic studies of obsessive-compulsive disorder and its future directions. *Yonsei Medical Journal, 47*(4), 443–454.

Lenane, M., Swedo, S., Leonard, H., Pauls, D., Sceery, W., & Rapoport, J. (1990). Psychiatric disorders in first degree relatives of children and adolescents with obsessive compulsive disorder. *Journal of the American Academy of Child Adolescence and Psychiatry, 29*(3), 407–412.

Lewis, A. (1935). Problems of obsessional illness. *Journal of the Royal Society of Medicine, 29*(4), 325–336.

Lipstiz, J. D., Mannuzza, S., Chapman, T. F., Foa, E. B., Franklin, M. E., Goodwin, R. D., & Fyer, A. J. (2005). A direct interview family study of obsessive-compulsive disorder II. Contribution of proband informant information. *Psychological Medicine, 35*(11), 1623–1631.

McDonald, R. J., & White, N. M. (1994). Parallel information processing in the water maze: Evidence for independent memory systems involving dorsal striatum and hippocampus. *Behavioral and Neural Biology, 61*(3), 260–270.

McGuffin, P., & Mawson, D. (1980). Obsessive-compulsive neurosis: Two identical twin pairs. *The British Journal of Psychiatry, 137*(3), 285–287.

Menzies, L., Achard, S., Chamberlain, S. R., Fineberg, N., Chen, C. H., del Campo, N.,...Bullmore, E. (2007). Neurocognitive endophenotypes of obsessive-compulsive disorder. *Brain, 130*(12), 3223–3236.

Mukhopadhyay, P., Dutt, A., Das, S. K., Basu, A., Hazra, A., Dhibar, T., & Roy, T. (2008). Identification of neuroanatomical substrates of set-shifting ability: Evidence from patients with focal brain lesions. In Rahul Banerjee & Bikas Chakrabarti (Eds.), *Models of brain and mind: Physical, computational and psychological approaches* (168, pp. 95–104.). Amsterdam: Elsevier.

Nestadt, G., Samuels, J., Riddle, M., Bienvenu, O. J., Liang, K. Y., LaBuda, M.,...Hoehn-Saric, R. (2000). A family study of obsessive-compulsive disorder. *Archives of General Psychiatry, 57*(4), 358–363.

Oldfield, R. C. (1971). The assessment and analysis of handedness: The Edinburgh inventory. *Neuropsychologia, 9*(1), 97–113.

Pauls, D. L. (1992). The genetics of obsessive compulsive disorder and Gilles de la Tourette syndrome. *Psychiatric Clinics of North America, 15*(4), 759–766.

Pauls, D. L., Alsobrook, J. P., Goodman, W., Rasmussen, S., & Leckman, J. F. (1995). A family study of obsessive-compulsive disorder. *The American Journal of Psychiatry, 152*(1), 76–84.

Peña, A., Kayashima, M., Mizoguchi, R., & Dominguez, R. (2011). Improving students' meta-cognitive skills within intelligent educational systems: A review. In D. D. Schmorrow & C. M. Fidopiastis (Eds.), *Foundations of augmented cognition: Directing the future of adaptive systems* (pp. 442–451). Berlin: Springer-Verlag.

Rajender, G., Bhatia, M. S., Kanwal, K., Malhotra, S., Singh, T. B., & Chaudhary, D. (2011). Study of neurocognitive endophenotypes in drug-naïve obsessive-compulsive disorder patients, their first-degree relatives and healthy controls. *Acta Psychiatrica Scandinavica, 124*(2), 152–161.

Rao, N. P., Reddy, Y. J., Kumar, K. J., Kandavel, T., & Chandrashekar, C. R. (2008). Are neuropsychological deficits trait markers in OCD? *Progress in Neuro-Psychopharmacology and Biological Psychiatry, 32*(6), 1574–1579.

Rasmussen, S. A., & Tsuang, M. T. (1984). The epidemiology of obsessive compulsive disorder. *Journal of Clinical Psychiatry, 45*(11), 450–457.

————(1986). Clinical characteristics and family history in DSM-III obsessive-compulsive disorder. *The American Journal of Psychiatry, 143*(3), 317–322.

Riddle, M. A., Scahill, L., King, R., Hardin, M. T., Towbin, K. E., Ort, S. I.,… Cohen, D. J. (1990). Obsessive compulsive disorder in children and adolescents: Phenomenology and family history. *Journal of the American Academy of Child and Adolescent Psychiatry, 29*(5), 766–772.

Solem, S., Haland, A. T., Vogela, P. A., Hansen, B., & Wells, A. (2009). Change in metacognitions predicts outcome in obsessive-compulsive disorder patients undergoing treatment with exposure and response prevention. *Behaviour Research and Therapy, 47*(4), 301–307.

Stuss, D. T., Levine, B., Alexander, M. P., Hong, J., Palumbo, C., Hamer, L.,…Izukawad, D. (2000). Wisconsin Card Sorting Test performance in patients with focal frontal and posterior brain damage: Effects of lesion location and test structure on separable cognitive processes. *Neuropsychologia, 38*(4), 388–402.

Vaghi, M. M., Hampshire, A., Fineberg, N. A., Kaser, M., Brühl, A. B., Sahakian, B. J.,…Robbins, T. W. (2017). Hypoactivation and dysconnectivity of a frontostriatal circuit during goal-directed planning as an endophenotype for obsessive-compulsive disorder. *Biological Psychiatry, Cognitive Neuroscience and Neuroimaging, 2*(8), 655–663

van Grootheest, D. S., Cath, D. C., Beckman, A. T., & Boomsma, D. I. (2005). Twin studies on obsessive-compulsive disorder: A review. *Twin Research and Human Genetics, 8*(5), 450–458.

Viswanath, B., Reddy, Y. J., Kumar, K. J., Kandavel, T., & Chandrashekar, C. R. (2009). Cognitive endophenotypes in OCD: A study of unaffected siblings of probands with familial OCD. *Progress in Neuro-Psychopharmacology and Biological Psychiatry, 33*(4), 610–615.

Wechsler, D., Wycherley, R. J., & Benjamin, L. (1997). *Wechsler Adult Intelligence Scale* (3rd ed.). San Antonio, TX: The Psychological Corporation.

Weissman, M. M., Bland, R. C., Canino, G. J., Greenwald, S., Hwu, H. G., Lee, C. K.,…Yeh, E. K. (1994). The cross national epidemiology of obsessive compulsive disorder: The Cross National Collaborative Group. *Journal of Clinical Psychiatry, 55*(Suppl), 5–10.

Wells, A., & Papageorgiou, C. (1998). Relationships between worry, obsessive-compulsive symptoms and meta-cognitive beliefs. *Behaviour Research and Therapy 36*(9), 899–913.

Wells, A., & Matthews, G. (1994). *Attention and emotion: A clinical perspective.* Hove: Erlbaum.

———(1996). Modelling cognition in emotional disorder: The SREF model. *Behaviour Research and Therapy, 34*(1–12), 881–888.

6

Impulsivity Versus Compulsivity

Personality Predisposition and Executive Functioning in OCD, OCSD and BPD

**Dinaz R. Jeejeebhoy,
Sreemoyee Tarafder,
Nilanjana Chatterjee and
Pritha Mukhopadhyay**

This chapter focuses on the compulsivity–impulsivity dimension of obsessive compulsive (OC) and other related disorders that comprise the OC spectrum. The term 'spectrum' has been widely used in literature to mean many things, and in this chapter, 'OC spectrum' refers to a group of disorders that are presumed to be distinct from, but related to, OCD, and which are characterized by repetitive thoughts and/or behaviours. Research evidence most strongly supports the inclusion of body dysmorphic disorder (BDD), Tourette's disorder and hypochondriasis (HYP), and there is also some support for the inclusion of obsessive compulsive personality disorder (OCPD) and eating disorders (Leckman et al., 2010). A debate of whether or not to include obsessive compulsive spectrum disorders (OCSDs) in the DSM-V led to a survey of 187 OCD experts from around the world (Mataix-Cols, Pertusa, & Leckman, 2007), and they mostly agreed that if a new category of OCSDs is included in DSM-V, it should be kept narrow. Support was greatest for including BDD (72% agreed), trichotillomania (71% agreed) and tic disorders (61% agreed) (Mataix-Cols, Pertusa, & Leckman, 2007). Support for including HYP (57% agreed) and OCPD (45% agreed) was more mixed. Relatively few experts agreed with including impulse control disorders (ICDs) (33%) (excluding trichotillomania) or eating disorders (28%), and very few agreed with including autism (9%) or addictions (5%) (Phillips, Stein, Rauch, Hollander, & Fallon, 2010).

The increased controversies of whether or not the OCSDs should at all be considered for inclusion in the then to be published DSM-V led to the conceptualization of the present study, where a need was felt to understand whether the underlying neuropsychological mechanism and the personality predisposition of individuals across the spectrum differed. It is especially relevant in the Indian scenario where literature regarding the spectrum is sparse.

In 1993, Hollander proposed the concept of an obsessive compulsive spectrum disorders as a dimensional model of risk avoidance in which impulsivity and compulsivity represent polar opposite psychiatric spectrum complexes that can be viewed along a continuum of compulsive and impulsive disorders. Compulsivity and impulsivity are natural behaviours that are essential for survival in all species and controlled by brain mechanisms and are greatly implicated in the concept of OCSDs. Pathological compulsivity and impulsivity characterize a broad range of mental disorders and are at the core of the most debilitating symptoms. Compulsivity refers to repetitive behaviours that are performed according to certain rules or in a stereotypical fashion (Grant & Potenza, 2006). The concept of impulsivity covers a wide range of actions that are poorly conceived, prematurely expressed, unduly risky or inappropriate to the situation and that often result in undesirable outcomes, or more simply put, a tendency to act prematurely and without foresight (Evenden, 1999). Impulsivity and compulsivity may be viewed as diametrically opposed or, alternatively, as similar, in that each implies a dysfunction of impulse control (Stein et al., 1996). Thus, although at first they seem to be polar opposites on a continuum of control—both control of the self and the control of others—impulsive behaviour seems to be characterized by inadequate or deficient control resulting in behavioural disinhibition and compulsive behaviour seems to be characterized by excessive overcontrol and behavioural inhibition. Such a simplistic division, however, does not appear to apply when the phenomenology of impulsive and compulsive behaviour is examined more closely.

Patients on the compulsive end of the spectrum tend to have an exaggerated sense of threat from the outside world and engage in rituals/routines, such as OC behaviours, to neutralize the threat or reduce the harm. This endpoint marks compulsive or risk-aversive behaviours characterized by overestimation of the probability of future harm, as exemplified by OCD. Patients on the impulsive end of the spectrum tend to underestimate the harm that is associated with behaviours such as aggression, excessive gambling or self-injury. This endpoint designates impulsive action generally characterized by a lack of consideration of the negative results of such behaviour and is exemplified by borderline and antisocial personality disorders (Hollander & Rosen, 2000).

The main focus of our study was to find out how OCD differed as a disorder from other disorders in the spectrum. For this purpose, two other study groups were selected, one on the complete opposite end of the spectrum, that is, BPD was selected and the other group comprised of persons suffering from BDD, HYP and OCPD. These disorders were selected as they lie midway between the impulsivity and compulsivity dimensions as proposed by Hollander (1993).

Hollander and colleagues (Hollander, 1993; Stein & Hollander, 1993) have suggested that compulsivity and impulsivity represent two ends of a continuum of restraint versus disinhibition. These authors suggest that OCD is the prototypic compulsive disorder and borderline personality disorder (BPD) is the prototypic impulsive disorder. The compulsive endpoint in this dimension involves a heightened estimation of harm and risk avoidance as seen in OCD. The impulsive endpoint in this dimension involves a decreased sense of one's behaviour along with elevated risk-seeking behaviour as is exhibited by individuals with BPD. Diagnostic criteria for BPD include items describing suicidal or self-mutilating behaviour, other potentially self-damaging impulsiveness, such as, rapid shifts in mood and frantic efforts to avoid abandonment. BPD has been shown by several investigators to be associated with substance use disorders (Links, Steiner, Offord, & Eppel, 1988; Zanarini, Gunderson, & Frankenburg, 1989) and bulimia (Hezrog, Keller, Lavori, Kenny, & Sacks, 1992; Skodol, Oldham, Hyler, Kellman, Doidge, & Davies, 1993). Impulsive behaviours generally have an element of pleasure, at least initially, although they may lose their pleasurable quality over time. This can be better understood through the following case:

Case 1

Akansha, a 34-year-old-female, second born of two sisters, who lives with her mother and lost her father when she was four, presented herself with high suicidal ideation and death wishes. She has not had any stable relationships as far as she can remember and has been in and out of romantic and sexual relationships. She feels that nobody understands her and she has a very deep feeling of emptiness within her despite being amongst many people. She can make friends easily but finds it hard to sustain the friendship. She goes to any length to establish relationships with the opposite sex and ultimately finds out that they are just using her. Nonetheless, she continues to persuade them into being with her with her, fearing that this is her last chance to be with someone and that if he does not stay she will be left alone forever. Her expectations from any relationship are far-fetched and seem utopian. She trusts very easily and invariably gets hurt. She is very attached to her mother and has repeatedly expressed that she would kill herself if anything should happen to her mother. She wants to marry and have children, and fears she is losing out on time and compares herself to her peers who are well settled in life. She holds a good job and performs well but does not save a penny for a rainy day.

This case demonstrates the cardinal features of BPD, with a pervading sense of vacuum and emptiness, frantic efforts to avoid real or imagined abandonment, unstable intense relationships and rapidly shifting and shallow expression of emotions. In some patients with ICD, we see them engaging in the behaviour to increase arousal, but there may be a compulsive component to their behaviour in which they continue to engage in the behaviour to decrease dysphoria.

Both OCD and BDD are characterized by recurrent, time-consuming, intrusive, persistent and unwanted thoughts (Phillips, McElroy, Keck Jr., Pope, & Hudson, 1993). This causes anxiety/distress and is usually resisted at least to some extent (Phillips, Gunderson, Mallya, McElroy, & Carter, 1998). It has been observed that BDD patients also engage in compulsive behaviours just as OCD patients do (e.g., mirror checking) (Phillips & Diaz, 1997; Phillips, Menard, Fay, & Weisberg, 2005; Phillips, Wilhelm, & Koran, 2010). These compulsions are repetitive, time-consuming, difficult to resist or control and not pleasurable. They are performed intentionally, in response to an obsession and aims to reduce anxiety or distress that the patient experiences (Phillips et al., 1998; Phillips & Kaye, 2007). Studies found that scores for preoccupations/obsessions and compulsive behaviours did not significantly differ for BDD vs. OCD, suggesting similarities in these symptoms (Phillips et al., 1998; Phillips et al., 2007). For instance, the following case of BDD highlights how people with body dysmorphic disorders are thoroughly preoccupied with their imagined deformities of their body parts.

178 / Dinaz R. Jeejeebhoy et al.

Twenty-five-year-old Sakshi was plagued with the doubt that her wisdom teeth were causing her face to look broad and square. She believed that she looked very ugly because of it, and no amount of reassurance from her parents, family, friends and even doctors could move this belief. There was no apparent disfiguration and she looked just as pretty as any other 25-year-old girl. She was distressed, and she believed that if all four wisdom teeth be removed she would feel good about herself again. She did get her wisdom teeth removed but still felt that she was not as pretty.

As can be seen from the aforementioned case study, the obsessions and compulsions in this case are limited to concerns about physical appearance. The overlap in symptom manifestation of BDD and OCD is that both engage in seeking reassurance and are excessively preoccupied with thoughts, but those with BDD are preoccupied with one or more perceived defects or flaws in their physical appearance. Clinical investigations have indicated that insight is poorer in BDD than in OCD, with 27% to 60% of BDD patients currently having delusional beliefs against only 2% of OCD patients (Eisen, Phillips, Coles, & Rasmussen, 2004; Mancuso, Knoesen, & Castle, 2010; Phillips, et al., 2006; Phillips, et al. 2007). Core beliefs in BDD appear to focus more on unacceptability of the self (e.g., being inadequate, worthless or unlovable) (Veale et al., 1996), and preliminary data suggests suicide rates may be higher in BDD than in OCD (Phillips et al., 1998; Phillips et al., 2007).

On comparing HYP with OCD, several studies have found that while both groups had similar levels of obsession component, anxiety and depression, HYP subjects had less compulsivity, less insight, more somatic fear and greater avoidance (Neziroglu, McKay, & Yaryura-Tobias, 2000). Another study pointed out that while the two groups had similar beliefs about the probability of falling ill, HYP patients had greater health anxiety and more catastrophic beliefs about disease (Abramowitz, Olatunji, & Deacon, 2007). The following case study will help in understanding the same:

> ### Case 3
>
> Sam, a 28-year-old man, visited many doctors with the hope that they would cure him of a terrible disease that he had contracted. Various doctors had run various tests and all results indicated that Sam was in good health. He was unduly alarmed with the slightest change in his body and would be convinced that he was suffering from a grave illness. The constant preoccupation caused personal distress and inability to function adequately in his social and occupational fields.

As is evident from the aforementioned case, people who suffer from HYP have high levels of bodily vigilance and intolerance of uncertainty but greater health anxiety and fewer OC symptoms. HYP entails a preoccupation with having or acquiring a serious, undiagnosed medical illness.

A discussion of OCPDs is not complete without taking into consideration anankastic personality or OCPD. The clinical presentation of OCPD indicates preoccupation with orderliness, perfectionism and mental and interpersonal control at the expense of flexibility, openness and efficiency, as manifested by eight specific criteria in the DSM (of which four or more are needed to make the diagnosis)—preoccupation with details, orderliness and rules; rigidity; perfectionism; excessive work devotion; reluctance to delegate; hypermorality; miserliness; and hoarding. Some of these features are demonstrated in the following case example:

> ### Case 4
>
> Kabir's parents reported that their son kept himself busy with details, orderliness and rules, was rigid and a perfectionist, worked overtime and did not believe that anybody but he himself could do any work perfectly. These behaviours were extreme in that because of the rigid rules and regulations that were self-imposed, work was always delayed and deadlines rarely met. Kabir (37 years old) did not think that he had a problem, and his parents were unable to convince him that he may require help.

As can be seen from the aforementioned case example, there are a few overlapping symptoms between OCD and OCPD such as preoccupation with orderliness, perfectionism, scrupulosity and behavioural (need for control) or cognitive (stubbornness) rigidity (Chamberlain, Blackwell, Fineberg, Robbins, & Sahakian, 2005; Nelson, Abramowitz, Whiteside, & Deacon, 2006; Rhéaume, Freeston, Dugas, Letarte, & Ladouceur, 1995). Due to this overlap, distinguishing the two disorders may be confusing (APA, 2000). OCPD is differentiated from OCD by the absence of strictly defined obsessions and compulsions (APA, 2000; WHO, 1992). However, behavioural manifestations of OCPD traits can have a compulsive quality being intentional, repetitive, time-consuming, difficult to resist or control, not pleasurable and associated with distress (APA, 2000; Rhéaume et al., 1995). In OCD, obsessions are intrusive, distressing and generally ego-dystonic. In contrast, OCPD traits and symptomatic behaviours are considered ego-syntonic, as they are viewed as correct (Fineberg, Sharma, Sivakumaran, Sahakian, & Chamberlain, 2007).

Thus, in general, while compulsivity may be driven by an attempt to alleviate anxiety or discomfort, impulsivity may be driven by the desire to obtain pleasure, arousal or gratification. Both types of behaviours share the inability to inhibit or delay repetitive behaviours (Hollander & Wong, 1995). Over time, impulsive behaviours may become compulsive (driven behaviours without arousal) and compulsive behaviours may become impulsive (reinforced habits).

Through the case studies just discussed, we may see that it all boils down to a unifying spectrum where there is impulsivity and compulsivity at the two ends. Considering the myriad aspects of the spectrum, we hypothesized that the patients suffering from OCD would differ from the extremely placed 'impulsive' individuals and the habitually compulsive individuals. Since there are major overlaps in the symptomatology of the OC spectrum, we were curious to look into the set shifting and personality patterns of these groups, when compared to one another.

Methods

Sample

The method of sampling used was purposive. The sample comprised of four groups—patients diagnosed with OCD (N=18); patients diagnosed with OCSD (N=18; 7 patients with HYP, 6 patients with OCPD and 5 patients with BDD); patients diagnosed with BPD (N=18) and the community sample (control group or CG) (N=18), matched on the basis of age, sex, education and handedness. The sample comprised of patients selected from different psychiatric outpatient services of hospitals/clinics located at different regions of Kolkata city. The patients were diagnosed by a consultant psychiatrist at the hospital/clinic and also by a clinical psychologist independently. The cases were selected only on the basis of agreement between the psychiatrist and the clinical psychologist, basing their diagnosis on the criteria listed in the DSM-IV-TR) (APA, 2000).

Patients who were included in the sample were those who matched their respective diagnostic criteria, of either sex within the age range of 18–45 years with a minimum level of education of standard X. Those who are not acquainted with this type of testing, that is, naive subjects, only right-handed subjects and those who agreed to partake in the study were included. However, patients having OCD with poor insight, those having history of co-morbid psychological disorders, with current serious/acute/chronic medical illness diagnosed by treating physician, with physical disability/neurological condition or with the history of developmental disorders were excluded from the study.

Rigorous one-to-one matching criteria with the OCD group was implemented for the selection of their corresponding clinical as well as nonclinical CG that was drawn from the community. Subjects with no history of any psychological disorders, who scored 4 or less on General Health Questionnaire (GHQ), who were not acquainted with this type of testing, that is, naive subjects, and those who agreed to partake in the study were included in the CG. Those with current serious/acute/chronic medical illness diagnosed by treating physician, with physical disability/ neurological condition and with the history of developmental disorders were excluded from the study. The tools used are listed in Table 6.1.

Procedure

Participants were included on the basis of the inclusion/exclusion criteria after receiving their consent. At the outset, a semi-structured socio-demographic and clinical data sheet was filled by the participants and the BPD group interviewed on the IPDE while the OCD group was administered the Y-BOCS and LOI and OCSD group administered the LOI. GHQ and the SAPAS were administered in case of the community sample. Following this Edinburgh Handedness Inventory and NEO-FFI were administered. This was further followed by administration of the WCST. From a total of 25 OCD patients identified, 6 patients were diagnosed with personality disorder, and one failed to complete the assessment schedule and was therefore not included in the present study. Out of 30 BPD patients identified, six patients being diagnosed with a co-morbid disorder could not be included in the study; five other subjects failed to complete the assessment schedule and one patient did not give consent and was excluded on that basis. From the 23 OCSD patients identified three patients failed to complete the assessment schedule as a whole and two patients did not give their consent and therefore not included in the study.

Statistical Analysis

For this study, non-parametric tests or distribution-free statistics were used since non-parametric statistics make no assumptions about the probability distributions of the variables being assessed and also for its wider applicability and increased robustness. The Mann–Whitney U Test was used to evaluate the difference between means among the four groups being studied. For

Sr No.	Tools	Purpose of Using Tool
	Table 6.1 *Correlation Table*	
1.	Semi-structured socio-demographic and clinical data sheet	Demographic details, case history
2.	Yale Brown Obsessive Compulsive Scale (YBOCS) (Goodman, Price, & Rasmussen, 1989)	Symptom severity (OCD group)
3.	Leyton Obsessional Inventory (LOI) (Cooper, 1970)	Obsessive symptoms and obsessive personality Trait (OCD and OCSD groups)
4.	International Personality Disorder Examination (IPDE) (Loranger, Janca, & Sartorius, 1997)	Screening criteria for patients with BPD
5.	GHQ (Goldberg & Hillier, 1979)	Selection criteria for the CG
6.	Standardized Assessment of Personality Abbreviated Scale (SAPAS) (Mann, Jenkins, Cutting, & Cowen, 1981; Pilgrim & Mann, 1990; Pilgrim, Mellers, Boothby, & Mann, 1993)	Selection criteria for CG
7.	Edinburgh Handedness Inventory (Oldfield, 1971)	Assess handedness
8.	NEO Five Factor Inventory (NEO-FFI) (Costa & McCrae, 1992)	Assess dimensions such as neuroticism, extroversion, openness, agreeableness and conscientiousness
9.	Wisconsin Card Sorting Test (WCST) (Heaton et al., 1993)	Perseveration and set shifting

Source: Authors.

analysis, 0.05 and 0.01 level of significance was accepted as critical level.

Result

The following section focuses on narration of the results obtained from our study. The results have been divided into two sections—personality variables and set shifting variables—to aid in understanding the similarities and dissimilarities between the study group and CG.

Section 1: Personality Variables

From Table 6.2, it is seen that there is a significant difference between the OCD group and the CG in the experience of subjective depression and neuroticism where the CG is better off on both measures. The OCD group patients are also significantly worse off from the OCSD group on their subjective experience of depression. Significant differences are seen between OCD and BPD in terms of openness, where the BPD group is more open to experiences than the OCD group. No differences have been seen in case of extraversion, agreeableness and conscientiousness between the groups.

Table 6.3 shows the similarities and dissimilarities between the study groups on the NEO-FFI scale. The pattern highlights the uniqueness of each patient group.

Section 2: Set Shifting Variables

From Table 6.4, it is evident that there is a significant difference between the OCD group and the CG on the measures of WCST such as percent error, PPR, PPE, PNPE, NOCC and FTMS where the CG is better off on all of them, and there is no significant difference on the measures of PCLR and TCFC. OCSD group is significantly worse off than the OCD group in terms of percent

Table 6.2 Mean (M) and Standard Deviations (SD) of OCD, OCSD, BPD and CG on BDI and NEO-Five Factor Inventory Along with Mean Difference (Mann–Whitney U Test) Comparing OCD with OCSD, BPD and CG

Variables	OCD		OCSD		BPD		CG		OCD – OCSD Mann–Whitney U Test	OCD – BPD Mann–Whitney U Test	OCD – CG Mann–Whitney U Test
	M	SD	M	SD	M	SD	M	SD			
Personality Variables											
BDI	29.72	9.404	19.94	7.13	28.77	13.89	3.44	2.35	64.50**	155.50	3.50**
Neuroticism	32.27	7.036	28.27	6.01	33.88	9.29	15.00	5.34	112.00	142.50	4.00**
Extraversion	24.94	6.62	25.50	9.28	29.00	8.45	23.00	8.08	152.50	104.00	135.00
Openness	24.33	3.06	23.22	5.01	28.00	6.32	23.83	7.42	134.50	99.00*	157.00
Agreeableness	26.38	5.54	22.83	6.77	25.33	3.00	22.55	7.31	126.00	151.00	106.00
Conscientiousness	27.72	7.37	30.88	4.41	26.66	8.26	26.33	8.85	123.50	153.00	144.50

Source: Authors.

Notes: *Level of significance $p > 0.05$, **Level of significance $p > 0.01$.
BDI = Beck Depression Inventory.

Table 6.3	NEO Style Analysis of the Three Study Groups, Namely, OCD, OCSD and BPD, Based on the Big Five Constellation Using NEO-FFI		
NEO Style Analysis	**OCD**	**OCSD**	**BPD**
Style of anger control: Temperamental (N high A low)	√	√	√
Style of impulse control: Undercontrolled (N high, C low)	√		√
Style of character: Undistinguished (A low, C low)	√		√
Style of well-being: Gloomy, pessimistic (N high E low)	√		
Style of activity: Lethargic (E low C low)	√		
Style of interactions: Competitor (E low, A low)	√		
Style of defence: Maladaptive (N high, O low)		√	
Style of attitude: Resolute believer (O low, A low)		√	

Source: Authors.

error, PCLR and NOCC, with no significant difference on the measures of PPR, PPE, PNPE, TCFC and FTMS. The BPD group is significantly worse off on WCST measures of percent error, PNPE and PCLR than the OCD group; the OCD group is significantly worse off from the BPD on measures of NOCC and FTMS on WCST, there being no significant difference in the two groups on the measures of PPR, PPE and TCFC.

Discussion

From the NEO-FFI style analysis of the study groups on Table 6.3, it becomes clear that each of the patient groups is unique in terms of their personality constellation. Their similarities also

Table 6.4 Mean (M) and Standard Deviations (SD) of OCD, OCSD, BPD and CG on Variables of WCST Along with Mean Difference (Mann–Whitney U Test) Comparing OCD with OCSD, BPD and CG, Respectively

Variables	OCD		OCSD		BPD		CG		OCD – OCSD Mann–Whitney U Test	OCD – BPD Mann–Whitney U Test	OCD – CG Mann–Whitney U Test
	M	SD	M	SD	M	SD	M	SD			
Set Shifting Variables											
Percentage Error	36.11	23.22	23.27	22.42	22.11	15.66	84.83	14.26	97.50*	95.50*	23.50**
PPR	28.77	26.42	21.77	22.25	22.27	18.53	74.16	23.09	131.50	142.50	29.50**
PPE	32.94	25.12	23.94	24.33	28.11	25.30	80.55	19.44	120.00	142.50	25.00**
PNPE	44.88	30.00	34.38	30.12	26.38	24.43	82.00	16.61	132.50	102.00*	54.50**
PCLR	40.00	28.49	18.11	18.08	18.22	16.66	77.83	20.83	76.00**	69.50**	52.50
NOCC	4.00	2.58	2.38	1.75	27.61	33.14	5.88	.4714	104.00*	53.50**	77.00**
TCFC	36.11	35.40	39.11	36.63	55.44	37.16	15.88	6.34	145.00	123.50	112.50
FTMS	3.94	10.20	1.16	1.42	54.05	37.07	.0556	.2357	129.50	10.00**	41.50**

Source: Authors.

Notes: *Level of significance $p > 0.05$, **Level of significance $p > 0.01$.

PPR = Percent perseverative response, PPE = Percent perseverative error, PNPE = Percent nonperseverative error, PCLR = Percent conceptual level response, NOCC = Number of categories completed, TCFC = Trials to complete first category, FTMS = Failure to maintain set.

are not suggestive of a similar pattern as each of the traits are working in conjunction with other domains/traits to make each of the groups behave separately, and it may be the reason why they manifest different symptoms. For example, all three groups are found to be temperamental that indicates that they are easily angered and tend to express anger directly. They are easily irritable and take offense readily, often overlooking the effects of their anger on others. These individuals are often at the mercy of their own impulses. The preceding description may ring true for the BPD group, but is questionable in the OCD and OCSD groups since they are not manifesting their impulsivities in the same manner. It may be explained from the fact that along with the presence of the said temperamental trait in OCD, they are also gloomy, pessimistic, lethargic and competitive by nature and will not express their anger reactions the way the patients of BPD tend to convey. Similarly, if we consider the profile of the OCSD group, we can find that in addition to being temperamental, they are resolute believers and maladaptive, highlighting their rigidity and making use of ineffective defences.

So even though all the three groups show high level of neuroticism, it needs to be interpreted differently, keeping in mind the group characteristics, symptom manifestation and their distinctive personality constellations.

OCD Group

High scores on neuroticism and its facets in OCD has also been observed by Rector, Cassin, Richter and Burroughs (2009), where they mention previous research (e.g., Rector, Hood, Richter, & Bagby, 2002; Samuels et al., 2000) on personality factors, which have demonstrated that individuals with OCD score higher on facets of neuroticism relative to control subjects. Their expression of this trait is reflected in them being more overtly apprehensive, being prone to worry, yet they experience anger, frustration and bitterness when things do not progress their way. They feel unable to cope with stress and perceive themselves as incapable of handling themselves in the face of stress. They are so preoccupied with self and distress that they are prone to sadness, hopelessness and loneliness as indicated in the present study through their significantly elevated scores on the BDI and gloomy pessimistic style of well-being on NEO-FFI. Their insight into the senselessness of their obsessions and compulsions increases their suffering. There is little that cheers them and much that causes anguish and distress, which is also (evident from the finding of temperamental anger control style) why they tend to easily succumb to depression and find life hard and joyless. Amongst the three clinical groups, it is to be noted that the OCD group is the only one that has low extroversion, indicating that they are introverted, reserved and serious, and may not be as sociable in their dealings with others. It may be surmised, therefore, that their anger expression, in spite of being temperamental and undercontrolled, will be expressed laced with gloomy pessimism and anhedonia. The present findings corroborate with Frost and colleagues' (1994) assertion that obsessive compulsives are more risk-aversive, perfectionistic and guilt-ridden than non-obsessive compulsives and that these characteristic traits are central features of the disorder.

OCSD Group

It is seen that the OCSD group are also high on neuroticism than the CG. Their expression of neuroticism is more akin to that of OCD where they too are more overtly anxious and are prone to distress and worry and preoccupied with certain rules and sets of behaviour. The OCSD group, however, has significantly lower level of subjective depression, greater extroversion and are more maladaptive and rigid as compared to the OCD group. This may be attributed to the fact that their symptoms are more ego-syntonic, and they have poor insight regarding their condition as assessed on mental status examination (MSE). Although they have a significantly lower level of subjective depression when compared to OCD, this level is significantly higher than that of the CG. The ego-syntonicity of their symptoms makes them feel that it is the people around them who do not understand them. Therefore, they feel distressed about not being supported and accepted which may have contributed to the increased levels of subjective depression as compared to CG. In addition to this, their maladaptive nature makes them use primitive and ineffective defences and also lack insight into distressing effects (Costa & McCrae, 1994). The reader may recall from the case studies mentioned in the beginning of the chapter that Sakshi, Sam and Kabir all displayed preoccupation, distress and anxiety, and their symptoms were more in sync with their ego. They find it difficult to appraise their own behaviour as the cause of distress. They feel that they are misunderstood and perceive their environment as non-supportive.

BPD Group

The BPD group also has significantly higher scores than the CG on neuroticism. Persistent disturbances in uncertainty about self-image, their aims in life and internal preferences (e.g., trouble deciding what is important in life) may lead to a grossly disturbed self-image and self-acceptance (DSM-IV-TR, 2000). Wiggins and Pincus (1989), conceptualized that personality disorders were strongly and clearly related to dimensions of normal personality traits including (but not limited to) a close relationship of borderline with neuroticism on the NEO-FFI. The finding of low agreeableness indicates that the patients with BPD are hardhearted, sceptical, proud and competitive who tend to express anger directly. Additionally, their low conscientiousness reflects that they are not well organized, are careless, easy-going and prefer not to make plans. Although both OCD and BPD groups reported their conscientiousness to be low, it is to be kept in mind that their clinical characteristics have much to do with it. The OCD group owing to their perfectionism and high standards report their conscientiousness to be low as their effort are followed with poor returns, they feel distressed and berate their level of conscientiousness. In our previous work (Tarafder & Mukhopadhyay, 2015), we have shown how the 'high standards' that the patient with OCD wishes to reach is indeed an idyllic benchmark and not just a preoccupation with details, rules, lists, order or organization to the extent that one forgets the major point of the activity, as is the case in OCPD. The distress is more palpable in patients with OCD and they suffer substantially because of the problem and wish to be rid of it. Whereas, patients suffering from OCPD are rarely uncomfortable about it and do not feel the need to change it (Hyman & Pedrick, 2005), which is evident from the OCD and OCSD comparison in the present study as well. The group of patients with BPD have also reported low levels of conscientiousness, but they do not have an exalted benchmark to reach (like the OCD) and owing to their unwillingness to make plans and poor goal-directedness, they report low levels of conscientiousness. Their low conscientiousness score is a reflection of their impulsivity, as they lack self-discipline and orderliness and are unprepared, lackadaisical, casual and inept at carrying out tasks that would help them to reach their goals.

The BPD group has high score on BDI and on extraversion domain of NEO-FFI. Despite being gregarious and having many people for company, their interpersonal relationships are grossly disturbed which is reflected in their reporting of a chronic feeling of emptiness and loneliness, leading to depression. This is a regular feature of BPD pattern where it is easy for them to establish relationships, but they are unable to maintain them as they tend to exert themselves unassertively. Furthermore, unrealistic expectations from others and their unstable capricious mood and impulsivity may be a source of instability in their relationships (Bilimoria, Mukhopadhyay, & Das, 2015). Although their openness scores are significantly higher as compared to OCD, indicating that they tend to have liberal views and prefer novelty over being conventional and traditional in their outlook and a narrower range of interests. For instance, Akansha did not have any stable relationships and felt that nobody understood her; this made her feel empty deep within. Her patterns in friendship were also similar to what has been explained here, and her primary fear of being left alone forever is also indicated.

The chart in Figure 6.1 highlights the different mechanisms present in the disorders (OCD, OCSD and BPD) that differ in overt expression.

Using diagrammatic representation, we have tried to explain that although the three groups are high on the trait of neuroticism (NEO-FFI) and have similar styles of anger control, their outward expression and their experience of personal distress (symptoms and clinical picture) differ greatly. Insight is a vital component that not only helps people to understand their problem, but also how the problem affects the individual's interaction with the outer environment, thereby influencing their attribution process.

Section 2: Set Shifting Variables

OCD and OCSD

In the present study, it has also been observed that the OCD and OCSD groups showed similar kind of executive dysfunction in terms of trials taken, errors made, perseverative responses, perseverative errors, nonperseverative errors, trials to complete the first category and the failure to maintain set. This finding is also in alignment with the evidence that OCSD show similar executive dysfunction as OCD (Hanes, 1998). But the OCSD differed significantly in terms of percent errors, conceptual level response and the NOCC, where OCSD performed poorly than OCD. It was seen overall that the number of errors made during the set shifting task was greater for the OCSD group which may be associated to the fact that they were unable to form a concept despite continuous feedback from the environment. In order to attain a concept, one needs to allocate adequate attention to internal as well as external cues, to accommodate them and then reproduce a response. The increased preoccupation with their thoughts has probably decreased their ability to deploy attention adequately to the task at hand which has subsequently increased errors, making it difficult for concept attainment and reduction in category completion. Impulsive and compulsive behaviours have in common a sense of urgency or pressure preceding the behaviours.

Figure 6.1 *Different Mechanisms Present in the Disorders (OCD, OCSD and BPD) that Differ in Overt Expression*

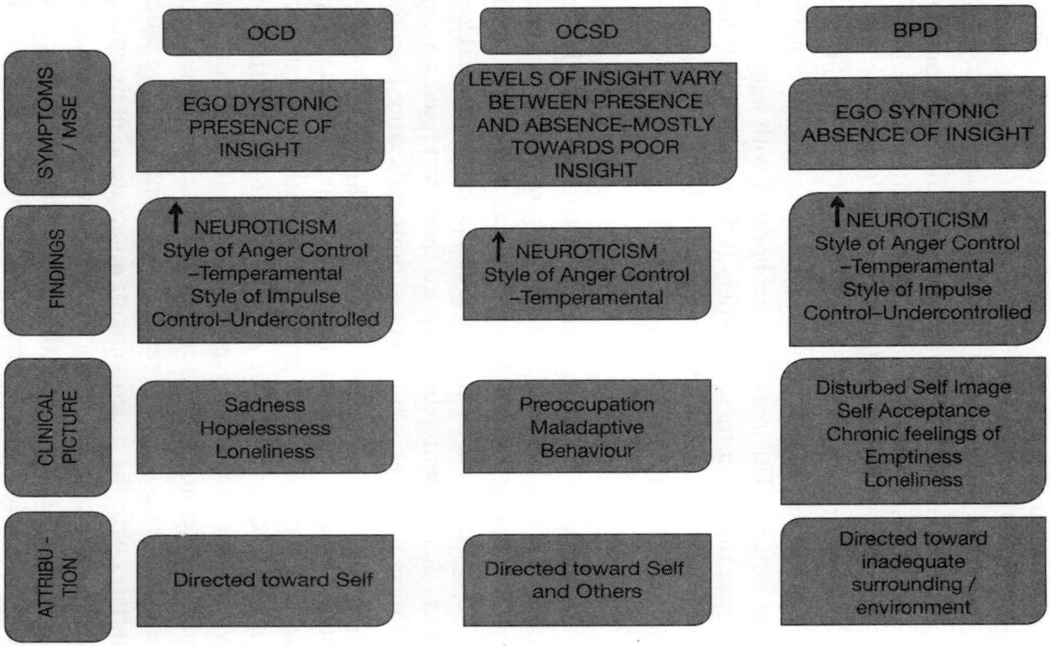

	OCD	OCSD	BPD
SYMPTOMS / MSE	EGO DYSTONIC PRESENCE OF INSIGHT	LEVELS OF INSIGHT VARY BETWEEN PRESENCE AND ABSENCE—MOSTLY TOWARDS POOR INSIGHT	EGO SYNTONIC ABSENCE OF INSIGHT
FINDINGS	↑ NEUROTICISM Style of Anger Control –Temperamental Style of Impulse Control–Undercontrolled	↑ NEUROTICISM Style of Anger Control –Temperamental	↑ NEUROTICISM Style of Anger Control –Temperamental Style of Impulse Control–Undercontrolled
CLINICAL PICTURE	Sadness Hopelessness Loneliness	Preoccupation Maladaptive Behaviour	Disturbed Self Image Self Acceptance Chronic feelings of Emptiness Loneliness
ATTRIBU- TION	Directed toward Self	Directed toward Self and Others	Directed toward inadequate surrounding / environment

Source: Authors.

The disorders in the OCSD group comprised of HYP, BDD and OCPD in the current study and although all three primarily show symptoms of compulsivity in terms of preoccupation, some behaviours may also reflect impulsivity, for example, the increased aggression in the OCPD when things do not go their way or in BDD where they go to lengths to reshape their imagined misshaped body part. Thus, although essentially compulsive, impulsivity in the OCSD group cannot be ruled out, and the failure to resist an impulse, drive or temptation to perform an act could also contribute to failure in concept formation. Therefore, it is seen that the dysfunction in OCD and OCSD is similar for set shifting but the OCSD are worse off on some of the dimensions of set shifting. This may be corroborated with neurobiological evidence that both these disorders (OCD and OCSD) have the frontostriatal and OFC involvement which makes their executive dysfunctions quite similar (Eisen, Phillips, Baer, Beer, Atala, & Rasmussen, 1998).

The tendency to focus excessive attention onto the thought processes is not only a distinctive feature of OCD, but is also observed among OCSD. This particular tendency in OCD and OCSD to emphasize intrinsic cues despite environmental feedback reflects their cognitive bias toward their own fixed assumptions and their resultant subsequent actions indicating that they are stuck in set (for detailed understanding, refer to Barceló & Knight, 2002) and disregard important environmental feedback. They remain constantly preoccupied with recurrent intrusive thoughts and fail to come out of it to cope with the dynamic environment, which is an index of difficulty in set shifting. The finding is in conformity with prevailing notion that when orbitofrontal cortex is overwhelmed by the potent obsessive thought, it interferes with the functioning of dorsolateral prefrontal cortex (DLPFC), which is the seat of executive functioning (Arciniegas & Beresford, 2001). It may be the reason why the OCD set a rule of their own to deal with the matching of the cards in WCST task, and fail to come out of the set in spite of feedback, culminating in poor conceptual-level responses and perseveration that gives a direct link to account for the underlying mechanism of the repetitive inappropriate and ritualistic compulsions as the most dominant feature in OCD.

OCD and BPD

Reviewing the performance of OCD with BPD on set shifting, it was seen that patients with BPD had significantly poor scores on the percent error, nonperseverative error and conceptual-level response in comparison to OCD. This reflects the ineffective use of the trial and error mechanism. It may be inferred that the patients with BPD use strategy-less random errors. Since they do not utilize insightful learning and flout external feedback, it results in turn in poor response selection, poor concept formation and poor category completion (Bilimoria, Mukhopadhyay, & Das, 2015). They show resistance to feedback utilization and get lost between relevant and irrelevant as observed by other researchers as well (Burgess, 1992; Ruocco, 2005). Implementation of a new response is a result of utilization of feedback to one's response when the stimulus–response task is based on trial and error mechanism. Poorer nonperseverative error percentile could also be explained as the error in feedback utilization, resulting in poor response selection, which results in poor conceptual-level response and poor category completion on WCST. Perseveration of previous inappropriate responses and difficulties in effectively utilizing feedback to adapt to changing conditions and environments is evident in both the groups. Impairment of set shifting capacity is an index of their difficulty in taking decision regarding response selection and shifting of attention (Bilimoria, Mukhopadhyay, & Das, 2015). Previous research revealed that patients with BPD make risky decisions significantly more often than the CG and show reduced capacities to advantageously utilize feedback (Svaldi, Philipsen, & Matthies, 2012). Moreover, where OCD is concerned, these findings are in line with numerous prior reports (Boone et al., 1991; Christensen, Kim, Dysken, & Hoover, 1992; Harvey, 1987; Head, Bolton, & Hyman, 1989; Lucey et al., 1997; Moritz et al., 2009; Mukhopadhyay et al., 2010; Tarafder et al., 2006). The feedback provided is the basis on which the performer takes the decision to shift set from one category to another based on either colour, form or number on WCST task (Goldman-Rakic, 1991).

It is seen that all the three clinical groups find it difficult to generate and select alternatives and therefore maybe we could look at it as a deficit in flexibility. Preoccupation of OCD and OCSD with their thoughts and impulsivity in the actions of the BPD may reduce the efficiency of the functioning of the set shifting function.

The finding may also be interpreted as poor attention allocation and a lack in the ability to use the 'think ahead' strategy, and in OCD and OCSD, it is their need for perfection that is emphasized upon, rather than the completion of the task. Poor mental flexibility and concept attainment in BPD is reflected through their implementation of random strategies, and OCD seem to follow internally made rigid rules and are thus 'stuck in their own set ways', therefore unable to shift between their own set and what is expected of them, displaying poor response inhibition and poor feedback utilization. In their quest of striving for unrealistic perfection, they eventually violate rules. BPD act on the basis of their present needs and feeling in combination with their impulsivity, and display poor response inhibition which is further reflected through violations in rules which indicates a gap between their knowledge and action.

Thus, we find that BPD, OCD and OCSD reflect similar errors on the different dimensions of executive functions but their underlying pathology leading to the same differs. OCD and OCSD follow a rather predictable pattern, whereas there appears to be no discernible pattern of behaviour for BPD as illustrated in Figure 6.2.

Figure 6.2 explains the orderliness in OCD and OCSD versus the randomness in BPD where although the underlying psychopathology is similar, the expression differs.

Figure 6.2 *Orderliness in OCD and OCSD Versus Randomness in BPD*

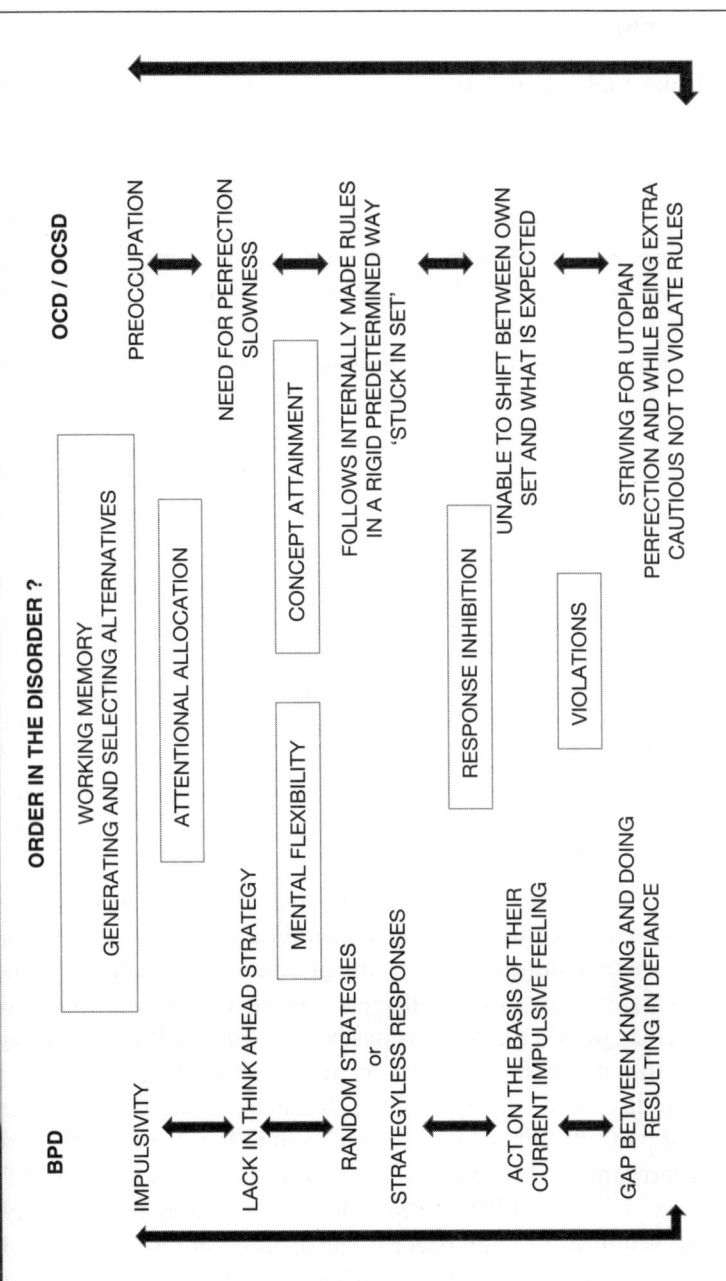

BPD

ORDER IN THE DISORDER ?

OCD / OCSD

IMPULSIVITY

PREOCCUPATION

WORKING MEMORY
GENERATING AND SELECTING ALTERNATIVES

LACK IN THINK AHEAD STRATEGY

NEED FOR PERFECTION
SLOWNESS

ATTENTIONAL ALLOCATION

CONCEPT ATTAINMENT

MENTAL FLEXIBILITY

RANDOM STRATEGIES
or
STRATEGYLESS RESPONSES

FOLLOWS INTERNALLY MADE RULES
IN A RIGID PREDETERMINED WAY
'STUCK IN SET'

RESPONSE INHIBITION

UNABLE TO SHIFT BETWEEN OWN
SET AND WHAT IS EXPECTED

ACT ON THE BASIS OF THEIR
CURRENT IMPULSIVE FEELING

VIOLATIONS

GAP BETWEEN KNOWING AND DOING
RESULTING IN DEFIANCE

STRIVING FOR UTOPIAN
PERFECTION AND WHILE BEING EXTRA
CAUTIOUS NOT TO VIOLATE RULES

Source: Authors.

Conclusion

While looking into the personality pattern of the groups, we found that even with similar characteristics they differed from each other because of the constellation of the Big Five Factors. Similarly, on WCST, we found similar yet differing patterns of errors. It goes on to show that test results alone cannot reflect the underlying pathology. For in-depth understanding of these varied groups of patients who in some way or the other reflect compulsivity and/or impulsivity, we need to corroborate the findings with our observations and thereby develop necessary insights into their problems.

The patients with OCD navigate the onslaught of potent thought in a ritualized order which has to be followed with utmost precision or else it would have to be repeated to perfection. This repetition reflects the rigidity with which the ritual has to be performed in order for it to be perfect. Reflection of this is seen in the set shifting task where their errors reflect a certain order further strengthening the base for OCD to be referred to as having an order in the disorder. From the NEO-FFI style analysis of the study groups in Table 6.3, it becomes clear that each of the patient groups is unique in terms of their personality constellation. Their similarities also are not suggestive of a similar pattern as each of the traits are working in conjunction with other domains/traits to make each of the groups behave separately, and it may be the reason why they manifest different symptoms. Although all three groups are found to have high neuroticism and are temperamental in terms of anger control, their personality patterns are vastly different from each other owing to the interplay of other factors, as has been discussed. It is additionally seen that the performance on the test of set shifting reveal that all three disordered groups exhibit executive dysfunction but their error patterns differ. In case of OCD and OCSD groups, the error pattern and response style follow a rather predictable pattern, whereas for the BPD group it is wayward and unpredictable. This is indicative of an order in the disorder of OCD and OCSD, who fare better on tasks assessing set shifting when compared to BPD, which may be corroborated with their personality style where impulsivity rules and overrides self-control.

References

Abramowitz, J. S., Olatunji, B. O., & Deacon, B. J. (2007). Health anxiety, hypochondriasis, and the anxiety disorders. *Behaviour Therapy*, *38*(1), 86–94.

Arciniegas, D. B., & Beresford, T. P. (2001). *Neuropsychiatry: An introductory approach*. Cambridge, MA: Cambridge University Press.

American Psychiatric Association. (1994). *Diagnostic and statistical manual of mental Disorders* (4th ed.). Washington, DC: American Psychiatric Association.

American Psychiatric Association. (2000). *Diagnostic and statistical manual of mental disorders-IV* (Text Revision). Washington, DC: American Psychiatric Association.

Aycicegi, A., Dinn, W. M., Harris, C. L., & Erkmen, H. (2003) Neuropsychological function in obsessive-compulsive disorder: Effects of comorbid conditions on task performance. *European Psychiatry*, *18*(5), 241–248.

Bannon, S., Gonsalvez, C., Croft, R., & Boyce, P. (2002). Response inhibition deficits in obsessive-compulsive disorder. *Psychiatry Research*, *110*(2), 165–174.

Barceló, F., & Knight, R. T. (2002). Both random and perseverative errors underlie WCST deficits in prefrontal patients. *Neuropsychologia*, *40*(3), 349–356.

Bilimoria, D. D., Mukhopadhyay, P., & Das, S. (2015). Psychopathology of emotionally unstable personality disorder: A neuropsychosocial perspective. *Indian Journal of Clinical Psychology*, *42*(1), 25–34. (ISSN0303-2582).

Boone, K. B., Ananth, J., & Philpott, L. (1991). Neuropsychological characteristics of nondepressed adults with obsessive-compulsive disorder. *Neuropsychiatry, Neuropsychology, and Behavioral Neurology*, *4*(2), 96–109.

Burgess, J. W. (1992). Neurocognitive impairment in dramatic personalities: Histrionic, narcissistic, borderline, and antisocial disorders. *Psychiatry Research*, *42*(3), 283–290.

Chamberlain, S. R., Blackwell, A. D., Fineberg, N. A., Robbins, T. W., & Sahakian, B. J. (2005). The neuropsychology of obsessive compulsive disorder: The importance of failures in cognitive and behavioural inhibition as candidate endophenotypic markers. *Neuroscience & Biobehavioral Reviews*, *29*(3), 399–419. (PubMed: 15820546).

200 / **Dinaz R. Jeejeebhoy et al.**

Christensen, K. J., Kim, S. W., Dysken, M. W., & Hoover, K. M. (1992). Neuropsychological performance in obsessive-compulsive disorder. *Biological Psychiatry, 31*(1), 4–18.

Cooper, J. (1970). The Leyton Obsessional Inventory. *Psychological Medicine, 1*(1), 48–64.

Costa, P. T., & McCrae, R. R. (1992). *Revised Neo Personality Inventory (NEO PI-R) and Neo Five-Factor Inventory (NEO-FFI): Professional manual.* Odessa, FL: Psychological Assessment Resources. Culberston, W. C., & Zilmer, E. A. (2001). *Tower of London – Drexel University.* Chicago, IL: Multi-Health Systems.

Eisen, J. L., Phillips, K. A., Baer, L., Beer, D. A., Atala, K. D., & Rasmussen, S. A. (1998). The Brown Assessment of Beliefs Scale: Reliability and validity. *The American Journal of Psychiatry, 155*(1), 102–108.

Eisen, J. L., Phillips, K. A., Coles, M. E., & Rasmussen, S. A. (2004). Insight in obsessive compulsive disorder and body dysmorphic disorder. *Comprehensive Psychiatry, 45*(1), 10–15. (PubMed: 14671731).

Evenden, J. L. (1999). Varieties of impulsivity. *Psychopharmacology (Berl), 146*(4), 348–361.

Fineberg, N. A., Sharma, P., Sivakumaran, T., Sahakian, B., & Chamberlain, S. R. (2007). Does obsessive-compulsive personality disorder belong within the obsessive-compulsive spectrum? *CNS Spectrums, 12*(6), 467–482. (PubMed: 17545957).

Frost, R. O., Steketee, G., Cohn, L., & Griess, K. (1994). Personality traits in subclinical and non obsessive-compulsive volunteers and their parents. *Behaviour Research and Therapy, 32*(1), 47–56.

Goldberg, D. P., & Hillier, V. F. (1979). A scaled version of the General Health Questionnaire. *Psychological Medicine, 9*(1), 139–146.

Goldman-Rakic, P. S. (1991). *Prefrontal cortical dysfunction in schizophrenia: The relevance of working memory.* New York, NY: Raven.

Goodman, W. K., Price, L. H., & Rasmussen, S. A. (1989) Yale-Brown Obsessive Compulsive Scale: I. Development, use and reliability. *Archives of General Psychiatry, 46*(11), 1006–1010.

Grant, J. E., & Potenza, M. N. (2006). Compulsive aspects of impulse-control disorders. *Psychiatric Clinics of North America, 29*(2), 539–551.

Harvey, N. S. (1987). Neurological factors in obsessive-compulsive disorder. *British Journal of Psychiatry, 150*(4), 567–568.

Hanes, K. R. (1998). Neuropsychological performance in body dysmorphic disorder. *Journal of the International Neuropsychological Society, 4*(2), 167–171.

Head, D., Bolton, D., & Hymas, N. (1989). Deficit in cognitive shifting ability in patients with obsessive-compulsive disorders. *Biological Psychiatry, 25*, 929–937.

Heaton, R. K., Chelune, G. J., Talley, J. L., Kay, G. C., & Curtiss, G. (1993). *Wisconsin Card Sorting Test manual.* Odessa, FL: Psychological Assessment Resources.

Hezrog, D. B., Keller, M. B., Lavori, P. W., Kenny, G. M., & Sacks, N. R. (1992). The prevalence of personality disorders in 210 women with eating disorders. *Journal of Clinical Psychiatry 53*(5), 147–152.

Hollander, E. (1993). *Introduction*. In E. Hollander (Ed.), *Obsessive-compulsive-related disorders* (pp. 1–16). Washington, DC: American Psychiatric Press.

Hollander, E., & Rosen, J. (2000). Impulsivity. *Journal of Psychopharmacology, 14*(2 Suppl 1), S39–S44.

Hollander, E., & Wong, C. M. (1995). Obsessive-compulsive spectrum disorders. *Journal of Clinical Psychiatry, 56*(Suppl 4), 3–6.

Hyman, B. M., & Pedrick, C. (2005). *The OCD workbook: Your guide to breaking free from obsessive-compulsive disorder* (2nd ed.). Oakland, CA: New Harbinger.

Leckman, J., Denys, D., Simpson, H., Mataix-Cols, D., Hollander, E., Saxena, S.,...Stein, D. J. (2010). Obsessive-compulsive disorder: A review of the diagnostic criteria and possible subtypes and dimensional specifiers for DSM-V. *Depression and Anxiety, 27*(6), 507–527.

Links, P. S., Steiner, M., Offord, D. R., & Eppel, A. (1988). Characteristics of borderline personality disorder: A Canadian study. *Canadian Journal of Psychiatry, 33*(5), 336–340.

Loranger, A. W., Janca, A., Sartorius, N., Korfine, L., & Neff, C. (1997). *Assessment and diagnosis of personality disorders: The ICD-10 international personality disorder examination (IPDE)*. Cambridge, MA: Cambridge University Press.

Lucey, J. V., Burness, C. E., Costa, D. C., Gacinovic, S., Pilowsky, L. S., Ell, P. J.,...Kerwin, R. W. (1997). Wisconsin Card Sorting Task (WCST) errors and cerebral blood flow in obsessive-compulsive disorder. *British Journal of Medical Psychology, 70*(Pt 4), 403–411.

Mancuso, S., Knoesen, N., & Castle, D. J. (2010). Delusional vs nondelusional body dysmorphic disorder. *Comprehensive Psychiatry, 51*(2), 177–182. (PubMed: 20152299).

Mann, A. H., Jenkins, R., Cutting, J. C., & Cowen, P. J. (1981). The development and use of a standardized assessment of abnormal personality. *Psychological Medicine, 11*(4), 839–847.

Mataix-Cols, D., Pertusa, A., & Leckman, J. F. (2007). Issues for DSM-V: How should obsessive-compulsive and related disorders be classified? *The American Journal of Psychiatry, 164*(9), 1313–1314. (PubMed: 17728412).

Moeller, G., Barratt, E. S., Dougherty, D. M., Schmitz, J. M., & Swann, A. C. (2001). Psychiatric aspects of impulsivity. *The American Journal of Psychiatry, 158*(11), 1783–1793.

Morein-Zamir, S., Fineberg, N. A., Robbins, T. W., & Sahakian, B. J. (2010). Inhibition of thoughts and actions in obsessive-compulsive disorder: Extending the endophenotype? *Psychological Medicine, 40*(2), 1–10.

202 / Dinaz R. Jeejeebhoy et al.

Moritz, S., Hottenrott, B., Randjbar, S., Klinge, R., Von Eckstaedt, F. V., Lincoln, T. M., & Jelinek, L. (2009). Perseveration and not strategic deficits underlie delayed alternation impairment in obsessive-compulsive disorder (OCD). *Psychiatry Research, 170*(1), 66–69.

Mukhopadhyay, P., Tarafder, S., Bilimoria, D. D., Paul, D., & Bandyopadhyay, G. (2010). Instinctual impulses in obsessive compulsive disorder: A neuropsychological and psychoanalytic interface. *Asian Journal of Psychiatry, 3*(4), 177–185.

Nelson, E. A., Abramowitz, J. S., Whiteside, S. P., & Deacon, B. J. (2006). Scrupulosity in patients with obsessive-compulsive disorder: Relationship to clinical and cognitive phenomena. *Journal of Anxiety Disorders, 20*(8), 1071–1086. (PubMed: 16524696).

Neziroglu, F., McKay, D., & Yaryura-Tobias, J. A. (2000). Overlapping and distinctive features of hypochondriasis and obsessive-compulsive disorder. *Journal of Anxiety Disorders, 14*(6), 603–614. (PubMed: 11918094).

Oldfield, R. C. (1971). The assessment and analysis of handedness: The Edinburgh inventory. *Neuropsychologia, 9*(1), 97–113.

Phillips, K. A., & Diaz, S. F. (1997). Gender differences in body dysmorphic disorder. *The Journal of Nervous and Mental Disease, 185*(9), 570–577. (PubMed: 9307619).

Phillips, K. A., Gunderson, C. G., Mallya, G., McElroy, S. L., & Carter, W. (1998). A comparison study of body dysmorphic disorder and obsessive-compulsive disorder. *Journal of Clinical Psychiatry, 59*(11), 568–575. (PubMed: 9862601).

Phillips, K. A., & Kaye, W. H. (2007). The relationship of body dysmorphic disorder and eating disorders to obsessive-compulsive disorder. *CNS Spectrums, 12*(5), 347–358. (PubMed: 17514080).

Phillips, K. A., McElroy, S. L., Keck, P. E., Jr., Pope, H. G., Jr., & Hudson, J. I. (1993). Body dysmorphic disorder: 30 cases of imagined ugliness. *The American Journal of Psychiatry, 150*(2), 302–308. (PubMed: 8422082).

Phillips, K. A., Menard, W., Fay, C., & Weisberg, R. (2005). Demographic characteristics, phenomenology, comorbidity, and family history in 200 individuals with body dysmorphic disorder. *Psychosomatics, 46*(4), 317–325. (PubMed: 16000674)

Phillips, K. A., Menard, W., Pagano, M. E., Fay, C., & Stout, R. L. (2006). Delusional versus nondelusional body dysmorphic disorder: Clinical features and course of illness. *Journal of Psychiatric Research, 40*(2), 95–104. (PubMed: 16229856).

Phillips, K. A., Pinto, A., Menard, W, Eisen, J. L., Mancebo, M., & Rasmussen, S. A. (2007). Obsessive-compulsive disorder versus body dysmorphic disorder: A comparison study of two possibly related disorders. *Depression and Anxiety, 24*(6), 399–409. (PubMed: 17041935).

Phillips, K. A., Stein, D. J., Rauch, S., Hollander, E., & Fallon, B. A. (2010). Should an obsessive-compulsive spectrum grouping of disorders be included in DSM-V? *Depression and Anxiety, 27*(6), 528–555.

Phillips, K. A., Wilhelm, S., Koran, L. M., Didie, E. R., Fallon, B. A., Feusner, J., & Stein, D. J. (2010). Body dysmorphic disorder: Some key issues for DSM-V. *Depression and Anxiety, 27*(6), 573–591.

Pilgrim, J., & Mann, A. (1990). Use of the ICD-10 version of the Standardized Assessment of Personality to determine the prevalence of personality disorder in psychiatric in-patients. *Psychological Medicine, 20*(4), 985–992.

Pilgrim, J., Mellers, J. D., Boothby, H., & Mann, A. H. (1993). Inter-rater and temporal reliability of the Standardised Assessment of Personality and the influence of informant characteristics. *Psychological Medicine, 23*(3), 779–786.

Rao, N. P., Reddy, Y. C., Kumar, K. J., Kandavel, T., & Chandrashekar, C. R. (2008). Are neuropsychological deficits trait markers in OCD? *Progress in Neuro-Psychopharmacological & Biological Psychiatry, 32*(6), 1574–1579.

Rector, N. A., Hood, K., Richter, M. A., & Bagby, R. M. (2002). Obsessive-compulsive disorder and the five-factor model of personality: Distinction and overlap with major depressive disorder. *Behaviour Research and Therapy, 40*(10), 1205–1219.

Rector, N. A., Cassin, S. E., Richter, M. A., & Burroughs, E. (2009). Obsessive beliefs in first-degree relatives of patients with OCD: A test of the cognitive vulnerability model. *Journal of Anxiety Disorders, 23*(1), 145–149.

Rhéaume, J., Freeston, M. H., Dugas, M. J., Letarte, H., & Ladouceur, R. (1995). Perfectionism, responsibility and obsessive-compulsive symptoms. *Behaviour Research and Therapy, 33*(7), 785–794. (PubMed: 7677716).

Rosenberg, D., Dick, E., OHearn, K., & Sweeney, J. (1997). Response-inhibition deficits in obsessive-compulsive disorder: An indicator of dysfunction in frontostriatal circuits. *Journal of Psychiatry & Neuroscience, 22*(1), 29–38.

Ruocco, A. C. (2005). The neuropsychology of borderline personality disorder: A meta-analysis and review. *Psychiatry Research, 137*(3), 191–202.

Samuels, J., Nestadt, G., Bienvenu. O. J., Costa, P. T., Riddle, M. A., Liang, K.-Y., Hoehn-Saric, R., Grados, M. A., & Cullen, B. A. M. (2000). Personality disorders and normal personality dimensions in obsessive-compulsive disorder. *The British Journal of Psychiatry, 177*(November), 457–462.

Skodol, A. E., Oldham, J. M., Hyler, S. E., Kellman, H. D., Doidge, N., & Davies, M. (1993). Comorbidity of DSM-III-R eating disorders and

204 / Dinaz R. Jeejeebhoy et al.

personality disorders. *International Journal of Eating Disorders, 14*(4), 403–416.

Stein, D. J., & Hollander, E. (1993). The spectrum of obsessive-compulsive-related disorders. In E. Hollander (Ed.), *Obsessive-compulsive-related disorders* (pp. 241–271). Washington, DC: American Psychiatric Press.

Stein, D. J., Trestman, R. L., Mitropoulou, V., Coccaro, E. F., Hollander, E., & Siever, L. J. (1996). Impulsivity and serotonergic function in compulsive personality disorder. *The Journal of Neuropsychiatry and Clinical Neurosciences, 8*(4), 393–398.

Svaldi, J., Philipsen, A., & Matthies, S. (2012). Risky decision-making in borderline personality disorder. *Psychiatry Research, 197*(1–2), 112–118.

Tarafder, S., Bhattacharya, P., Paul, D., Bandyopadhyay, G., & Mukhopadhyay, P. (2006). Neuropsychological disposition and its impact on the executive functions and cognitive style in patients with obsessive-compulsive disorder. *Indian Journal of Psychiatry, 48*(2), 102–106.

Tarafder, S., & Mukhopadhyay, P. (2015). Exploring the possibility of shared familial diathesis for personality in OCD probands. *Psychological Studies, 4*(60), 455–461.

Veale, D., Boocock, A., Gournay, K., Dryden, W., Shah, F., Willson, R., & Walburn, J. (1996). Body dysmorphic disorder: A survey of fifty cases. *The British Journal of Psychiatry, 169*(2), 196–201. (PubMed: 8871796).

Wiggins, J. S., & Pincus, A. L. (1989). Conceptions of personality disorders and dimensions of personality. *Psychological Assessment: A Journal of Consulting and Clinical Psychology, 1*(4), 305–316.

World Health Organization. (1992). *ICD-10 classification of mental and behavioural disorders: Diagnostic criteria for research.* Geneva: World Health Organization.

Zanarini, M. C. (1993). Borderline personality disorder as an impulse spectrum disorder. In J. Paris (Ed.), *Borderline personality disorder: Etiology and treatment* (pp. 67–85). Washington, DC: American Psychiatric Press.

Zanarini, M. C., Gunderson, J. G., & Frankenburg, F. R. (1989). Axis I phenomenology of borderline personality disorder. *Comprehensive Psychiatry, 30*(2), 149–156.

7

Slowness in Obsessive Compulsive Disorder
A Comparative Study

Sreemoyee Tarafder, Parmeet Kaur Soni and Pritha Mukhopadhyay

Introduction

Obsessive Compulsive Disorder (OCD) is a very heterogeneous group with varied types of symptom manifestation. A common shared feature in them is slowness—slowness in thinking, action, such as grooming, and processing information. Obsessive slowness has been described as a syndrome of extreme slowness or tardiness in the way various tasks are performed (e.g., Singh, Sharan, & Grover, 2003). The preoccupation of OCD patients with unwanted, intrusive, recurrent thoughts, impulses, repetitive behaviours or mental acts, carried out in relation to these obsessions, suggests how preoccupation with an unproductive yet personally significant thought, image or action interferes with their engagement in another meaningful task in hand. Equal demands of cognitive resources by both the tasks make it difficult for them to concentrate and act upon the given task in this conflicting situation, which is described as ambivalence in OCD.

APA, thereby, finds the impact of the disease process as debilitating by consumption of unusually more time leading to marked distress and impairment in terms of socio-occupational functioning (DSM-IV, 1994). Rachman (1974) introduced it as syndrome and termed it 'primary obsessive slowness' which is characterized by such prominent debilitating reduction in processing speed. However, obsessive slowness has been considered as an integral part of OCD (Singh et al., 2003), which is evident from the research outcome of several researchers (Basso, Bornstein, Carona, & Morton, 2001; Moritz et al., 2002; Schmidtke, Schorb, Winkelmann, & Hohagen, 1998), and its claim for an independent syndrome has been challenged by Singh et al. (2003). But observation of obsessive slowness in patients with obsessive compulsive spectrum disorders (OCSDs) and even among the first-degree relatives (FDRs) of OCD also raises a question towards that assertion.

Many theorists and researchers have studied the phenomena of slowness and tried to cognize and comprehend it through faulty decision-making, ambivalence, perfectionism, intrusive thoughts and so on. Roth, Baribeau, Milovan and O'Connor (2004) stated that obsessive slowness could be ascribed to intrusive thoughts or meticulousness. Sawamura, Nakashima, Inoue and Kurita (2005) posit that failure to develop organizational strategies owing to their tendency to not leave any variables unattended to reach a conclusion, results in their inability to complete task within time. Through our work with patients of OCD, we found how processing speed is related to intrusive thoughts pertaining to sexuality (Mukhopadhyay, Tarafder, Bilimoria, Paul, & Bandyopadhyay, 2010). We took into consideration the Processing Speed Index (PSI) of patients with OCD and also observed that during digit symbol task patients with OCD took a lot of care in copying the symbols and concentrating on accuracy, thereby compromising upon the speed aspect to complete the task within the specified period of time. The finding was explained in terms of the psychopathology of maladaptive perfectionism which is in agreement with Rhéaume, Freeston, Dugas, Letarte and Ladouceur (1995) and Hwang, Kwon, Shin, Lee, Kim and Kim (2007). The preoccupation of the OCD with unresolved ego dystonic intrusive instinctual thoughts explains the dysexecution in organizing and processing new thoughts giving rise to perseveration and slowness (Mukhopadhyay et al., 2010). The causal factors related to perseveration and slowness have been depicted in Figure 7.1 that shows how forbidden thoughts of sexuality and inability to modulate hostile thoughts lead to unresolved ego-dystonic thoughts, leading to cognitive resource allocation to ward off

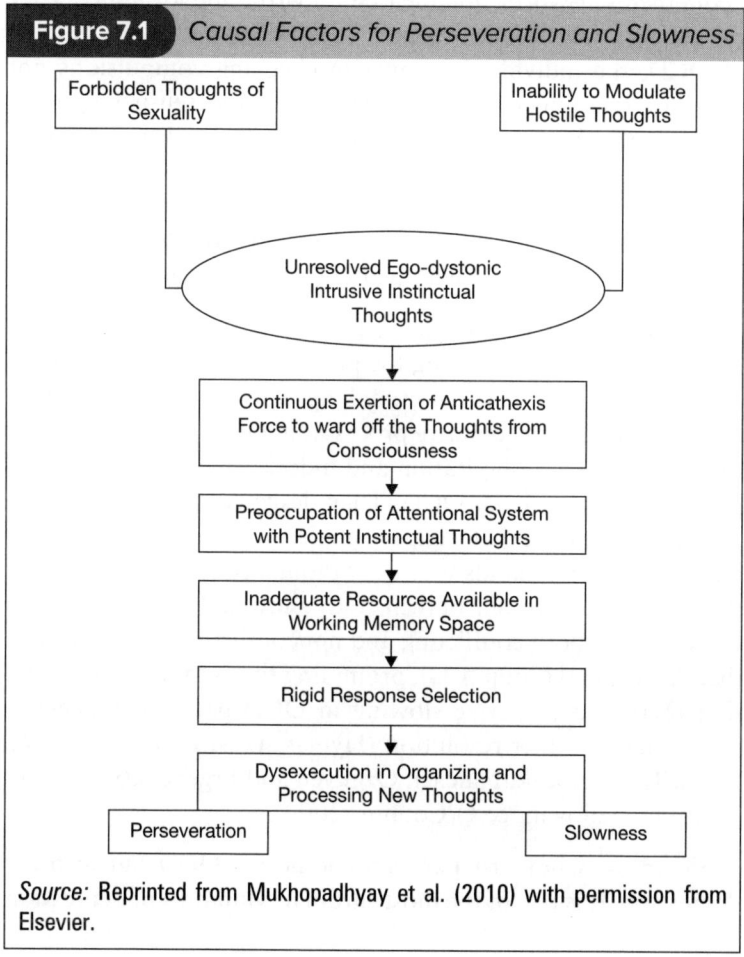

Figure 7.1 *Causal Factors for Perseveration and Slowness*

Forbidden Thoughts of Sexuality

Inability to Modulate Hostile Thoughts

Unresolved Ego-dystonic Intrusive Instinctual Thoughts

Continuous Exertion of Anticathexis Force to ward off the Thoughts from Consciousness

Preoccupation of Attentional System with Potent Instinctual Thoughts

Inadequate Resources Available in Working Memory Space

Rigid Response Selection

Dysexecution in Organizing and Processing New Thoughts

Perseveration

Slowness

Source: Reprinted from Mukhopadhyay et al. (2010) with permission from Elsevier.

impulses. This in turn creates a dearth of resources in working memory space, giving way to rigid response selection, leading to dysexecution reflected through perseveration and slowness. (Refer to Mukhopadhyay et al., 2010, for a detailed discussion on instinctual impulses and its link with dysexecution).

While explaining slowness in patients with OCD, Fenichel (1945) correlated it to their characteristic ambivalence. Cognitive theorists Guidano and Liotti (1983) have also pointed out those individuals prone to obsessionality hold highly ambivalent beliefs about their self-worth, and their moral virtue and lovability. They refer to this as 'self-ambivalence'. In Guidano and Liotti's model of OCD, the individual engages in checking compulsions not only to avert danger, but also to avoid negative self-perceptions. According to this perspective, compulsions primarily try to bridge the gap between the concept of self with images of self that are valued and idealized by the individual. The feeling that they are not being able to live up to the requisite standards makes them ambivalent and slows down their cognitive processes.

The ambivalence may also be attributable to shallow processing of information regarding the given stimulus, which causes a continual conflict in decision-making. Citing studies that have reported slowing of cognitive processes in OCD patients interpret slowing in terms of hesitation and indecisiveness on part of the patients suffering from OCD. They designed an experiment to simulate a situation that triggered anxiety and obsessions in OCD patients, and commands with or without a conflict were given to the participants. Results of their study showed that OCD patients responded to both conflicting and nonconflicting stimuli slower than the control group (CG), prompting the authors to speculate that there is a cognitive slowing in OCD patients, independent of their conflict resolution (Hymas, Less, Bolton, Epps, & Head, 1991; Koçak, Nalcacı, Özgüven and Ergenc, 2010; Roth, Baribeau, Milovan, & O'Connor, 2004).

Slowness is not just pathognomonic for OCD but also for depression. It is one of the most cardinal symptoms of depression that results in psychomotor retardation in depression. It seems to be interesting to probe whether the nature of slowness is different in these two disorders although it may have apparent similarities. For example, depressive rumination has been proposed to be characterized by cognitive rigidity (Meiran, Diamond, Toder, & Nemets, 2011) like in OCD. In OCD, patients suffer from obsessions that are recurrent, persistent and distressing intrusive thoughts, impulses or images, which are difficult to suppress (APA, 1994) and in unipolar depression, patients tend to ruminate, that is, repetitively think about the causes, consequences and symptoms of their negative affect (Nolen-Hoeksema & Morrow, 1991). Meiran and colleagues (2011) assessed patients with depression and OCD on a battery of executive tests, such as task switching, Stroop, working memory updating and post-conflict adaptation. They found that although patients were different from their controls, the patient groups did not differ from one another. They reported that in both disorders while patients were able to (more or less) successfully adopt or engage in a switching mode, they were less able to disengage from, or inhibit a previous mode when it became irrelevant. Patients also required more trials to adjust to single-task conditions after experiencing task switching, reflecting slow disengagement from switching mode. Their findings substantiated similar cognitive rigidity in both the groups. We hypothesize that this rigidity may result in cognitive slowness.

With the keen desire to get the answer, we focused on identifying specific factors contributing to this slowness in three groups, namely, OCD, depression and community samples (CG), to study them across factors as delineated in the following. We hypothesized that slowness can be owing to certain neuropsychological factors operating in the two groups.

The premises that we wish to assess are:

1. An individual can be slow in terms of his reaction and processing speed, which can be looked at through his performance on reaction time (RT).

2. An individual may be otherwise preoccupied and therefore not concentrating on the work at hand, resulting in slowness, which may be assessed by looking at his response inhibition and cognitive interference factor.
3. Time as a paradigm may be ill judged with deficiency in time perception resulting in slowness, which needs to be looked into.
4. Deficit in decision-making may delay the process of cognition and result in slowness making it necessary to inspect decision-making.
5. The task demand of processing may require utilization of feedback to complete it on time and therefore studying feedback utilization is essential as well. It is hypothesized that the OCD group cannot incorporate feedback well.

The thrust areas of neuropsychological functioning that need to be addressed while studying slowness are as follows:

- Reaction time
- Cognitive interference
- Time perception
- Decision-making
- Feedback utilization

Methodology

Study Design

The study was a comparative study designed to investigate the RT, cognitive interference, time perception, decision-making and the extent of feedback utilization in OCD patients and depressive patients (DEP) in comparison to normal controls (CG), based on purposive sampling.

Sample

Purposive sampling technique was used to select the sample and data were collected from patients with OCD, depression and normal controls (CG) for the selected domains. A total of 72 participants were selected. OCD group consisted of 12 males and 12 females. DEP consisted of 11 males and 13 females, while the CG consisted of 12 males and 12 females. Patient groups were recruited from psychiatric outpatient services of government hospitals, Kolkata, after diagnosis by a consultant psychiatrist as well as a clinical psychologist after they satisfied the ICD-10 Diagnostic Criteria for Research (WHO, 1993). Only right-handed subjects were chosen, as it is a factor that affects the performance on neuropsychological tests and in order to ensure homogeneity. Education till standard X, domicile urban/suburban was kept as inclusion criteria. Exclusion criteria kept common for three groups were developmental or neurological disorders, serious head injury, substance abuse and epilepsy.

Group I: Patients Diagnosed with OCD

Patients with all subtypes of obsessions and compulsions were included with the exception of hoarding. The primary issue effecting OCD research is the heterogeneity of the syndrome itself. Dividing patients into mutually exclusive subtypes is difficult as patients are rarely monosymptomatic (Mataix-Cols, do Rosario-Campos, & Leckman, 2005). All patients in the clinical groups were primarily being treated with selective serotonin reuptake inhibitors (SSRIs), for at least two months prior to the initiation of the study.

Group II: Patients Diagnosed with Depression (DEP)

The sample comprised of 24 patients with a diagnosis of depressive episode (mild to moderate) and who had received pharmacological intervention at least two months prior to the beginning of the study.

Group III: Community Control Group (CCG)

The matching criteria for the CCG were age, sex, educational level and handedness. The community sample that matched the OCD and DEP patients in terms of predetermined matching criteria was selected through the snowballing technique and screened on the General Health Questionnaire (GHQ).

Tools Used

The following tools were used in the present study:

1. Semi-structured socio-demographic and clinical data sheet
2. Yale-Brown Obsessive Compulsive Scale (YBOCS)
3. Leyton Obsessional Inventory (LOI) (Cooper, 1970)
4. Beck Depression Inventory (BDI) (Beck, Ward, Mendelson, Mock, & Erbaugh, 1961)
5. Hamilton Depression Rating Scale (HDRS) (Hamilton, 1960)
6. Edinburgh Handedness Inventory (EHI) (Oldfield, 1971)
7. General Health Questionnaire (GHQ) (Goldberg & Hillier, 1979)
8. Stroop Neuropsychological Screening Test (SNST) (Trenerry, Crosson, DeBoe, & Leber, 1989)
9. Iowa Gambling Task (IGT) (Bechara, 2007)
10. Sumon's Responsoscope (Mukhopadhyay, 2003): The instrument is designed to measure RT. The mode of presentation of the stimulus was visual (neutral stimuli-white light) with intensity of stimulus being set at 6 volts and the fore-period fixed at 1.5 seconds based on study conducted in the Department of Psychology, University of Calcutta. After the fore-period, the experimenter produced the white light, followed by which the participant had to respond.

Instructions for RT-Control: 'You will hear a "beep" sound, followed by a light. When you see the light glow, you are to react by pressing subject's push button. Try and do your best. You are to continue doing so until asked to stop. In case, you face any difficulty please report to me immediately'.

Instructions for Reaction Time-Knowledge of Result (RT-KOR): 'You will hear a "beep" sound, followed by a light. When you see the light glow, you are to react by pressing subject's push button. In this condition, after every trial you will be informed exactly how much time you took to react to the stimuli (your RT). The knowledge of your result will be provided to you each time. Try and do your best. Continue doing so until you are asked to stop. In case, you face any difficulty please report to me immediately'.

Scoring: Each subject was given both the conditions. Fifteen trials were completed for each condition. Average RT (mean) and standard deviation (SD) for each condition was calculated.

11. Sumon's Apparentimer (Mukhopadhyay, 2003): The instrument with an audiovisual display time reproducer (AVDTR) panel, where the estimated time is displayed, was used to assess time perception, using method of reproduction, using filled and unfilled time. The experimenter presented a standard time interval of 1.5 seconds and the subject attempted to judge and reproduce the same time interval.

Scoring: Fifteen trials were completed for each condition. The constant error was calculated for each condition, following the formula: Constant **error**=Mean of subject's reproduction – Mean of the experimenter's presentation (Standard).

Procedure

Subjects were selected on the basis of the inclusion/exclusion criteria mentioned earlier. At first, the nature and the purpose of this research was explained to them. A semi-structured socio-demographic and clinical data sheet was filled by the subjects. Initially, the YBOCS, LOI, BDI and HDRS were administered to the clinical groups as well as to the CCG group for the purpose of screening and assessing the level of severity of the symptoms. The CCG was also administered GHQ. Each group consisted of 24 subjects. Following the standardized procedure, the tests were administered to all three groups.

Analysis of Data

Statistical analysis of the data was done with the help of Statistical Package for Social Sciences (SPSS), Windows Version 20 (SPSS 20). The means and SDs were calculated. The obtained data were checked for equality of variances using Levene's Test. As the data showed homogeneity of variance, parametric statistics were considered. Thereafter, general linear model (repeated measures) was used to conduct 3×2 factorial designs for RT and time perception. The independent sample t-test was used as a post-hoc analysis to determine the differences in the three groups. The paired sample t-test was used to obtain the mean difference, if any, in the OCD, DEP and CG, respectively, in the two conditions of RT—to assess the extent to which each group has gained from the given feedback–knowledge of results. Since the effect of feedback was to be seen, the condition without knowledge of result formed the control condition and paired-t was computed. To find out the relationship between RT, time perception, interference, decision-making, obsessive traits, obsessive symptoms and depression in OCD and DEP groups, the Pearson rank coefficient correlation was computed. Stepwise Multiple Regression Analysis (SMRA) was computed to determine the relative contribution of obsessive traits, obsessive symptoms, subjective distress and severity of obsessive and depressive symptoms on different variables (RT, time perception, interference, decision-making and feedback utilization) in OCD and DEP. For analysis, 0.05 and 0.01 level of significance were accepted as critical levels.

Result

The domains that were assessed, namely, (a) reaction time, (b) cognitive interference, (c) time perception, (d) decision-making and (e) feedback utilization, showed group differences, significant at 0.01 level in RT ($F = 19.38$), Stroop interference task (colour word total time $F = 18.25$) and in feedback utilization ($F = 7.61$) using Analysis of Variance. However, the groups did not differ in terms of time perception and decision-making.

Table 7.1 depicts the mean, SD and mean differences between the pathological groups and the community controls. The t-test has been used to analyse the differences between the groups: comparing OCD and depression, OCD and community controls, and depression and community controls.

The hypotheses that we tested revealed the following:

(a) Our hypothesis of slower RT and processing speed was retained by our results. Significantly higher mean scores in RT was obtained by the OCD and DEP compared to CG.

(b) The hypothesis that preoccupation may result in poor response inhibition and cognitive interference was also supported by the findings. On the subdomain of colour t/time and colour–word t/time on Stroop test, the scores were higher in OCD compared to both groups, and DEP group showed greater interference as compared to CG. For the subdomain of colour–word error, both the clinical groups made greater number of errors with respect to CG. One interesting observation is that all three groups showed greater variability in error scores of Stroop interference task.

(c) No differences were observed among the groups in terms of time perception, which indicates that the OCD is at par with others in terms of estimating time.

(d) It was hypothesized that decision-making may be deficient in the OCD group, but our findings did not support the

Table 7.1 Mean, SD and t-values Showing Significance of Differences Between the OCD, Depression and Control Groups

Domains	Subdomains	OCD		DEP		t	OCD		CG		t	DEP		CG		t
		M	SD	M	SD		M	SD	M	SD		M	SD	M	SD	
(i) Reaction time	RT	0.32	0.14	0.40	0.17	1.73	0.32	0.14	0.21	0.06	3.75**	0.40	0.17	0.21	0.06	5.33**
(ii) Interference	Colour t/time	81.08	27.50	61.67	10.26	3.24**	81.08	27.50	47.25	11.12	5.59**	61.67	10.26	47.25	11.12	4.67**
	Colour–word (CW t/time)	177.75	57.05	150.79	25.21	2.12*	177.75	57.05	112.75	17.79	5328**	150.79	25.23	112.75	17.79	6.04**
	Colour–word (CW error)	3.83	4.61	5.13	7.13	0.75	3.83	4.61	1.54	2.28	2.18*	5.13	7.13	1.54	2.28	2.34*
(iii) Time perception	Filled time (F-time)	−0.47	0.34	−0.39	0.26	0.94	−0.47	0.34	−0.42	0.19	0.70	−0.39	0.26	−0.42	0.19	0.40
	Unfilled time (F-time)	−0.075	0.53	−0.18	0.32	0.84	−0.075	0.53	−0.19	0.20	1.02	−0.18	0.32	−0.19	0.20	0.16
(iv) Decision-making	Advantageous decks (C+D)	28.25	8.50	29.04	4.34	0.41	28.25	8.50	29	6.66	0.34	29.04	4.34	29	6.66	0.03
	Disadvantageous decks (A+B)	31.83	8.42	30.79	4.61	0.53	31.83	8.42	30.63	7.2	0.54	30.79	4.61	30.63	7.2	0.10
(v) Feedback utilization	RT-Knowledge of results	0.30	0.12	0.31	0.11	0.35	0.30	0.12	0.19	0.03	4.56**	0.31	0.11	0.19	0.03	5.34**

Source: Authors.

Note: *$p < 0.05$ level, **$p < 0.01$, level df = 23.

claim on IGT. The OCD group did not differ from the control or DEP group on IGT in terms of decision-making.
(e) In terms of feedback utilization, although simple analysis of knowledge of results between the two pathological groups do not show any difference, the paired-t outcome, which determines the gain in terms of their own performance, shows no changes in the OCD group (paired-t$=0.79$; $p<0.05$), signifying their incapacity to utilize and gain from feedback. But the significant difference between the two conditions in both DEP (paired-t$=2.44$; $p>0.05$) and CG (paired-t$=2.42$; $p>0.05$), with significantly lower score in the RT-KOR condition, signifies greater rate of decline in RT in both the groups, indicating efficient feedback utilization in them.

We also wanted to look at the correlation between the slowness factors and symptom severity and found symptom severity to be directly related to interference errors ($r=0.526, p>0.01$) and negatively with total score on decision-making task ($r=-0.440, p>0.05$).

Summary of SMRA for variables predicting factors related to slowness are provided in Table 7.2. Among the potential predictors, symptom severity of OCD (YBOCS) and obsessive traits (LOI) emerged as significant predictors of slowness among the OCD group. Depressive symptom ratings significantly predicted RT. Taken together, these findings draw attention to effect of depression and OCD symptoms and traits over slowness prevalent among OCD patients.

Table 7.2 reveals that in the OCD group, HDRS predicts RT-control and explains 63.5% of the total variance ($p>0.01$, $\beta=0.807$) while their symptom severity predicts Stroop interference error by explaining 24.4% of the total variance ($p>0.01$, $\beta=0.526$). The symptom severity also showed a negative impact on decision-making (A+B) – (C+D), explaining 15.7% of the total variance ($p>0.05$, $\beta=-0.44$). Finally, OC traits negatively influenced utilization of knowledge of results, accounting for 13.1% of the total variance ($p>0.05$, $\beta=-0.411$).

Table 7.2 *Results of Stepwise Multiple Regression Analysis (SMRA) Showing Impact on the DV Domains by the Predictors in the OCD Group*

DV	Predictors	Adjusted R^2	Significance	Beta value
RT-CONTROL	HDRS	0.635	0.001**	0.807
Stroop interference error	Symptoms severity (YBOCS)	0.244	0.01**	0.526
Decision-making (A + B) −(C + D)	Symptoms severity (YBOCS)	0.157	0.03*	−0.44
Feedback utilization	OC trait	0.131	0.05*	−0.411

Note: $*p > 0.05$ level, $**p > 0.01$ level, df = 22.

Source: Authors.

The summary of the results obtained from the study, in terms of the factors relating to slowness, are listed as follows:

(i) **Reaction time:** The poor status of both OCD and DEP in comparison to the CCG in RT suggest impairment in RT in both the study groups. And, the two study groups did not differ with each other in terms of baseline RT.

(ii) **Response inhibition and cognitive interference factor:** Both OCD and DEP in comparison to the CCG scored poorly on Stroop test. OCD took greater time than DEP group to produce colour–word responses with greater variability indicating greater vulnerability to interference and lesser scores than DEP group on C–W error indicate greater response inhibition in them.

(iii) **Time Perception:** All the groups underestimated filled time and DEP and OCD performed at par with each other in terms of time estimation.

(iv) **Decision-making:** Decision-making was found to be adequate in all the groups as the study groups were at par in terms of their performance on IGT.

(v) **Feedback utilization:** Maximal utilization of knowledge of result could be made by the DEP group, whereas OCD group could not utilize the feedback provided to them.

Discussion

The importance of the results obtained from the study needs discussion in detail, highlighting each domain that could have influenced the speed of processing in the clinical groups and resulted in slowness. The poor status of both OCD and DEP, in comparison to the CCG in RT, suggests impairment in RT in both the clinical groups that may be attributable to their psychomotor slowness and/or cognitive rigidity. The direct correlations between RT and depressive symptoms in DEP and OCD groups and additionally with the obsessive traits and symptoms for OCD group indicate that basal RT is keenly linked to the underlying psychopathology of the clinical groups. The OCD and the DEP groups differ in terms of the nature of their slowness. The DEP group is affected primarily by the depressive symptoms and distress, but the OCD group is additionally afflicted by their obsessive traits and symptoms, resulting in slower processing. Thus, a greater RT in OCD than CCG could be due to their slower cognitive processing speed which is in congruence with the previous research report (Mukhopadhyay et al., 2010), where processing speed of 20 OCD patients was significantly worse compared to their matched controls on Processing Speed Index (PSI). Significantly longer response latency in the DEP than CCG could be due to difference in their processing speed, which is perhaps part of their psychopathology and their delayed information processing.

The test of decision-making (IGT) does not have a demand on speed, which could be the reason why it did not discriminate the three groups in terms of decision making. No strict time frame and the delay thereof could have facilitated their decision making task. However, this premise needs further research to be definitive.

The task demand of Stroop control condition is to focus upon one's ability to direct attention towards task-relevant information. Only in the second condition it becomes more complex as it makes the client focus on task-irrelevant information of naming the ink in which the word is written and provide the response by suppressing the interference caused by the same. In case of OCD, the attention is literally captured by the potent internal thought mechanism that is operative within them. For them even the primary demand of colour naming is difficult to fulfil as there is a response competition that is operating simultaneously. The Stroop task calls for increased attentional demands that involves the anterior cingulated cortex (Pardo, Pardo, Janer, & Raichle, 1990), which acts as a conduit between lower, more impulse-driven brain regions and higher, more thought-driven behaviours. These results may reflect abnormality in the anterior cingulate cortex associated with these psychopathologies (e.g., Elliot & Dolan, 1998; Ullsperger & Von Cramon, 2006), a brain region believed to subserve performance monitoring (Botvinick, Braver, Barch, Carter, & Cohen, 2001). The cognitive mechanism at work in this process is called directed attention. This mental resource is used to manage our thoughts by inhibiting one response in order to say or do something else (De Young, 2014).

This directed attention is at stake in the OCD group who takes significantly more time to respond even to the simple demand of reading out a list of colour names. They are vulnerable to distractibility as there is interference that is inherent in them. The source of distraction is within them and that is the reason why even a simple reading out of words (as in Stroop control condition) takes so much time. Meiran and colleagues (2011) reported that cognitive rigidity is characteristic of OCD and DEP on comparing the performance of 17 patients (9 suffering from unipolar depression [UD] without OCD and 8 suffering from OCD without UD) and 17 matched controls on Stroop. Their results indicated similar cognitive rigidity in OCD and UD.

From our findings, we can see that the slowness that is present in the OCD group differs with the nature of slowness in DEP owing to the different neuropsychological underpinnings at play. The OCD group habitually exerts control that is directed at suppressing their prepotent obsessive thought that explains their disposition for habitual response of taking longer time to respond to any given stimulus. Observation also revealed that OCD group could comprehend the demand of the given task but exhibited a complete failure in its execution as is evident from poor performance on C–W naming in Stroop test. The OCD top-down information processing makes them sieve out each and every response and makes them disregard the bottom-up cues.

Since this obsessive slowness is the reflection of inhibition due to interference and not a deficit in appraisal of time, their estimation of both the filled and unfilled time was at par with CCG. OCD group is even more deficient in its performance as it cannot utilize the given feedback adequately, due to impact of the OC trait (as seen in regression analysis) on the knowledge of results. The behavioural observation shows that OCD group gives more premature responses or 'false alarms', an index of poor response inhibition (that corroborates with findings on Stroop task of present study) and impaired self-monitoring ability (Lezak, 1995).

Regarding feedback utilization, in contrast to the DEP and CCG, the present test findings indicate no effect of feedback (i.e., the knowledge of results) on RT measure of OCD group. It is evident from the result of gaining from feedback utilization that both the DEP and CCG are able to pick up relevant information from the environment and process and utilize the given feedback. Maximum utilization of information by DEP group indicates their intact capacity for adequate bottom-up processing and top-down monitoring, whereas inefficiency in feedback utilization by OCD group suggests their deficit in feedback utilization owing to their imbalance in distribution of attention between intra- and extrapersonal spaces (Tarafder, 2012). In spite of acknowledgement of the presence of feedback, they have deficit in capacity for monitoring of top-down processing to accommodate bottom-up information. The finding suggests that they are biologically programmed to respond in a speed which is equivalent to one's predisposition of 'inhibition due to interference'. They are unable to come out of it in spite of environmental demand. The present test findings of regression analysis further reveal that the feedback utilization in OCD group gets compromised by their OC trait.

For the DEP group who had the longest response latency and highest ceiling response latency in the RT-control condition, their RT declined maximally with a steeper slope after the feedback was provided, while the CCG had the lowest ceiling response latency in RT-control condition and their decline in response latency after feedback was the least. This is probably due to the fact that even without feedback, CCG performed the best as they were self-motivated enough to take initiative to perform and could focus on task at hand, but the DEP group in the RT-control condition, where no feedback was provided, failed to take initiation enough to focus on the task at hand. But the rapid rate of decline in time taken to respond with receiving the knowledge of their performance after each trial suggests that they had difficulty neither in feedback utilization per se nor in associating the bottom-up and top-down processing, rather they had volitional error which they could overcome with feedback.

Thus, when the gain from given feedback of each group is compared, it is seen that the DEP group has gained the maximum. The findings of a significant relationship between the level of subjective distress experienced by DEP group and their latency to respond in RT-control condition, and that of prediction of response latency by severity of depression, indicates the debilitating effect of depression on RT. It is interesting that reception of feedback that acted as reinforcement could improve their response to a significant level within such a short period of time. The finding corroborates with the notion of Lewinsohn, Yongren and Grossup (1979) who theorized the importance of poor reinforcement in life that leads to depression.

Conclusion

It is an interesting finding in this study that in spite of OCD's slowness, their estimation of time is comparable to the CCG, signifying their problem is not in appraisal of time as such but rather the reflection of time taken to overcome the intrinsic interference. Failure in feedback utilization on RT task suggests how their attention bias towards obsessive thought interferes with bottom-up cue utilization necessary for optimal performance.

References

American Psychiatric Association. (1994). *Diagnostic and statistical manual of mental disorders* (DSM-IV) (Revised 4th ed.). Washington, DC: American Psychiatric Association.

Basso, M. R., Bornstein, R. A., Carona, F., & Morton, R. (2001). Depression accounts for executive function deficits in obsessive-compulsive disorder. *Neuropsychiatry, Neuropsychology and Behavioral Neurology. 14*(4), 241–245.

Bechara, A. (2007). *Iowa Gambling Task*. Lutz, FL: Psychological Assessment Resources.

Beck, A. T., Ward, C. H., Mendelson, M., Mock, J., & Erbaugh, J. (1961). An inventory for measuring depression. *Archives of General Psychiatry, 4*(6), 561–571.

Botvinick, M. M., Braver, T. S., Barch, D. M., Carter, C. S., & Cohen, J. D. (2001). Conflict monitoring and cognitive control. *Psychological Review*, *108*(3), 624–652.

Cooper, J. (1970). The Leyton Obsessional Inventory. *Psychological Medicine*, *1*(1), 48–64.

De Young, R. (2014). Using the Stroop effect to test our capacity to direct attention: A tool for navigating urgent transitions. Retrieved from: www.snre.umich.edu/eplab/demos/st0/stroopdesc.html (accessed on 8 March 2018).

Elliott, R., & Dolan, R. J. (1998). Activation of different anterior cingulate foci in association with hypothesis testing and response selection. *NeuroImage*, *8*(1), 17–29.

Fenichel, O. (1945). *The psychoanalytic theory of neurosis* (Vol. 3). New York, NY: W. W. Norton and Co.

Goldberg, D. P., & Hillier, V. F. (1979). A scale version of the General Health Questionnaire. *Psychological Medicine*, *9*(1), 39–145.

Guidano, V., & Liotti, G. (1983). *Cognitive processes and emotional disorders*. New York, NY: Guilford Press.

Hamilton, M. (1960). A rating scale for depression. *Journal of Neurological and Neurosurgical Psychiatry*, *23*(1), 56–62.

Hwang, S. H., Kwon, J. S., Shin, Y. W., Lee, K. J., Kim, Y. Y., & Kim, J. (2007). Neuropsychological profiles of patients with obsessive-compulsive disorder: Early onset versus late onset. *Journal of the International Neuropsychological Society*, *13*(1), 30–37.

Hymas, N., Less, A., Bolton, D., Epps, K., & Head, D. (1991). The neurology of obsessional slowness. *Brain*, *114*(5), 2203–2233.

Koçak, M. O., Nalcacı, E., Özgüven, D. H., & Ergenc, I. (2010). Evaluation of cognitive slowing in OCD by means of creating incongruence between lexicon and prosody. *Psychiatry Research*, *179*(3), 306–311.

Lewinsohn, P. M., Yongren, M. A., & Grossup, S. J. (1979). Reinforcement and depression. In R. A. Depue (Ed.), *The psychobiological of depressive disorders: Implications for the effect of stress*. New York, NY: Academic Press.

Lezak, K. (1995). *Neuropsychological assessment*. Oxford: Oxford University Press.

Mataix-Cols, D., do Rosario-Campos, M. C., & Leckman, J. F. (2005). A multidimensional model of obsessive-compulsive disorder. *The American Journal of Psychiatry*, *162*(2), 228–238.

Meiran, N., Diamond, G. M., Toder, D., & Nemets, B. (2011). Cognitive rigidity in unipolar depression and obsessive compulsive disorder: Examination of task switching, Stroop, working memory updating and post-conflict adaptation. *Psychiatry Research*, *185*(1), 149–156.

Moritz, S., Birkner, C., Kloss, M., Jahn, H., Hand, I., Haasen, C., & Krausz, M. (2002). Executive functioning in obsessive-compulsive disorder, unipolar depression, and schizophrenia. *Archives of Clinical Neuropsychology, 17*(5), 477–483.

Mukhopadhyay, P., Tarafder, S., Bilimoria, D. D., Paul, D., & Bandyopadhyay, G. (2010). Instinctual impulses in obsessive compulsive disorder: A neuropsychological and psychoanalytic interface. *Asian Journal of Psychiatry, 3*(4), 177–185.

Nolen-Hoeksema, S., & Morrow, J. (1991). A prospective study of depression and posttraumatic stress symptoms after a natural disaster: 1989 Loma Prieta earthquake. *Journal of Personality and Social Psychology, 61*(1), 115–211.

Oldfield, R. C. (1971). The assessment and analysis of handedness: The Edinburgh inventory. *Neuropsychologia, 9*(1), 97–113.

Pardo, J. V., Pardo, P. J., Janer, K. W., & Raichle, M. E. (1990). The anterior cingulate cortex mediates processing selection in the Stroop attentional conflict paradigm. *Proceedings of the National Academy of Sciences, 87*(1), 256–259.

Rachman, S. (1974). Primary obsessional slowness. *Behaviour Research and Therapy, 12*(1), 9–18.

Rhéaume, J., Freeston, M. H., Dugas, M. J., Letarte, M. H., & Ladouceur, H. (1995). Perfectionism, responsibility and obsessive-compulsive symptoms. *Behaviour Research Therapy, 33*(7), 785–794.

Roth, R. M., Baribeau, J., Milovan, D. L., & O'Connor, K. (2004). Speed and accuracy on tests of executive function in obsessive-compulsive disorder. *Brain and Cognition, 54*(3), 263–265.

Sawamura, K., Nakashima, Y., Inoue, M., & Kurita, H. (2005). Short-term verbal memory deficits in patients with obsessive-compulsive disorder. *Psychiatry and Clinical Neurosciences, 59*(5), 527–532.

Schmidtke, K., Schorb, A., Winkelmann, G., & Hohagen, F. (1998). Cognitive frontal dysfunction in obsessive compulsive disorder. *Biological Psychiatry, 43*(9), 666–673.

Singh, G., Sharan, P., & Grover, S. (2003). Obsessive slowness: A case report. *Indian Journal of Psychiatry, 45*(1), 60–61.

Sumon Apparentimer (2006). Devised by Sumon Mukherjee, Dept. of Psychology, University of Calcutta, West Bengal, India.

Sumon's Responscope (2006). Devised by Sumon Mukherjee, Dept. of Psychology, University of Calcutta, West Bengal, India.

Tarafder, S. (2012). *A search for an endophenotypic model of obsessive compulsive disorder: A study with OCD probands & their unaffected first degree relatives.* (Unpublished doctoral thesis). University of Calcutta, Kolkata.

Trenerry, M. R., Crosson, B., DeBoe, J., & Leber, W. R. (1989). *Stroop Neuropsychological Screening Test.* Odessa, FL: Psychological Assessment Resources.

Ullsperger, M., & Von Cramon, D. Y. (2001). Subprocesses of performance monitoring: A dissociation of error processing and response competition revealed by event-related fMRI and ERPs. *NeuroImage, 14*(6), 1387–1401.

World Health Organization (1993). *The international statistical classification of diseases and related health problems* (Tenth Revision) (IDC-10), Diagnostic Research Criteria. Geneva: WHO.

8

Obsessive Compulsive Disorder

Psychoanalytic and Neuropsychological Interface

Pritha Mukhopadhyay and Sreemoyee Tarafder

The culmination of our overall understanding of obsessive com-pulsive disorder (OCD) is delineated in this book. Throughout this book, our mode of mental status examination and psycho-logical understanding of OCD demonstrates it as a neuropsychi-atric condition. There are many references of viewing obsessive inflexibility as a function of frontostriatal circuit. Time and again, we have agreed with recent studies that point out the structural involvement of brain in the neurobiology of OCD. Most studies have suggested the involvement of the prefrontal cortex, the basal ganglia and the thalamus in the pathogenesis of OCD. But as psy-chologists we feel that it is not strictly a neurobiological construct that can do full justice to understanding a complex disorder like OCD. We are tempted to stretch our understanding to include Freudian theorization of anal characteristics (Freud, 1909) with the view that it is a heritable and debilitating neuropsychiatric condition (Chamberlain & Menzies, 2009).

Over a century has passed since Freud's publication of the Rat Man case (*Notes Upon a Case of Obsessional Neurosis*, 1909) and needless to say our understanding of OCD has undergone sea change since. We have been presented with unerring evidence base that suggests that specific executive dysfunction may be a primary deficit in OCD (Bannon, Gonsalvez, Croft, & Boyce, 2006; Demeter, Csigó, Harsányi, Németh, & Racsmány, 2008; Martínez-González & Piqueras-Rodríguez, 2008; Rao, Reddy, Kumar, Kandavel, & Chandrashekar, 2008), implicating the cortico-striatal-thalamic-cortical circuits (Purcell, Maruff, Kyrios, & Pantelis, 1998; Rosenberg & Keshavan, 1998). Does the current emphasis on neuropsychological findings strengthen the part played by innate personality traits in the pathogenesis of this complex disorder? Can we adopt an empirical approach to address the psychological construct underlying OCD as proposed by Freud?

In this concluding chapter, we will try to arrive at a holistic understanding of OCD, where we will look at the Freudian anal or obsessive compulsive (OC) traits through the lens of cognitive neuropsychologists. Perhaps the identified cortico-striatal-thalamic-cortical circuits that explain inflexibility resemble core anal characteristics as propounded by Freud in 1909. In the previous chapters, we have investigated neurocognitive functions including myriad aspects of executive functions (EFs) along with personality traits (refer to Chapter 4 for detailed discussion) that will be referred to here for developing an understanding of this disorder more comprehensively.

Anal character traits or obsessive compulsive personality traits (OCPTs) are defined as rigid adherence to rules and procedure, extreme orderliness, obstinacy, perfectionism, cleanliness, punctuality and miserliness. In Freud's paper 'Character and Anal Erotism', published in 1908, he outlined how a specific type of personality stems from unresolved conflicts during the anal stage of psychosexual development and how people with an anal character typically shows traits of orderliness (or excessive neatness), frugality (or stinginess) and obstinacy (which is an inability to be flexible). Anal eroticism makes the child treat faeces in a contradictory manner, expelling the matter from the body and at the same time retaining it as if it were a loved object and forms the root cause of anal ambivalence (Fenichel, 1945). These anal characteristics and their association with OC neurosis have dominated the psychoanalytic conceptualization of OCD since 1908. Otto Fenichel (1945) points out how frugality is a continuation of the anal habit of retention motivated by the fear of losing; orderliness is the expression of obedience to the environmental requirements covering the regulations of excretory functions, whereas obstinacy is the rebellion against the same. Pollak (1987) also affirmed that individuals who demonstrate obsessive personality traits are strongly invested in control and this control is but a reflection of their obstinacy and highlights the rigidity in their character. Pollak (1979, 1987) points out that the basic construct of obsession is characterized by emotional constriction with severe superego structures as furnished by Freud.

Although there are a substantial number of studies investigating the neurocognitive correlates of OCD (see reviews by Kuelz, Hohagen, & Voderholzer, 2004; Olley, Malhi & Sachdev, 2007), there are few studies examining the association of executive function in OCD with OCPTs. A recent study by Aycicegi-Dinn, Dinn and Caldwell-Harris (2009) identified a group of university students demonstrating pronounced OCPTs and a comparison group, and reported that students presenting with pronounced OCPTs exhibited performance deficits on the complex figure task which led the authors to conclude that performance deficits on a non-verbal measure of executive control and working memory were related to OCPTs, but were not associated with classic OCD symptoms in a nonclinical sample. We were intrigued as to how OCPTs correlate with EFs in the clinical population, thereby trying to bring together two differing perspectives or rather different schools of thought.

Freud's conceptualization has been criticized owing to high content of subjective bias in his theoretical constructs which he developed based on analysis of free association of his patients. Moreover, Freudian concepts are not falsifiable, which additionally poses a hurdle to undertake an empirical research from Freudian perspective, owing to the difficulty in testing the psychological constructs developed by him. In accordance with Freud, OCPT comprises extreme orderliness, obstinacy, perfectionism, cleanliness, punctuality and miserliness, and we now understand that assessment of each of these traits as a separate construct is scientifically not very pragmatic. However, the anal characteristics as understood by Freud could be measured today with psychological tools that are validated to assess obsessive personality traits as a constellation which fulfils the demand of scientific precision. Obsessive trait subscale of Leyton Obsessional Inventory (LOI) is a measure of obsessive trait that measures the anal characteristics in totality, making the hypotheses framed by Freud testable. According to Stanley et al. (1993), trait items of LOI address associated personality characteristics such as punctuality, hoarding, conscientiousness and irritability. Wellen et al. (2007) through factor analysis identified five factors, namely, obsessional ruminations and compulsions, ordering and arranging, organizing activities, contamination and parsimony, underlying the traits assessed through LOI. Therefore, we can see that the obsessive traits noted on LOI corroborate the anal characteristics mentioned by Freud.

Seen through the psychoanalytic lens, impairment in set shifting could be seen not just as an index of cognitive or neuropsychological dysfunction, but also as Freudian 'frugality' that incapacitates them from generating essential alternative responses. Frugality may be viewed as the expression of constricted energy. 'Obstinacy' too may be considered as the psychological underpinning of set shifting deficit as may be seen on poor perseverative scores in patients with OCD (Chapter 4). It suggests that their ability to shift sets utilizing the feedback to cater to test demand is rather poor. Under certain circumstances, obstinacy may become so extreme that the person in question is compelled to do the exact opposite of what is required of him (Fenichel, 1945), similar to their failure in searching new way to resolve the problem in an ambiguous set-up (perseverative response [PR]) and also an inability to shift response styles (perseverative error [PE]) even when the instructor is hinting towards the same. It is as if the stance of the OCD group is passive aggressive, to hold onto one's position to spite of somebody, refusing to process the command to alter task response.

OCD group's slower performance on tasks (explored in Chapter 5) in which processing speed is compromised has been ascribed to intrusive thoughts or meticulousness (Roth, Baribeau, Milovan, & O'Connor, 2004) and the single-minded focus upon the accuracy aspect of the task is akin to maladaptive perfectionism (Moretz & McKay, 2009) since it fails to take the time factor into account. Koçak, Nalçacı, Özgüven, Nalçacı and Ergençd (2010) designed an experiment to simulate a situation that triggered anxiety and obsessions in OCD patients, and commands with or without a conflict were given to the participants. Results of their study showed that OCD patients responded to both conflicting and nonconflicting stimuli slower than the control group, prompting the authors to speculate that there is a cognitive slowing in OCD patients, independent of their conflict resolution. This kind of indecisiveness reminds one of Freudian anal ambivalence, when the same faecal object in the anal stage may be either preserved or expelled, in accordance to or against parental disciplining over toilet training. Their effort to reach accuracy with prolonged time may be represented as an index of conformity to the rule vis-à-vis authority. The factor of accuracy is so prioritized in them and their cognitive bias towards it is so bold that they only assimilate bottom-up information regarding accuracy and ignore the information regarding the time frame to be followed for test performance. Since they follow their own internal rule, their disregard for the external instruction (from bottom-up sources) does not arouse a feeling of guilt in them, in spite of them being guilt-prone by nature. Their maladaptive perfectionism may therefore be interpreted keeping in mind the anal trait of orderliness where tidiness, meticulousness and propriety signify a displacement of the compliance with environmental requirements in regard to defecation. Subsequently, through generalization this ambivalence becomes an automatized response pattern resulting in it becoming a character trait.

Our findings also revealed planning deficit on Tower of London (TOL) task with the OCD patients performing worse than controls in terms of correct scores, move scores, execution time and time violations (refer to Chapter 4). The finding is in agreement with previous researchers who attribute the lengthened latency times on the TOL task as consequences of strategy failures, attentional problems and/or chronic doubting. An alternate explanation might emerge from the dynamic perspective whereby time violation may perhaps be viewed as a reflection of a means of passive aggression on part of the subject, who disregards the administrator's instructions pertaining to time limits. This fails to induce guilt as it is not a direct expression of aggression towards the examiner, as stubbornness is a passive type of aggressiveness—a habitual combative method in the struggle for self-esteem (Fenichel, 1945).

In our work with FDRs of OCD probands, we have seen that they too are pretty finicky about perfectionism (for detailed discussion, see Chapter 4). Perhaps during the psychosexual development, the accuracy aspect is prioritized by the parents of OCD probands. People with OCD typically receive positive feedback for perfectionism and severe reprimand in case of a failure to reach absolute accuracy. As children they learn to prioritize perfectionism at the cost of time and other parameters. They fail to see this imposed overemphasis of perfectionism as a violation, but compromise in accuracy induces guilt in them. If we draw a parallel between the Freudian premise and the neuropsychological understanding of the disorder, it will be as depicted in Figure 8.1.

In our research, we saw symptom severity (as assessed on Yale Brown Obsessive Compulsive Scale [YBOCS]) being significantly

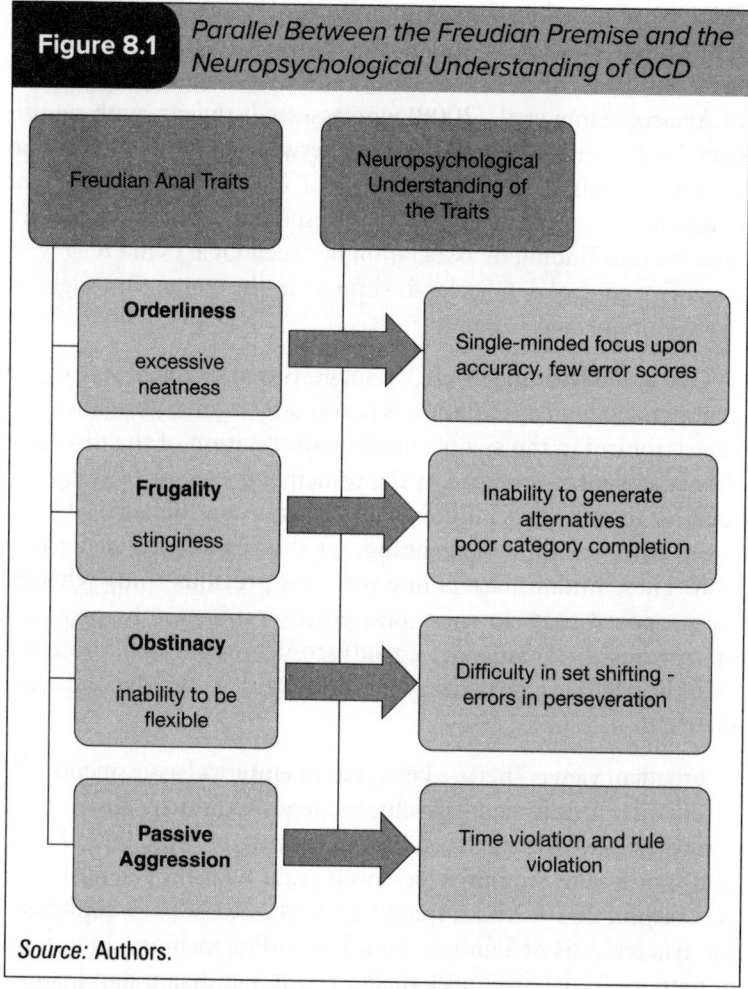

Figure 8.1 *Parallel Between the Freudian Premise and the Neuropsychological Understanding of OCD*

Freudian Anal Traits

Neuropsychological Understanding of the Traits

Orderliness

excessive neatness

Single-minded focus upon accuracy, few error scores

Frugality

stinginess

Inability to generate alternatives poor category completion

Obstinacy

inability to be flexible

Difficulty in set shifting - errors in perseveration

Passive Aggression

Time violation and rule violation

Source: Authors.

correlated with obsessive personality traits (assessed on LOI) and not with the obsessive symptoms. It reiterates the high degree of association between maladaptive personality factors and the severity of psychopathology in the OCD group. In our empirical studies, we have additionally found inverse correlation of obsessive personality traits with conceptual-level responses and category completion on Wisconsin Card Sorting Test (WCST). It firmly supports the claim of Bannon et al. (2006) and Rao et al. (2008) that specific executive function deficits in OCD, such as set shifting, are trait-like in nature. Our findings replicate those of Aycicegi-Dinn et al. (2009) who assessed students with significant OCPT and found association between executive tasks and OCPT, and claimed that specific OCPTs may in part represent compensatory tactics that evolve in response to executive control deficits. Our finding of association between OCPTs in OCD with executive control deficits lends support to the contention suggesting the importance of anal traits.

Our understanding of OCPT suggests that a crucial role of the anal personality constellation is marked by rigidity, frugality and perfectionism in the symptomatic manifestation of the disorder. Processing speed emerged as the principal predictor of symptom severity in our work, highlighting it as a core deficit in OCD, along with variables of planning, set shifting and divided attention. These findings are in line with our previous study wherein we proposed that slowness and perseveration are by-products of intrusive, unresolved, ego-dystonic instinctual thoughts (Mukhopadhyay, Tarafder, Bilimoria, Paul, & Bandyopadhyay, 2010).

Freudian viewpoints are being put to empirical assessments and recent advances in neuropsychiatric (e.g., Centonze, Siracusano, Calabresia, & Bernardi, 2005; Northoff et al., 2007; Pugh, 2002) and neurocognitive research (e.g., Moritz, Peters, Larøi, & Lincoln, 2010; Mukhopadhyay et al., 2010) have confirmed the crucial ideas of Sigmund Freud regarding memory, long-term potentiation, defence mechanism, latent aggression and instinctual impulses. Far from disproving the claims of Freud, our present understanding shows that OCPTs are core deficits in OCD, which bring about impairment in executive control characterized by cognitive inflexibility and slowness. Our findings contribute to understanding anal traits and ambivalence from a neurocognitive perspective. The present findings have implications for better eclectic understanding of the pathogenesis of executive dysfunction in OCD.

At the very end of this book, we arrive at a juncture that brings us to a holistic understanding of OCD. It is not a disorder that is explained by just a collection of obsessive traits or a fixated psychosexual development, nor a disorder that is only mediated by executive dysfunctions, but an amalgam of complex neuro-bio-psycho-social processes. We have also understood that OCD is facilitated by beliefs, and if beliefs are targeted remission is possible. Through our work, we have seen that biological relatives with equal status in terms of obsessive traits have not manifested the symptoms of OCD simply owing to their better metacognitive understanding whereby they have been able to stave off the psychopathology.

There are a significant proportion of people who are suffering from OCD all over the world. The more we arm ourselves with the knowledge about the disease process, the more we equip ourselves to fight back the disorder by building competencies. We also urge researchers to continue studying the disease from different perspectives, no matter what the constraints are. In India, we do not have the best of research facilities and infrastructure, yet we have tried in our humble way to empirically understand what the cognitive and neuropsychological underpinnings of the disorder are. Although a lot of promising research is carried out in India, not many are published. There is also a need to publish the research data from the rest of the subcontinent.

References

Aycicegi-Dinn, A., Dinn, W. M., & Caldwell-Harris, C. L. (2009). Obsessive-compulsive personality traits: Compensatory response to executive function deficit? *International Journal of Neuroscience, 119*(4), 600–608.

Bannon, S., Gonsalvez, C. J., Croft, R. J., & Boyce, P. M. (2006). Executive functions in obsessive-compulsive disorder: State or trait deficits? *Australian and New Zealand Journal of Psychiatry, 40*(11–12), 1031–1038.

Centonze, D., Siracusano, A., Calabresia, P., & Bernardi, G. (2005). Long-term potentiation and memory processes in the psychological works of

Sigmund Freud and in the formation of neuropsychiatric symptoms. *Neuroscience, 130*(3), 559–565.

Chamberlain, S. R., & Menzies, L. (2009). Endophenotypes of obsessive-compulsive disorder: Rationale, evidence and future potential. *Expert Review of Neurotherapeutics, 9*(8), 1133–1146.

Demeter, G., Csigó, K., Harsányi, A., Németh, A., & Racsmány, M. (2008). Impaired executive functions in obsessive compulsive (OCD): Review. *Psychiatria Hungarica, 23*(2), 85–93.

Fenichel, O. (1945). *The psychoanalytic theory of neurosis*. New York, NY: W. W. Norton & Company.

Freud, S. (1909). Notes on a case of obsessional neurosis. In J. Strachey (Ed.), *The standard edition of the complete psychological works of Sigmund Freud* (Vol. 10, pp. 153–318). London: Hogarth Press.

Koçak, O. M., Nalçacı, E., Özgüven, H. D., Nalçacı, E. G., & Ergençd, I. (2010). Evaluation of cognitive slowing in OCD by means of creating incongruence between lexicon and prosody. *Psychiatry Research, 179*(3), 306–311.

Kuelz, K., Hohagen, F., & Voderholzer, U. (2004). Neuropsychological performance in obsessive-compulsive disorder: A critical review. *Biological Psychology, 65*(3), 185–236.

Martínez-González, A. E., & Piqueras-Rodríguez, J. A. (2008). Neuropsychological update on obsessive-compulsive disorder. *Revista de Neurologia, 46*(10), 618–625.

Moretz, M. W., & McKay, D. (2009). The role of perfectionism in obsessive-compulsive symptoms: 'Not just right' experiences and checking compulsions. *Journal of Anxiety Disorders, 23*(5), 640–644.

Moritz, S., Peters, M. J., Larøi, F., & Lincoln, T. M. (2010). Metacognitive beliefs in obsessive-compulsive patients: A comparison with healthy and schizophrenia participants. *Cognitive Neuropsychiatry, 15*(6), 531–548.

Mukhopadhyay, P., Tarafder, S., Bilimoria, D. D., Paul, D., & Bandyopadhyay, G. (2010). Instinctual impulses in obsessive compulsive disorder: A neuropsychological and psychoanalytic interface. *Asian Journal of Psychiatry, 3*(4), 177–185.

Northoff, G., Walter, M., Schulte, R. F., Beck, J., Dydak, U., Henning, A.,...Boesiger, P. (2007). GABA concentrations in the human anterior cingulate cortex predict negative BOLD responses in fMRI. *Nature Neuroscience, 10*(12), 1515–1517.

Olley, A., Malhi, G., & Sachdev, P. (2007). Memory and executive functioning in obsessive-compulsive disorder: A selective review. *Journal of Affective Disorders, 104*(1–3), 15–23.

Pollak, J. M. (1979). Obsessive-compulsive personality: A review. *Psychological Bulletin, 86*(2), 225–241.

Pollak, J. (1987). Relationship of obsessive-compulsive personality to obsessive-compulsive disorder: A review of the literature. *The Journal of Psychology, 121*(2), 137–148.

Pugh, G. (2002). Freud's 'problem': Cognitive neuroscience and psychoanalysis working together on memory. *International Journal of Psychoanalysis, 83*(6), 1375–1394.

Purcell, R., Maruff, P., Kyrios, M., & Pantelis, C. (1998). Neuropsychological deficits in obsessive-compulsive disorder. *Archives of General Psychiatry, 55*(5), 415–423.

Rao, N. P., Reddy, Y. C., Kumar, K. J., Kandavel, T., & Chandrashekar, C. R. (2008). Are neuropsychological deficits trait markers in OCD? *Progress in Neuro-Psychopharmacology & Biological Psychiatry, 32*(6), 1574–1579.

Rosenberg, D. R., & Keshavan, M. S. (1998). Toward a neurodevelopmental model of obsessive-compulsive disorder. *Biological Psychiatry, 43*(9), 623–640.

Roth, R. M., Baribeau, J., Milovan, D. L., & O'Connor, K. (2004). Speed and accuracy on tests of executive function in obsessive-compulsive disorder. *Brain and Cognition, 54*(3), 263–265.

Stanley, M. A., Prather, R. C., Beck, J. G., Brown, T. C., Wagner, A. L., & Davis, M. L. (1993). Psychometric analyses of the Leyton Obsessional Inventory in patients with obsessive-compulsive and other anxiety disorders. *Psychological Assessment, 5*(2), 187–192.

Wellen, D., Samuels, J., Bienvenu, O. J., Grados, M., Cullen, B., Riddle, M.,...Nestadt, G. (2006). Utility of the Leyton Obsessional Inventory to distinguish OCD and OCPD. *Depression and Anxiety, 24*(5), 301–306.

ABOUT THE EDITORS AND CONTRIBUTORS

Editors

Pritha Mukhopadhyay is Professor at the Department of Psychology, University of Calcutta. She has been a brilliant and meritorious student right from the beginning of her student life. She was awarded national scholarship by the Government of India for her performance at higher secondary and graduation examinations. She was the recipient of the gold medal at the postgraduation level at the Department of Psychology, University of Calcutta in 1980. She went on to join the Department of Psychology, University of Calcutta as a lecturer in 1986. She was awarded her doctoral degree in 1991. For her postdoctoral work, she received the J. William Fulbright Scholarship and visited the School of Medicine at Temple University, USA in 1994. She is an avid researcher and her primary interests lie in the areas of psychophysiology and neuropsychology. She is the Coordinator of the UGC-funded Centre with Potential for Excellence in Particular Area, University of Calcutta, since 2011, and is carrying out cutting-edge work at her laboratory there with quantitative electroencephalogram and brain training programmes. She has received several research projects awarded by University Grants Commission, Indian Council of Social Science Research, All India Council for Technical Education and Department of Science & Technology. She has around 60 journal publications to her credit, both at national and international levels, and has authored 10 book chapters in various publications. She lives in Kolkata with her husband and daughter and loves reading books and travelling. Former head of the Department of Psychology, University of Calcutta, she is widely acclaimed and respected for her academic and administrative brilliance.

Sreemoyee Tarafder, is at present an Assistant Professor and Coordinator of the Department of Psychology, West Bengal State University, Barasat. A promising student of psychology right from her undergraduate days, she is a gold medalist in MPhil in Clinical Psychology from the University of Calcutta where she also received the G. G. Prabhu Award for topping her class. She completed her PhD from University of Calcutta, under Prof. Pritha Mukhopadhyay and was felicitated with the Durganand Sinha Memorial Award for her doctoral work on OCD from the National Association of Psychology (NAOP). She is also a corporate trainer and a consultant clinical psychologist who is specialized in areas related to personality disorders and anxiety disorders with specific expertise in OCD. She has established scientific liaisons with University of Haifa, Israel, BRAC University and Dhaka University in Bangladesh and University of Bath, UK. She has published around 20 papers in journals of national and international repute. She is a known face on mass media and frequently appears for mental health-related shows on regional and national channels of television and radio to promote awareness of mental health at community level. She lives in Kolkata with her husband and family, and apart from her passion for films, art, theatre and dance, she loves travelling, reading and socializing.

Contributors

Suvosree Bhattacharya, MPhil (Clinical Psychology) is clinical psychologist and Assistant Professor at the Department of Applied Psychology, The Neotia University, Kolkata. She obtained her MPhil in Medical and Social Psychology from Central Institute of Psychiatry, Ranchi, in 2006. After obtaining her MPhil, she worked at the Memory Disorder Research Group, Department of Neurology, Copenhagen University Hospital, Denmark, and at the Goodwill Industries of East Texas (USA) as a counsellor and workforce development trainer in the workforce development (WFD) department. After she returned to India, she worked as clinical psychologist at the Department of Clinical

Psychology, Institute of Psychiatry, IPGMER, Kolkata. She also has wide teaching experience, having taught as a visiting faculty at the Department of Psychology, West Bengal State University and Department of Applied Psychology, University of Calcutta. She knows Danish and Japanese languages, and learning new languages is her passion.

Nilanjana Chatterjee is a school psychologist and refers to herself as a health and wellness teacher at South Point High School. She obtained her master's degree from the Department of Psychology, University of Calcutta. She is also associated with different organizations as a psychologist and trainer. She is an avid photographer, with a keen interest for photography and travelling.

Sujata Das is consultant neuropsychologist at Fortis Hospital, Kolkata. She obtained her doctoral degree in 2009, having studied cognitive functions in obsessive compulsive disorder (OCD), paranoid schizophrenia and idiopathic Parkinson's disease. She is a sincere researcher and practitioner, with over 15 publications in peer-reviewed journals, both national and international. She was associated with the Department of Psychology, West Bengal State University, as a visiting faculty, teaching courses on biopsychology and cognitive studies. She loves to read and travel and has a special interest in folk music, especially *baul gaan*.

Shyamal Kumar **Das**, MBBS, MD, DM, is professor and head of the Department of Neurology, Bangur Institute of Neurosciences, Institute of Post Graduate Medical Education & Research (IPGMER), Kolkata. He is a renowned researcher with over 150 international and national publications in indexed journals. He received a movement disorder fellowship from University of Calgary, Canada. He specializes in neurodegenerative disorders, clinical sciences, neurogenetics, neuromedicine and neurophysiology. He has undertaken significant research projects related to dementia and dystonia. He is known for his avid interest in research and academic rigour.

Dinaz R. Jeejeebhoy, MPhil (Clinical Psychology), PhD, is Assistant Professor, Loreto College, Kolkata, and also a practising clinical psychologist. She has been a meritorious student all through her academic career. She was awarded with the national scholarship for achievement at BSc level by the University of Calcutta to pursue MSc in psychology for the batch 2003–2005. She was the recipient of the Debarpita Mukhopadhyay Book Prize for 2003 (for topping BSc examination) and the Dr G. Bose Memorial Prize for 2002 (for topping BSc Part I examination), awarded by the Department of Psychology, University of Calcutta. She has presented a number of papers at seminars and conferences and was recently awarded the S. C. Gupta Best Paper Award in 2015 by the Indian Association of Clinical Psychology for her work on borderline personality disorder. She is actively involved with an NGO that works for the upliftment of women and children. An avid sportswoman, she continues to play basketball at the club level and trains guides and bulbuls.

Parmeet Kaur Soni, MSc, MPhil (Clinical Psychology), is consultant clinical psychologist at Mental Health Foundation, Kolkata. She is a registered clinical psychologist, qualified in 2010, and has been working in mental health and research settings since 2012. She works mainly with children, adolescents and young adults in the area of emotional and behavioural disorders and has extensive experience in conducting psychodiagnostic assessments and providing psychotherapy using evidence-based methods. She provides parent training as well as works in liaison with schools to recommend viable management solutions for children. She has a special interest in clinical training and supervision, participating in clinical-based research, and in the area of substance abuse disorders and dual diagnosis in adolescents and young adults.

INDEX